PRESIDENTIAL LEADERSHIP

★

15
DECISIONS THAT CHANGED THE NATION

PRESIDENTIAL LEADERSHIP

★

15
DECISIONS THAT CHANGED THE NATION

NICK RAGONE

FOREWORD BY
ALI VELSHI
CNN ANCHOR & CHIEF BUSINESS CORRESPONDENT

PB **Prometheus Books**
59 John Glenn Drive
Amherst, New York 14228-2119

$28.00

Published 2011 by Prometheus Books

Inquiries should be addressed to
Prometheus Books
59 John Glenn Drive
Amherst, New York 14228–2119
VOICE: 716–691–0133
FAX: 716–691–0137
WWW.PROMETHEUSBOOKS.COM

15 14 13 12 11   5 4 3 2 1

Library of Congress Cataloging-in-Publication Data

Ragone, Nick.
   Presidential leadership : 15 decisions that changed the nation / by Nick Ragone.
      p. cm.
   Includes bibliographical references and index.
   ISBN 978–1–61614–237–7 (cloth : alk. paper)
   1. Presidents—United States—History. 2. Presidents—United States—Case studies 3. Political leadership—United States—Case studies. 4. United States—Politics and government—Case studies. 5. United States—Politics and government—Decision making—Case studies. I. Title.

E176.1.R228 2011
973.09/9 22—dc22
                                                                                        2010044250

Printed in the United States of America on acid free paper

For Tyan, Frankie and Mona,
my guiding lights

And in memory of the original Frank T. Ragone,
who is surely watching down with prideful eyes

CONTENTS

ACKNOWLEDGMENTS

Like everything in my life, this book was the product of many helping hands. I owe a special debt of gratitude to my wonderful agent, Barb Doyen. I'm still perplexed as to why she took a chance on me over a decade ago, but eternally grateful that she did. I hope I've repaid her confidence and look forward to our next project. Editor Linda Reagan's gentle suggestions made for a dramatically better read. Several chapters in particular—I won't tell you which ones!—wouldn't have been nearly as compelling without her sound guidance. Perhaps we'll get the chance to work together again. Good friend, accomplished journalist and author, and unhinged Mets fan Ken "Kenny Boy" Belson's enthusiasm for the project kept me going when things were ready to stall. His quirky insights and vast knowledge of historical minutiae added the right touch of levity where it was needed. Jen Reinhard turned out to be an invaluable and informal copy editor for the very, very rough first draft. Her meticulous attention to detail saved me from turning in a manuscript riddled with grammatical atrocities. Alan Miller found time in his busy schedule to review most of the chapters with his typical candor and irreverence. "What would you do without me?" became his standard refrain throughout the project. The listeners of Ralph Bailey's daily radio show on KNZR 1560 in Bakersfield, California, tolerated my frequent book tangents during my weekly segment on his show. Chatting with the listeners forced me to think closely about some of the narratives. Hal Walker, Clark Hare, Rob Flaherty, Jane Wells, Paul Sullivan, and Roy Martin were generous and helpful in their feedback. A hearty salute, as always, to the Rutgers University Library staff. I would still be roaming the stacks were it not for their tireless assistance. Special thanks to Ali Velshi for writing the foreword. I look forward to returning the favor someday. And I would be remiss (and exiled to the couch in perpetuity!) in overlooking the heartiest and most important thanks for my beautiful wife, Tyan, for making this all possible. One part cheerleader, one part taskmaster, full-time parent to two curious kids—I would still be talking about writing a book someday were it not for her encouragement. Her name belongs above the fold with mine.

FOREWORD

When my good friend Nick Ragone asked me to write the foreword to this book, I was pleasantly surprised but also a bit baffled.

As many of you reading this know, I'm neither a historian nor an expert on presidential decision making. In fact, I'm not even an American citizen. And while I have a deep appreciation for and interest in American history, the presidency, and the study of leadership, I suppose others do as well. Certainly, there are scores more qualified to speak to the subject than I am.

But then it dawned on me why Nick sought my testimonial: we're both storytellers. Every day I'm challenged to gather, digest, and synthesize information from all reaches of the globe and distill it into a narrative—sometimes no more than a minute or two long—that makes sense to my viewers. It needs to be accurate, informative, objective, and instructive. Hopefully, it's empowering in some way, too. And on a good day, it's compelling.

I've spent a career trying to shed light on and simplify complicated topics, provide broader context for events and news, bring clarity to developments that yearn to be unclear. It's my life's work—a genuine passion. I hope it comes across that way to viewers.

You're going to find the same thing with this book. You won't get two pages into the first chapter before experiencing the utter joy he brings to his craft; it practically radiates from the pages. In his mind, it's not enough to simply recite interesting stories laced with a learning moment or two. He wants you to feel his excitement and appreciation for these men, their decisions, and the legacy they left behind: Andrew Jackson's decision to take on his Southern brethren over nullification; Lincoln's realization that emancipation and union were inextricably linked together; Wilson's zealous devotion to the concept of a league of nations; Roosevelt's skilled maneuvering in coming to Great Britain's aid in their hour of greatest need. These aren't lessons to be learned so much as they are moments to be relived. And it reads that way.

It seems like every conversation I've ever had with Nick somehow comes back to American history—usually the presidency—in the form of a parallel, or analogy, or some kind of odd tidbit that makes for a more lively and informed discussion. To him, there's very little in our daily lives that isn't relatable to the presidency, one way or another. If there's a connection to be made, he'll find it.

Leadership, of course, is a great place to start. It's impossible to walk into a bookstore and not be greeted by dozens of tomes on the subject from myriad points of view. The same holds true for the presidency. While historians and others have tackled the office from every conceivable angle, I'm convinced that this book will shed new light on the men and their decisions that shaped the America we see today. I know it did for me.

Above all else, I think you're going to be riveted by the characters and their actions. Great storytelling is at the heart of this book. I'm not sure there's a better narrative accounting of Truman's decision to drop the bomb, for instance, or Reagan's decision to call the Soviet Union an "evil empire," or Kennedy's decision to shoot for the moon. It's a great way to reconnect with America's past.

Ali Velshi
CNN Anchor & Chief Business Correspondent

INTRODUCTION

Leadership is something of a lost art. One only has to turn on the television, pick up a newspaper, or go online to see its failure up close. And it's not just politicians and elected officials. The sight of business executives being led away in cuffs, athletes tearfully confessing to years of using performance-enhancing drugs, and celebrities behaving boorishly has become all too common. Even the pope has come under fire for his handling of the church's alleged sex-abuse scandal.

True enough, there is nothing particularly new about public figures misbehaving. It's practically a time-honored tradition in politics. But it seems to have reached epidemic proportions. Whereas poor judgment, faulty decision making, and lack of discretion were once the exception to the rule, sadly today it has become the rule.

One could argue that at the heart of the matter, what's driving this systemic failure is a lack of principled, difference-making leadership. If only boards of directors hadn't abdicated their oversight responsibilities, perhaps the economy wouldn't have been brought to its knees. If only the commissioner of baseball hadn't turned a blind eye to the rampant steroid abuse, perhaps the record books wouldn't be riddled with asterisks. If only church leaders had vigorously investigated suspected pedophiles, perhaps it wouldn't be staring into a reputational abyss. But we know that wasn't the case.

This book is a study of leadership at the highest level, the presidency. There's arguably no position on the planet more demanding, transparent, or documented than president of the United States. Surely there are valuable lessons to be gleaned from understanding the hows and whys of the office. Why did the president tackle a particular issue? How did he come to a decision? What made it successful (and in the case of Woodrow Wilson and the League of Nations, a failure)? What does it tell us about the nature of leadership?

This is not an academic treatise. Rather, it's narrative storytelling with analysis mixed in. My first goal is to tell a good story and keep your attention. History doesn't have to be dull or arid to be thoughtful; the two aren't mutually exclusive. Hopefully, the pages will turn quickly and insights will jump from the text.

My other goal is to spark debate, create conversation, and encourage readers to seek out additional literature on the topics. My analysis is just that—mine. It's not intended to be the sole or last voice on the matter. It's simply where the story took me. Maybe it will take you somewhere else.

Why these fifteen decisions? What was the selection process? Do they all have something in common?

Well, they had to be impactful. *Transformative* might be too strong a word, but *defining* is not. In my opinion, each action stretched the office, changed the landscape, élucidated a principle, and helped define their respective legacy. Readers will notice an absence of crisis responses, such as the Cuban Missile Crisis, Nixon's resignation, or the attempted rescue of the Iranian hostages. That was purposeful. Those are great subjects, but not for this book. The focus is on proactive, not reactive, decisions.

Readers will also notice that there is little judgment about the overall legacies of the presidents chronicled in the book. That, too, was purposeful. The book is not an evaluation of their entire tenure in office. There are plenty of wonderful biographies to choose from for that. The focus is on their particular decision, and that alone. Just because there is a chapter on Nixon and China doesn't mean I believe Nixon was a great president. It simply means that it's a decision that I believe is worth exploring. Same with Lyndon Johnson, Harry Truman, and all the others.

As it turns out, there is some connective tissue between the decisions, at least in a broad sense. The theme for the first four chapters—Washington puts down the Whiskey Rebellion, Jefferson signs the Louisiana Purchase, Jackson prevents nullification, Lincoln signs the Emancipation Proclamation—is the tension between federal and state power. It culminates in the Civil War, where the issue is essentially put to rest. The next batch—Roosevelt builds the Panama Canal, Wilson creates the League of Nations, FDR passes Lend-Lease, Truman drops the atomic bomb—speaks to America's emergence as a world power. In a fifty-year period, the nation went from committed isolationist to world superpower, the bombs at Hiroshima and Nagasaki marking the final transformation. The chapters on Truman firing MacArthur, "Ike," Kennedy and the space race, Nixon going to China, and Reagan and the "evil empire" take root in the Cold War. The flow gets interrupted with

LBJ and Civil Rights and Ford pardoning Nixon, but even then there's still some commonality: both decisions were politically ruinous (in the case of civil rights, it cost the Democrats their grip on the South). It's too soon to tell where Obama's healthcare reform fits into the mix.

It's important to keep in mind that while some of the topics are well known, others are not. Where the material was a bit more obscure—the Whiskey Rebellion, nullification, Truman and MacArthur, and so on—readers will notice more narrative and less analysis. Likewise where the opposite holds true, the emphasis is on insights, not storytelling. It should make for a better read.

Readers will also notice extended "back stories" in some of the chapters. Knowing that Nixon was a ferocious anticommunist in the 1950s is necessary for putting his decision to go to China in proper perspective. Lincoln's nuanced position on slavery during the 1850s makes the Emancipation Proclamation seem all the more remarkable. It's impossible to appreciate FDR's struggle to pass Lend-Lease without understanding the depth of isolationist feeling in the country. In many chapters, this context is critical to understanding the narrative.

It only makes sense that a book about presidential leadership and decision making draw liberally from the president's own words. It was a conscious decision to give primacy to the letters, speeches, memoir reflections, and other documents written by the men themselves. It's their decisions, their struggles. Of course, others played a role—no action or policy occurs in a vacuum. But the voice heard most often is the one at the center of the action.

In the end, this book is meant to be a companion on your journey for a deeper understanding—and perhaps appreciation—of the presidency, its occupants, and the decisions that shaped the nation. It is my hope that you'll enjoy reading it as much as I did writing it.

Chapter 1

WASHINGTON PUTS DOWN THE WHISKEY REBELLION

Used with permission of the National Guard Bureau.

Why has government been instituted at all? Because the passions of man will not conform to the dictates of reason and justice without constraint.
—Alexander Hamilton, *Federalist Paper* No. 15.

A little rebellion now and then is a good thing. The tree of liberty must be refreshed from time to time with the blood of patriots and tyrants.
—Thomas Jefferson, 1786

In the summer of 1794, an angry mob of seven thousand people gathered outside Pittsburgh, Pennsylvania, to convene an ad hoc "convention" of sorts to determine their responses to the federal government's attempts to collect the taxes imposed on distilled spirits. Tensions between distillers and the government had been on the rise in western Pennsylvania since 1791 when the whiskey tax was first instituted. There had been intermittent bursts of violence every time federal agents tried to collect tax revenues from the distillers, and by July of

1794, many in the government feared that mass violence, insurrection, and
even the overthrow of the capital in Philadelphia was imminent. At the prod-
ding of Treasury Secretary Alexander Hamilton, President George Washington
summoned thirteen thousand armed militia from neighboring states and per-
sonally led the effort to put down the rebellion. It was a defining moment for the
young Republic—its first constitutional crisis—and would remain the largest
domestic disturbance until the Civil War some sixty-five years later.

* * *

Armed resistance and protest was not uncommon during the early
years of the Republic. There had been minor uprisings
throughout the thirteen colonies immediately following the Revolutionary War, the largest and most serious being "Shays's Rebellion" of
1786, where one thousand armed protesters in central Massachusetts
surrounded the capital in search of debt relief and tax fairness from the
local courts. A private army was formed to put down the rebellion—
which it easily did—but the prospect of having to organize private armies
to defeat future insurrections convinced political leaders that the Articles
of Confederation were simply not tenable as a governing charter.

Shays's Rebellion highlighted the weakness in the loose confederation approach. In the summer of 1787, the second Continental Congress
convened in Philadelphia with the intent to amend the Articles of Confederation, which favored a weak central government and reserved great
powers to the states. The Founding Fathers decided to scrap the articles
altogether, and instead wrote a new charter for the United States, which
was ratified the following summer. The hope was that a new constitution
with a strong central government would bring greater stability and cohe-
sion to the fledgling country.

George Washington was unanimously selected as the first president
of the United States under the newly ratified Constitution, in part
because he was universally regarded as the most capable and trustworthy
person to guide the new country through its formative years. Nobody
was quite certain how a strong chief executive—something the Articles
of Confederation did not have—would relate to Congress and the states,
or how his powers would be interpreted and used. In many ways, the
political establishment was counting on Washington to carefully and

deliberately define the position and the office. Their logic was simple if not unassailable: if there was one person who could strike the right balance between respecting popular sovereignty and providing firm authority, it was George Washington.

The Whiskey Rebellion was the first test for President Washington and the new Republic. It was particularly complicated because the crisis represented not only a physical threat—for a brief time, an assault on the capital was a real possibility—but an intellectual one as well. Was it the duty of a responsive government to simply accede to the protestors' demands and repeal the tax? Did the president need the assent of Congress to raise an army and put it down? Would an aggressive reaction from the federal government pose a threat to liberty itself? Nobody really knew for certain. Antifederalists—those who supported a weak central government—had one point of view, federalists held another, and many farmers and merchants throughout the colonies sympathized with the rebels. The president's own cabinet was split on the issue while Congress was preoccupied with other matters. This was Washington's decision alone, and with it rested the fate of the country.

Hamilton's Tax

Many historians consider Alexander Hamilton the father of the US economy, and with good reason: as the nation's first treasury secretary, Hamilton helped found the first National Bank, established the United States Mint, created a national system of tax collectors, promoted a stable paper currency, and generally transformed what had been a regional, disorganized financial system under the Articles of Confederation into a rigorous and highly structured national economy.[1]

He did it, in part, because he could. Hamilton was a brilliant political philosopher and financial theorist with few equals. Given that President Washington's first order of business was to stabilize the economy (in order to quell any lingering domestic unrest as well as protect the country from foreign encroachment), Hamilton was given free rein to reshape commerce—and create the institutions necessary to do it—to his liking. It was an opportunity he met with zeal.

But it went beyond just merely following Washington's agenda and implementing his orders. Hamilton was an ardent believer in a strong central government. During the Constitutional Convention of 1787, in fact, he argued—quite passionately—that the president should have a life term, a position that caused many to suspect that he secretly desired a monarchy. Writing as "Publius" in the *Federalist Papers*, Hamilton was at his most persuasive when defending the notion of a strong executive and central government. "A feeble Executive implies a feeble execution of the government," he writes in *Federalist Paper* no. 70. "A feeble execution is but another phrase for a bad execution; and a government ill executed, whatever it may be in theory, must be, in practice, a bad government." It's not surprising then that Hamilton viewed the president's directive to create a robust economy as something of an invitation to consolidate the power of the federal government—and he wasn't about to pass that up.

In January of 1790, Alexander Hamilton put forward his plan to reorganize the economy and straighten out the nation's finances. Called the "Report on Public Credit," the fifty-one-page document was startling for its complexity and ambition; few members of Congress were able to adequately comprehend it, let alone debate it. The plan did three things: paid interest on (and ultimately paid off) the foreign and private debt incurred during the Revolutionary War; assumed the debts that the state governments had also incurred during the war; and raised revenues through a series of tariffs and duties on imported goods as well as an excise on whiskey—the first-ever domestic tax.

Hamilton's plan was shrewd. By paying off the foreign debt, it established the government's credit worthiness and enabled it to borrow money from foreign powers that could be used to fund his ambitious federal programs, something that Thomas Jefferson—who was also in the cabinet—and James Madison opposed.[2] But even more importantly, by assuming the states' debts, it gave creditors—most of whom resided in the states—a reason to support his national agenda since it resulted in the funding of their war bonds. In effect, Hamilton bought their loyalty and in the process lessened their fealty to the states. "The debt of the United States," Hamilton reasoned, "was the price of liberty."[3] He would later refer to the assumption of debt as a "national blessing."[4]

Of course, in order to assume and finance all this debt, the federal government needed to collect revenues, and that's where their whiskey tax came in. Hamilton somehow convinced Congress that a tax on whiskey was both desirable from a public health standpoint (he had the Philadelphia College of Physicians testify that whiskey consumption had become a "plague" on the laboring class) and equitable from a fairness standpoint because it would disproportionately tax the wealthy who could afford to consume whiskey. "A source of national extravagance and impoverishment" is how he described whiskey to the Congress, and after little debate, the whiskey tax was passed.[5] The fact that he knew that both assumptions were patently false hardly mattered. His real goal in passing a federal excise tax was that it would necessitate the creation of a national network of federal tax collectors—something that had never existed before—who would round up revenues from whiskey distillers and any future taxes, too. Up to that point, the federal government had relied upon the states to collect taxes, which made predicting government revenues a difficult proposition. But not anymore. In one fell swoop, Hamilton had strengthened the federal government by adding a network of tax men, created a predictable and consistent revenue stream to fund the growing federal government, and lessened the authority of the states by assuming their debt. Everything was in place for national commerce to flourish, or so he thought.[6]

Tar and Feather

In the early fall of 1791, not long after the whiskey tax became law, a newly appointed federal tax collector for western Pennsylvania named Robert Johnson was making his way through the dense forests of the back country when he was met by a gang of musket-toting locals. The group represented something of a "welcoming committee" to the westernmost counties of the state; the dozen or so men had been instructed by county leaders to advise Johnson to leave at once or face the consequences. They were in no mood to negotiate.[7]

The earnest taxman, looking to complete his task and collect revenues from the local distillers, refused to yield or run. And for it he was rewarded with a shaved head, scalding hot tar, and a body full of feathers. The rabble stripped him of his clothes, horse, and supplies and left him stranded twenty miles in the forest to walk his way back to civilization in shame. Somehow Johnson survived the ordeal and eventually made his way back to Philadelphia, where he recited his humiliating tale. For the first time Alexander Hamilton experienced a hint of doubt as to whether his plan to nationalize the economy would actually succeed. It was a portent of things to come.[8]

Throughout 1791 and 1792, similar tales of abuse were reported from all corners of the country. The details varied here and there but the basic story was the same: tax collector enters county; tax collector met by local vigilantes; tax collector is abused or tortured. In North Carolina, one wild-eyed distiller locked the taxman in his barn for three days. Another unfortunate soul had his nose ground off from a grinding wheel.[9]

Western Pennsylvania, and in particular four counties—Washington, Allegheny, Westmoreland, and Fayette—represented the epicenter of the growing civil unrest. It wasn't because the inhabitants were particularly ornery or more rebellious than their neighbors—though being frontiersmen, they certainly enjoyed a more rigorous existence than their city brethren. It was a simple numbers game: of the eight thousand Americans who distilled whiskey for a living, a quarter of them resided in those four counties. And the whiskey tax represented a direct assault on their way of life.

In some respects, Alexander Hamilton planned it that way. His dream of creating a thriving merchant class required the transfer and consolidation of wealth and resources to the cities, the federal government, and the educated elite in order to create manufacturing jobs along the coastline and the transportation infrastructure to support it. It was in direct contrast to Thomas Jefferson's competing vision of an agrarian-based economy, which Hamilton found detestable. In that sense, the whiskey tax had the added benefit of undermining Jefferson's ambitions. If Hamilton could raise government revenues through the tax and force laborers off the farms—all the better.

Of course, Hamilton never came out and said this; to the contrary, he positioned the tax as equitable—the burden would be shared by distillers both big and small everywhere. But with Hamilton, the devil was always in the details, and in this case the fine print told a different story. He deliberately placed the tax burden on the point of distillation, not sale, so that he could create a two-tier payment system: one for large distilleries located in big cities and one for rural distilleries out in the hinterlands. Since the government could monitor the big distilleries in the cities and nearby towns, those businesses paid a tax on the *actual* whiskey produced, while the rural distilleries paid an annual flat fee based on the total *estimated* capacity of their stills. Hamilton structured it this way because he knew full well that small stills could only distill a fraction of the assumed capacity outlined in his onerous law—the impact being that their net tax burden would be substantially higher than the larger distilleries. What made matters worse for them, the law required that the tax be paid at the point of whiskey creation (literally at the still) in coin or paper currency—something westerners had very little of—with the failure to pay resulting in a stiff fine and an appearance at a Philadelphia court. Why Philadelphia? Hamilton chose it because it meant a difficult, ten-day trip over the mountains for the aggrieved distillers in the western counties. And he knew that many would rather forfeit their stills to the government than leave their families and make the dangerous journey to the east. He had thought of everything.

At the end of the day, the whiskey tax placed an enormous burden on the entire system of commerce in the "frontier" counties because, in addition to consuming it, whiskey was also used as currency. Unlike paper currency, which tended to fluctuate wildly in value, and coins, which were hard to come by, whiskey was commonplace and very stable in value. It was simple to make, easy to transport, and didn't easily perish. Landlords accepted it as rent; laborers preferred it as pay; and merchants recognized it as tender. Doctors used it as anesthesia and a remedy for common ailments. It was the life-blood of rural farmers everywhere, and the tax on it reminded many aggrieved patriots why they had supported independence from England in the first place. "A breath in favor of the law is sufficient to ruin any man," is how renowned novelist and protest sympathizer Hugh Henry Brackenridge described it. "It was considered a badge of toryism."[10] An insult, no doubt, that Hamilton took with delight.

Oddly enough, while most in Congress didn't pick up on Hamilton's ulterior motives or lopsided mathematics, the illiterate masses in the backcountry weren't fooled for a second; they understood the dire implications of the whiskey tax from the moment it was enacted. Some distillers toyed with the idea of simply selling their raw grain—which wasn't taxed—to the markets back east instead of converting it to whiskey, but the cost of transporting bundles of grain by pack mule over the mountains was simply greater than the revenues it would generate. Whiskey in barrels was much lighter than grain, and therefore cheaper and easier to get to market—the reason why so many farmers became distillers in the first place.

Throughout the fall of 1791 and the winter of 1792, organized mobs in the western counties continued to harass and brutalize tax collectors at every turn. The goal was to make collection both impossible for the federal agents and undesirable for the local inhabitants. For "cooperating" residents—those citizens who actually tried to register their stills and pay the tax—it meant physical abuse and torture for them, too. And anyone who dared to assist the tax collectors by renting them office space or publishing their notices were guaranteed to be victimized. In modern parlance, it was a 360-degree approach to vigilantism: anyone remotely associated with the tax-collecting process would be abused.[11] Threats, harassment, intimidation, and public humiliations became so commonplace that by the early spring of 1792, federal collectors simply quit attempting to register the distilleries and closed shop. It was time to go back to the drawing board.

Enter Washington

For a brief while, it looked like the westerners had prevailed. Federal agents stopped trying to collect the tax; local residents didn't dare consider voluntarily complying with the law; and anyone associated with the federal government was practically shunned from the county. Commercial activity returned to normal as small distillers again sold their whiskey tax free at market.

Alexander Hamilton knew that he had a problem. His ambitious plan to redesign the economy was dependent upon nearly a million dollars in whiskey tax revenues, but the government had collected only a fraction of it—most of it coming from the big distilleries in the east. Hamilton didn't mind running a federal deficit; he was concerned, however, that creditors would eventually lose faith in treasury bonds if the government appeared incapable of collecting revenues.

None of this was lost on George Washington. Hamilton had kept the president apprised of the difficulties in collecting the whiskey tax revenue and encouraged Washington to address it in his State of the Union address in the fall of 1791. "The impression with which this law has been received by the community," Washington told Congress, "has been upon the whole such as were to be expected among enlightened and well-disposed citizens from the propriety and necessity of the measure. The novelty, however, of the tax in a considerable part of the United States and a misconception of some of its provisions have given occasion in particular places to some degree of discontent; but it is satisfactory to know that this disposition yields to proper explanations and more just apprehensions of the true nature of the law, and I entertain a full confidence that it will in all give way to motives which arise out of a just sense of duty and a virtuous regard to the public welfare." He concluded by stating that he was amenable to removing any "well-intentioned objections that may happen to exist" in the law if it would further "lay the foundations of the public administration in the affections of the people."[12]

At Washington's insistence, Hamilton offered several modifications to the tax law, which Congress happily passed. His hope was that by reducing the tax by a penny, and giving distillers the option to pay on either capacity or actual production, it would convince the rural counties to register their stills with their local excise office and end their resistance. The revised law even allowed for a monthly license for those smaller distillers who weren't interested in year-round production—an important concession, or so he thought. Washington and Hamilton hoped that it would do the trick.

It didn't. Though the violence slowed during the summer months, it was only because collection had become all but impossible. Federal agents were scarcely able to set foot in the hostile counties, and those who did were physically run out of town. On September 15, 1792, Washington issued a presidential proclamation admonishing the tax resisters for their unlawful behavior and exhorting them to comply with the law. But perhaps more importantly, he prevailed on the "courts, magistrates, and officers whom it may concern . . . to exert the powers in them respectively vested by law . . . to tender the welfare of their country, the just and due authority of government, and the preservation of the public peace, to be aiding and assisting therein according to law."[13]

Washington was losing his patience—with the hostile distillers, the recalcitrant county officials in western Pennsylvania, even with Hamilton himself. In an earlier draft of the proclamation, Hamilton had made explicit the threat of federal troops against the rabble rousers, but the president struck the reference out. Even so, Hamilton pushed the matter, hoping that Washington would relent and send in the army—something Washington did not want to do. "It may be necessary to look forward in time to ulterior arrangements," he lectured Hamilton, "and here not only the Constitution and laws must strictly govern, but employing the regular troops to be avoided, if it is possible to effect order without their aid; otherwise there would be a cry at once 'the cat is let out; we now see for what purpose an army was raised.'"[14]

It was not unusual for Hamilton to push Washington or for Washington to scold his younger colleague. The two had an odd relationship, one that spanned two decades and at times resembled a father-son rivalry. As Washington's self-appointed chief of staff during the Revolutionary War, Hamilton had proved himself invaluable to the general; so much so that Washington refused to give him his own command until the very end of the war because he was so indispensable—a perceived slight that Hamilton carried with him. Hamilton later baffled his mentor when he tried to draw the general into a potential army mutiny (in Newburgh, New York) over the issue of back pay for the soldiers. Hamilton thought the threat of insurrection (just weeks before the end of the war as it turned out) would force the Continental Congress to finally pay the broke soldiers after years of neglect, but Washington would have none of it. He coldly admonished Hamilton in several testy letters and ultimately stamped out the mutiny himself with a personal appearance before the aggrieved soldiers.

Nonetheless, Washington was fully aware of Hamilton's genius. He brought him into the cabinet, in part, to act as a counterweight to Thomas Jefferson—for whom Washington didn't always see eye-to-eye—as well as for his financial acumen, which was unparalleled. He trusted Hamilton and gave him copious license to shape the nation's economy. But it wasn't a blank check. In matters of federalism, civil enforcement, and popular sovereignty—delicate issues that could undermine the young country—Washington had his own ideas, and didn't hesitate to disregard Hamilton's counsel when it became too strident. It was beginning to approach that point.

Showdown at Pittsburgh

It was a reluctant George Washington who at the beginning of 1793 agreed to a second term as president, in part because he remained concerned about the threat of insurrection in the western territories. While things had been quiet for most of the year, the fundamental problem still existed: the US government was incapable of enforcing federal laws across all the states. Washington was not a political philosopher like Jefferson or Madison. He was through and through military—a man of action. He drew inspiration by leading men, seizing moments, charting history. He left it to others to ponder the larger meaning of it all.

But with insurrection still fomenting in Pennsylvania, Washington knew that there was a greater principle at stake than merely tax collection. The Articles of Confederation had failed miserably, in part, because the federal government and its laws didn't take primacy over the states. It essentially collapsed under the weight of its own ineffectiveness. The Founding Fathers remedied that by creating a system of federalism whereby federal law now superseded state law. While few disputed that the federal government had the power to pass laws for which the states were bound to comply, enforcement was another matter altogether. And as Washington was beginning to realize, without the ability to enforce national laws, federalism amounted to little more than a hollow theory— no different than the Articles of Confederation.

But as his letters to Hamilton and others suggest, Washington was hesitant to raise an army to enforce the law, even though it was well within his power. From the very beginning in 1791, Hamilton had been in favor of military intervention to force the frontiersmen to comply with the tax. To him, it was a clear-cut case of insurrection, and he felt comfortable counseling the president to quickly put it down by force. Washington didn't quite see it that way. Just because he had the power to use military force didn't mean it was appropriate. He was acutely aware that many of his countrymen—particularly those living on the frontier—were already fearful of this new, stronger, central government. The use of force against civilians would simply confirm their worst fears—that they had replaced one form of tyranny (the king) with another (the president). Washington wasn't about to let that happen.[15]

Events were conspiring against him, however. In June of 1794, the federal tax officials somehow found the courage to attempt again the collecting of the whiskey tax in the four western counties of Pennsylvania, only to be met with a wave of attacks, reprisals, and condemnation from the frontiersmen. But unlike the humiliating tar and feather incidents from several years earlier, which were mostly random acts of intimidation, the latest wave of resistance was highly organized, coordinated, and, in fact, much more violent. During the intervening years, the westerners had formed a professional militia, in essence, which was trained to move swiftly and decisively against the tax collectors from the moment they tried to set up shop in the county. Burned houses and offices, armed assault, and outright torture were the typical fates awaiting the federal agents, while residents caught complying with the law fared no better.[16] Even the top tax inspector for the state, General John Neville, wasn't immune from the violence: the Revolutionary War hero's mansion was burned to the ground shortly after he took on the assignment.

What had started as an episodic protest against an unpopular tax was quickly morphing into a full-blown insurrection. In late July, seven thousand insurgents gathered outside Pittsburgh to hold a "Constitutional Convention" of their own to decide whether western Pennsylvania should become a separate state—perhaps even a separate country. Not content with merely seceding from the Union, some of the more radical elements were advocating for an overthrow of the entire federal government, beginning with the ransacking of Pittsburgh, which sat defenseless just a few miles away. With Pittsburgh under control, reasoned many of the insurgents, it would be easy to overrun the capital in Philadelphia. They were probably right.

Word quickly reached President Washington that things were spiraling out of control. And yet, even with Pittsburgh hanging in the balance, the president still wasn't convinced that calling in the troops was the best solution. Hamilton was pushing hard for it—without letup—but Washington wasn't ready to make that call. He much preferred to repel the mob and restore order through a proclamation, confessing as much to his friend and former aide-de-camp, Colonel Burgess Ball, who was much closer to the situation on the ground. "What is said, or thought, as far as it has appeared to you, of the conduct of the People in the Western Counties of this state [Pennsylvania] towards the excise Officers? Does there seem to be a disposition among those with whom you converse, to bring them to a Sense of their duty, and obedience to law, by coercion, if, after they are fully notified by the proclamation and other expedients . . . in a word, would there be any difficulty, as far as the matter has passed under your observation, in drawing out the militia to quell this rebellious spirit, and to support order and good government?"[17]

On August 7, Washington gave a peaceful solution one last chance when he issued a lengthy proclamation ordering the insurgents to disband by September 1. Should they refuse, the proclamation read, the troops would be sent in. It was lengthy, in part, because it recited many of the atrocities committed by the rebels—a smart ploy by Washington to turn public sentiment against the frontiersmen.[18]

Washington was doubtful that the proclamation alone would end the standoff. He made a formal request of Governor Thomas Mifflin of Pennsylvania to send in the state militia to quell the unrest. Mifflin, who was a Jefferson supporter and devout antifederalist, refused to get involved. It was a federal matter, not a state problem, said Mifflin to Washington in a face-to-face meeting. Should he be ordered to summon the state militia as part of the federal response, Mifflin lectured the president, he would have to consult with the state legislature first.[19]

For Washington, this was the last straw. An intransigent rabble holding an impromptu convention outside Pittsburgh was one thing; having a sitting governor reject the concept of federal supremacy was quite another. In some ways, the latter was more disturbing than the former. Washington made one last attempt to avoid armed confrontation when he sent a three-person commission to negotiate a peaceful resolution with the insurgents. Not surprisingly, the commissioners got nowhere. Their counsel to Washington was to send in the troops—there was nothing left to be done.[20]

After three years and countless meetings, letters, memos, proclamations, and discussions, George Washington did exactly what he had hoped to avoid: summoned a militia to put down the rebellion. It was the option of last resort, but when he finally committed to a military response, it came with two important addendums: it would be an overwhelming force (in this case, thirteen thousand troops) and he would personally lead it. Washington knew that failure to end the insurrection could be a fatal blow to the country, and it was a chance he wasn't about to take. By personally leading the troops, and at double the size of the insurgents' force, Washington felt confident that he could end the sordid episode without any bloodshed. It was a huge gamble—he was putting his personal prestige and the concept of federal supremacy on the line—but he knew that a bloodless victory would be a credit to both. It was worth the risk.

Fortunately for George Washington, his instincts were correct. In late September, he donned his old military uniform, saddled up, and spent the next few weeks commanding the troops through western Pennsylvania in a show of brute force meant to intimidate the protestors. By this time word had reached the insurgents that the great man himself was commanding the effort, and their resolve quickly dissolved. Most of them disbanded. What few holdouts remained were rounded up, arrested, and extradited to Philadelphia to stand trial. What began as a tense and uncertain expedition quickly turned into a valedictory lap for the president as the westerners welcomed him as a conquering hero. It was a rather anticlimactic ending to what many historians consider the greatest constitutional threat prior to the Civil War.

* * *

After all the tar and featherings, violence, and the threat of secession, only twelve insurgents were tried and just two convicted. In a magnanimous gesture befitting his character, Washington quickly pardoned the two rebels. And with it, the matter was put to rest. The Constitution had triumphed; the rebellion was squelched. Washington was pleased with the outcome.

As for the tax collectors, though they no longer feared for their lives, their jobs were not made easier. Many of the distillers changed their tactics from resistance to hiding and simply sold their moonshine on the black market. And so began a long and contentious relationship between the federal government and the burgeoning moonshine industry.

President Thomas Jefferson wasted little time in repealing the tax—something he never supported in the first place. He thought it unfairly penalized farmers and he was happy to do away with it. Ironically, the task fell to his treasury secretary, Albert Gallatin, who happened to be one of the leading instigators of the insurrection. Gallatin would call his involvement with the rebels the greatest regret of his career. Jefferson's successor, James Madison—another opponent of the original tax—briefly brought it back in 1812 to help finance the war against England; it was repealed again in 1817, this time until the Civil War.

For George Washington, the Whiskey Rebellion has mostly been an overlooked triumph in his long and brilliant career. The preponderance of Washington biographies focus on the colonial and revolutionary years, with less examination given to his presidential terms. But it could be argued that quelling the insurrection and enforcing the tax law were the defining actions of his eight years in office. He certainly viewed it as critical to the success of the Republic. "What may be the consequence of such violent and outrageous proceedings is painful in a high degree even in contemplation," he wrote a friend at the height of the Pittsburgh gathering, "but if the Laws are to be so trampled upon, with impunity, and a minority (a small one, too) is to dictate to the majority there is an end put, at one stroke, to republican government; and nothing but anarchy and confusion is expected thereafter."[21]

Chapter 2

THOMAS JEFFERSON PURCHASES THE LOUISIANA TERRITORY

Courtesy of the holdings of the National Archives and Records Administration, Washington, DC.

This little event, of France's possessing herself of Louisiana, is the embryo of a tornado which will burst on the countries on both sides of the Atlantic and involve in its effects their highest destinies.

— Thomas Jefferson

[The Louisiana Purchase] makes no alteration in the Constitution, it only extends the principles of it over a larger territory, and this certainly is within the morality of the Constitution.

—Thomas Paine

It [the Louisiana Purchase] resulted solely from a fortuitous concurrence of unforeseen and unexpected circumstances, and not from any wise or vigorous measures on the part of the American government.

—Alexander Hamilton

In the summer of 1803, Thomas Jefferson doubled the size of the United States with the stroke of a pen. The unexpected purchase of the entire Louisiana Territory from France was met with celebration and near-universal praise by the American people and press. In an instant, Jefferson had secured the critical Mississippi River passageway to the Gulf of Mexico, brought the United States one step closer to fulfilling its "manifest destiny" of extending the nation across the continent, and greatly retarded the expansionist desires of France, England, and Spain in the hemisphere. And most impressively, he did it without firing a single shot, a feat practically unknown during that era. While Jefferson was hailed for his accomplishment, he struggled mightily with the decision. He knew that acquiring the land was a monumental opportunity for the United States—one that was simply too good to pass up. From every angle it made perfect sense. His dilemma was an intellectual one, for the very act of unilaterally purchasing the expanse without consulting Congress or seeking a constitutional amendment seemed to violate Jefferson's deepest and most cherished principles about republicanism and limited government. It was a dramatic instance where political philosophy stood in violent conflict with pragmatic reality. And in this case, pragmatism won out.

* * *

Thomas Jefferson holds a special place with the American people among the pantheon of Founding Fathers who helped give birth to the nation. He has been studied, conjectured, written about, and consequently mythologized more than any American figure save Abraham Lincoln. If George Washington is revered for being the father of our country, Ben Franklin for defining American values and spirit, James Madison for drafting the Constitution and Bill of Rights, and Alexander Hamilton for creating the economy, then Thomas Jefferson may be best remembered as America's first and greatest political philosopher.

Few figures in American history can boast a résumé of accomplishments as robust as Thomas Jefferson's. Even if he never served a minute as president, vice president, or secretary of state, his list of achievements would still rival that of any founder. In fact, Jefferson believed that his greatest contributions came outside of elected office. On his tombstone inscription, which he wrote, he's recognized as the author of the Declaration of Independence and the Virginia Statute for Religious Freedom, and founder of the University of Virginia. Nowhere does it mention that he was president of the United States, which speaks volumes about his regard for the office in the greater scheme of things.

In some ways, his lack of regard for his time in the White House was shaped by his lack of regard for the office of the presidency in general. Unlike John Adams, Alexander Hamilton, and to a lesser extent George Washington, Thomas Jefferson considered Congress—not the presidency—the dominant branch of government, particularly the House of Representatives. He considered the House as the true repository of a representative government, or republicanism, as well as democracy, and as such that it should drive the political agenda for the nation. He believed so firmly in that notion, as well as the principle of state sovereignty and the limited province of the federal government, that he formed the first-ever political party to advance those ideas, the Democratic-Republicans (the forerunner of the modern-day Democratic Party).

This feat makes Jefferson's actions involving the Louisiana Purchase all the more interesting. For someone who adhered to a strict interpretation of the Constitution and its powers, and viewed the presidency as a weak executive office, Thomas Jefferson's decision to purchase the Louisiana Territory seemingly stood in direct contrast to that philosophy. And yet he went ahead with it, principles notwithstanding. As one Jefferson biographer put it, the purchase was "unquestionably the greatest achievement of the Jefferson presidency and, with room left for scholarly quibbling about Abraham Lincoln in 1861, Franklin Roosevelt in the 1930s and Harry Truman in 1945, one of the most consequential executive actions in all of American history."[1]

"The Revolution of 1800"

Thomas Jefferson suffered a bumpy tenure in appointed and elected office during the first dozen years of the Republic. As George Washington's first secretary of state, he was consistently outmaneuvered by Treasury Secretary Alexander Hamilton on critical issues of policy and precedent. It was his frustration with Hamilton and Hamilton's growing influence over Washington that chased Jefferson from the cabinet and left him disillusioned about the direction of the young nation. In 1796, he was coaxed out of retirement to oppose John Adams for the presidency he was coaxed out of retirement to oppose John Adams for the presidency and lost, but thanks to a quirk in the Constitution, he became vice president (a situation that was later rectified by the Twelfth Amendment, which mandates that the president and vice president run as a ticket).

The vice presidency was a miserable time for Thomas Jefferson. He and Adams agreed on almost nothing, and, to make matters worse, the Federalists (Adams's party) controlled both houses of Congress. Jefferson was particularly galled by the passage of the Alien and Sedition Acts of 1798, a series of four laws that dramatically reduced civil liberties, including the ability to criticize the government. He viewed them as an affront to freedom and blatantly unconstitutional. He used the unpopular acts as a rallying point for the Democratic-Republican Party, which vehemently opposed the use of government power to restrict personal liberty. Evidently the country felt similarly, and in 1801 the Democrats took control of both Congress and the presidency with Jefferson's election. Years later he would refer to it as the "revolution of 1800," which he considered "as real a revolution in the principle of our government as that of 1776 was in its form; not effected indeed by the sword, as that, but by the rational and peaceable instrument of reform."[2]

Hyperbole? Perhaps a little. But it was the first time that the party in power had been replaced by the opposition, so in that sense it represented a "revolution in spirit" if not governance. And there's no denying that Jefferson and the Democrats viewed the Constitution, the role of the federal government, and the sanctity of personal liberty much differently than Adams, Hamilton, and the other Federalists. "The true theory of our Constitution is that the states are independent as to everything within themselves, and united as to everything respecting foreign nations," he wrote a fellow Democrat weeks before his inauguration—a notion that Hamilton and Adams would have rejected out of hand.[3]

As his swearing-in approached, there was real concern among Federalists that Jefferson would dismantle the federal government and possibly even call for a convention that would replace the Constitution with something resembling the old Articles of Confederation. One leading Federalist said he would not be surprised if it happened during the first term. Jefferson's inaugural address put some of the wilder conspiracies to rest—he wasn't about to scrap the Constitution—but it also left little doubt that he was embarking on a dramatically different path than his predecessors.[4] "The sum of good government," said Jefferson, was "a wise and frugal government, which shall restrain men from injuring one another, which shall leave them free to regulate their pursuits of industry and improvements, and shall not take from the mouth of labor the bread it has earned."[5]

What did that mean in practical terms? For starters, Jefferson was determined to end the government's deficit spending and eliminate the national debt, which had grown to $17 million over the preceding dozen years. Jefferson's old nemesis Hamilton was primarily responsible for the debt, which he considered a "national blessing" because, in his estimation, it strengthened the federal government, nationalized the economy, and spurred the need for government revenues. Jefferson saw it the other way: it dangerously centralized the government power, practically invited intrusive taxes and government corruption, and created an economy that favored manufacturing and industry over farming. As one historian put it, Jefferson considered the national debt America's "original sin" and made its elimination the focal point of his administration.

Jefferson's plan to tackle the debt was relatively simple: cut spending by reducing the number of federal jobs (which totaled only 130 when he took office); put the navy in dry dock and dramatically scale back the army; and curtail most internal improvements that could be otherwise managed by the states. Many Federalists, and even some moderate Democrat-Republicans, believed that Jefferson's single-mindedness about eliminating the debt was excessively severe, bordering on draconian. They were especially concerned about his dismantling of the navy. This, after all, was a function that the states could not pick up. Doing away with it, they argued with Jefferson, would stunt America's development and put it at the mercy of the European powers. It would turn out to be one of the worst decisions of his presidency.

Thomas Jefferson's election was a revolution in style as much as it was in substance. Jefferson deplored the pomp and pageantry that had steadily grown around the presidency and was determined to put an end to it; he was concerned that it bore too much resemblance to the monarchy and celebrated the primacy of the federal government and its power. Jefferson believed that simplicity of style would help diminish the importance of government and was more than happy to practice what he preached. He walked alone to his own inaugural and dressed in casual clothes instead of the military garb favored by Washington and Adams. He did away with the customary inaugural party afterward, opting to dine in the cafeteria of the boarding house he was staying at. At social events and state dinners at the White House, he went to great lengths—comically so, as one observer put it—"to inculcate upon the people his attachment to a republican simplicity of manners and his unwillingness to admit the smallest distinction, that may separate him from the mass of his fellow citizens."[6]

So why does all this matter? For the simple reason that Jefferson's political philosophy and approach to government serves as a necessary prism to understanding and appreciating his decision to acquire the Louisiana Territory. As biographer John Ellis put it, "Jefferson regarded his ascendance to power as a mandate to purge the American government of all the excess institutional baggage it had acquired since its pristine birth a quarter century earlier."[7] In light of this, purchasing a tract of land that doubled the size of the country, doing it in secret without consulting Congress, and then deciding not to go forward with a planned constitutional amendment for reasons of political expediency seems all the more remarkable.

Napoleon, Haiti, and the Mighty Mississippi

The territory of Louisiana was first settled by French explorers in 1682 and named after King Louis XIV. It remained a French colony until 1763, when they ceded the entire territory to Spain after their defeat in the French and Indian War.

As American frontiersmen continued to push farther and farther west across the Appalachian Mountains, the Mississippi River became an increasingly central artery for the transportation of goods back east and abroad. "The Hudson, the Delaware, the Potomac, and all the navigable rivers of the Atlantic, formed into one stream," is how Jefferson typically described the Mississippi.[8] Within short order, New Orleans had become one of the busiest ports in the hemisphere. By the end of the century, American merchants were shipping over a million dollars' worth of goods a year through the city, an enormous sum in those days. So vital had it become to settlers that in 1795 the United States and Spain entered into the treaty of San Lorenzo, which secured the southernmost border between the United States and Spanish Louisiana, provided Americans with navigation rights on the Mississippi River, and established a duty-free "right to deposit" goods at the port of New Orleans. The treaty was hailed as a diplomatic coup for the infant Republic and encouraged even more adventurers to head west.

French dictator Napoleon Bonaparte, who had come to power shortly before Jefferson took office, wanted desperately to reestablish the French empire in the Western Hemisphere. It began with retrocession of the Louisiana Territory back to France, which he forced from the Spanish government in 1800 in the secret treaty of San Ildefonso. Using the French colony in Haiti as a launching point, Napoleon's strategy was to surround the United States from the west and the south by controlling the Mississippi River, New Orleans, the Gulf of Mexico, the Caribbean Sea, and at some point Florida, which Spain was struggling to hold on to. It was a daring, if not brilliant plan, and if successful, would leave America hostage to his whims.

Like his predecessors, Thomas Jefferson could live with Spanish control of the Mississippi and New Orleans. Considered a second-rate power by most, their presence on the continent bothered few. But the return of the Louisiana Territory to France was a different matter entirely: living next door to the bumbling Spanish empire was one thing; having Napoleon as a neighbor was quite another.

As rumor of the retrocession made its way across the Atlantic, Thomas Jefferson became increasingly alarmed about the prospects of Napoleon controlling the Mississippi River. It was feared that should France take legal possession of New Orleans, it would give them the right to restrict access to the mighty river and the port, a potentially crippling prospect for the United States. "According to the law of nations," wrote the British foreign minister to the US ambassador in England, Rufus King, "in the event of the district of Louisiana being ceded to the French, that country would come into possession of its subject to all the engagements which appertained to it at the time of cession . . . and consequently, allege no colorable pretext for excluding His Majesty's subjects, of the citizens of the United States, from the navigation of the river Mississippi."[9]

Jefferson reluctantly agreed with that assessment. "There is on the globe one single spot, the possessor of which is our natural and habitual enemy," is how he described New Orleans. He knew that French possession of New Orleans would force the United States to ally itself with England, a prospect he found equally unappealing. "From the moment [the French take possession] we must marry ourselves to the British Fleet and nation," he wrote to Robert Livingston, the American ambassador in France. "This is not a state of things we seek or desire."[10]

It was at this point that Jefferson opened a back-channel communication with Napoleon through his old friend Pierre du Pont de Nemours, a French aristocrat and leading statesman. Jefferson wanted Napoleon to understand the grave consequences should he take possession of New Orleans—but without formally threatening war. He mischievously asked Du Pont to courier a letter, written in that vein, to Ambassador Livingston in Paris on the condition that he personally read, seal, and then hand deliver it to Livingston. He knew that Du Pont would relay the contents of the letter—and its thinly veiled threats—to Napoleon, which is exactly what happened. The message to Napoleon, however informal, was unmistakable: take possession of New Orleans at your own peril.[11]

How much did this back-channel threat influence Napoleon's decision to sell the territory? It's difficult to say. In the short run, it didn't seem to change much. In early 1802, Napoleon sent 25,000 soldiers to Haiti under the command of his brother-in-law, General Charles Leclerc. Their mission was to re-enslave the island's black population and then proceed to New Orleans, where they would take possession of the city.

It didn't work out that way. The fighting in Haiti was brutal, and Leclerc and his men were no match for the indigenous peoples, who fought vigorously to retain their freedom, or for the rampant malaria. By the early fall, the entire French contingent had been slaughtered or expelled, and with it French rule of the island had come to an ignominious and bloody end. "Damn sugar, damn *coffee*, damn *colonies*!" was Napoleon's only response.[12]

Around the same time that Leclerc was making his way to Haiti, Jefferson came up with the idea of buying New Orleans from Napoleon, which he floated past his friend Du Pont in a series of letters. Comparing

French possession of the city to an "embryo of a tornado that . . . will burst on the countries on both sides of the Atlantic," Jefferson prevailed upon Du Pont to take his offer to Napoleon or face "a war which will annihilate her [France]."[13] Du Pont agreed that it was a good idea, and practically handed Jefferson a roadmap for negotiating with his country. "France will ask you the highest she can," he wrote in the spring of 1802, "and you will offer the lowest you can. But offer enough," he coached Jefferson, "in order to incite her to make up her mind before taking of possession because the interest of the governors, of the prefects and of the commercial companies would become strong obstacles. These treaties," he prophetically warned, "must be concluded quickly: the more one bargains, the less one makes a good deal; the worst of all would be a break."[14]

And so the negotiations went back and forth for the next twelve months. So critical was keeping New Orleans out of Napoleon's hands that Jefferson made the unusual move of nudging Secretary of State James Madison out of the picture so that he could orchestrate the discussions directly. To help with this, Jefferson sent his protégé, James Monroe, to Paris to assist Ambassador Livingston with the complicated maneuverings. He wasn't convinced that Livingston was capable of handling the delicate situation on his own.

While Monroe was making the trip to France, the Spanish intendant (or ruler) of New Orleans decided, without warning, to close the port to US goods and products. It was a baffling move—nobody knew who had ordered it—with potentially devastating consequences for western settlers. Without the ability to deposit goods in New Orleans, the western economy would grind to a standstill. The Federalists in Congress demanded immediate war against Spain, but Jefferson resisted. He believed that Napoleon, not the Spanish government, was behind the order. He viewed it as a negotiating tactic—and a good one—meant to drive up the price for the city. With the Federalists screaming for war and Napoleon behaving erratically, Jefferson had little time to act. A deal would have to be struck quickly.[15]

Monroe was originally charged with purchasing New Orleans and Florida from the French, which Jefferson believed was part of the retrocession. Jefferson authorized him to pay as much as $9 million for the territories, an amount that would nearly double the debt that he hated so dearly. Still stinging from the crushing defeat in Haiti, and in desperate need of funds to crank up his war machine against England again, Napoleon hastily offered to sell the entire Louisiana Territory for $15 million. "Irresolution and deliberation are no longer in season," exclaimed Napoleon. "I renounce Louisiana. It is not only New Orleans that I cede; it is the whole colony, without reserve."[16]

The offer caught Livingston and Monroe by surprise. Though they didn't have the authorization to spend $15 million, and weren't even sure if the United States could raise it, they agreed to the terms anyway. It was simply too good a deal to pass up. "An acquisition of so great an extent was, we well know, not contemplated by our appointment," Livingston and Monroe wrote to Secretary of State Madison, "but we are persuaded that the circumstances and considerations which induced us to make it will justify us in the measure to our government and country."[17]

On May 2, 1803, a treaty was signed and the sale was complete. Napoleon gave the US government exactly six months to ratify the treaty and transfer the funds or the deal would be off. Thomas Jefferson had his work cut out for him.

"From this day the United States take their place among the powers of the first rank"

News of the treaty reached Washington on July 4, of all dates. It was universally hailed as a magnificent triumph for the president and the nation, save for a few cranky Federalists who refused to acknowledge the obvious. The *National Intelligence* newspaper rejoiced over Jefferson's triumph and boldly predicted that he would be the recipient of "the widespread joy of millions at an event which history will record among the most splendid in our annals."[18]

For the most part, he was. Jefferson's popularity skyrocketed as terms of the deal became known. Without jeopardizing a single American life, the United States had acquired roughly 828,000 square miles of land (565 million acres) for $15 million, or three cents per acre. The territory that doubled the size of the United States would come to include all or parts of fourteen future states. Robert Livingston may have captured the sentiment best: "From this day the United States take their place among the powers of the first rank," he prophetically remarked at the signing ceremony in Paris.[19]

While the rest of the nation celebrated the acquisition, Jefferson quietly fretted. The terms weren't the issue—he knew the price was a steal. And even though it piled on more debt (something he absolutely abhorred), and would mean deeper cuts in the Navy and other federal expenditures, Jefferson put those concerns aside, too. He instructed Treasury Secretary Albert Gallatin to retire the notes as quickly as possible so as to minimize interest payments over the life of the bonds.[20]

The more troubling aspect was a philosophical one: did the Constitution authorize the purchase of foreign lands, or would an amendment be required? There's no doubt how Hamilton, Adams, or the other Federalists would have answered that question (were they the ones to have acquired the territory, of course): unequivocally yes. Being the strict constitutionalist that he was, Jefferson saw it differently. It was anathema to his "pure Republicanism" beliefs to act outside the literal words of the Constitution for a matter of such importance. He had spent an entire career railing against this very behavior; it's what drove him from Washington's cabinet and later brought him out of retirement to oppose John Adams. He simply couldn't turn his back on everything he believed for sheer political expediency.

In dozens of correspondences with Gallatin, Madison, Livingston, and others, Jefferson reiterated his desire to amend the Constitution to sanction the deal. As early as January of 1803, while negotiations were still taking place, he expressed as much to Albert Gallatin, noting that it would be "safer not to permit the enlargement of the Union but by amendment of the Constitution." Gallatin assured him that "the United States as a nation has an inherent right to acquire territory" and that "the treaty-power is vested with a constitutional right to sanction the acquisition," but Jefferson wasn't buying it. [21]

To John Dickerson, an old friend and delegate at the constitutional convention, he wrote: "Our Confederation is certainly confined to the limits established by the revolution. The general government has no powers but such as the Constitution has given it; and it has not given it a power of holding foreign territory . . . an amendment of the Constitution seems necessary for this." He confessed to having acted "beyond the

Constitution" in a letter to Senator John Breckinridge of Kentucky, one of his closest allies. Jefferson felt so strongly about the need for an amendment that he drafted two proposed versions himself, which he gave to Attorney General Levi Lincoln for review. He asked Lincoln to keep the drafts to himself, observing "that the less that is said about any constitutional difficulty, the better."[22]

Jefferson's instincts were correct in one regard: if word got out that he was struggling over the need for a constitutional amendment, it could sink the whole deal. As the summer wore on, Napoleon began having second thoughts about honoring the treaty. Capricious and unpredictable, it wouldn't be out of character for him to void it on a whim, a sentiment that Robert Livingston echoed in a letter to Jefferson. "He appears to wish the thing undone," he cautioned the president.

It was the prospect of losing the acquisition, more than anything else, that convinced Jefferson to drop the notion of a constitutional amendment. With the Democrat-Republicans outnumbering the Federalists two to one in the Senate, he knew that the treaty would be easily ratified without the amendment. He reluctantly came to the conclusion that amending the Constitution was simply too impractical and would put the purchase at risk, though he clung to the belief that it was the right thing to do. In a long, thoughtful, soul-searching letter to his friend Senator Wilson Nicholas of Virginia, he lamented that an overly broad interpretation of the treaty power could easily reduce the Constitution to a "blank paper," but conceded that should "our friends think differently, certainly I shall acquiesce with satisfaction; confiding that the good sense of our country will correct the evil of construction when it shall produce ill effects."[23]

It bothered Jefferson that he didn't follow through with a constitutional amendment. On some level, he knew that it was a betrayal of his Republican beliefs for mere political gain. The "revolution of 1800" that had ushered him into power was about reducing the influence of the federal government, subordinating the chief executive to the legislative branch, and adhering strictly to the enumerated powers of the Constitution. The acquisition violated all those tenets and then some: it deepened the national debt, exerted the president's preeminence, and broadly interpreted the language of the Constitution. "What is practicable must often control what is pure theory," he confessed to a friend, "and the habits of the governed determine in a great degree what is practicable."[24]

Jefferson likely took comfort in the words of fellow revolutionary Thomas Paine, who wrote his friend just weeks before the Senate's ratification vote to reassure him of his decision. Paine reminded the president that the framers of the Constitution thought nothing about the acquisition of new territories. That silence, he believed, allowed for considerable flexibility in contemplating unforeseen circumstances such as the Louisiana Purchase. "The cession makes no alteration in the Constitution," Paine noted, "it only extends the principles over a larger territory, and this certainly is within the morality of the Constitution, and not contrary to, nor beyond, the expression of intention of any of its articles."[25]

* * *

Did Jefferson's decision to bypass a constitutional amendment in order to quickly ratify the treaty constitute a betrayal of his Republican principles? In some regards, it represented an evolution more than an abandonment, for it forced him to reexamine long-held beliefs that were mostly philosophical conjecture to that point. It could be argued that Jefferson rejected a strict construction of the Constitution—something he had advocated for since the day it was written—in order to find "permission" to ratify the treaty without an amendment. But in his mind, and in the view of many Democratic-Republicans, this broader interpretation was permissible because it occurred within the realm of foreign policy, where the president had unquestioned dominion. Had it been a purely domestic issue—one where Congress played the central role—there's little doubt that Jefferson would have remained true to his strict constructionalist approach. This was not the case. The Constitution was silent on land acquisition, but clear that the president had primary responsibility for conducting foreign relations. It was a subtle but important distinction for Jefferson.

Several years after leaving office, and with plenty of time on his hands to contemplate the more philosophical issues of his presidency, Thomas Jefferson offered what may be the clearest explanation for his decision to put policy ahead of principle. In response to a friend's query about whether it was ever permissible for office holders to assume authority "beyond the law," Jefferson admitted that in theory the question was easily answered but was "sometimes embarrassing in practice."

What he meant by that, he wrote, was that "a strict observance of the written law is *one* of high duties of a good citizen, but it is not *the highest*. The laws of necessity, or self preservation, of saving our country when in danger are of higher obligation." Jefferson wasn't speaking specifically of the Louisiana Purchase, but he might as well have been. "To lose our country by a scrupulous adherence to written law, would be to lose the law itself . . . thus absurdly sacrificing the end to the means." In the end, said Jefferson, the "*Salus Populi* [Latin for "let the welfare of the people be the supreme law"] was paramount over the written law."[26] When considered in that light, Jefferson's decision regarding the Louisiana Purchase makes perfect sense.

Chapter 3

ANDREW JACKSON REJECTS NULLIFICATION

Courtesy of the Library of Congress Prints and Photographs Division, Washington, DC.

If the sacred soil of Carolina should be polluted by the footsteps of an invader, or be stained with the blood of her citizens, shed in her defense, I trust in Almighty God that no son of hers . . . who has been nourished at her bosom . . . will be found raising a parricidal arm against our common mother.
—Governor Robert Y. Hayne of South Carolina

Please give my compliments to my friends in your State, and say to them, that if a single drop of blood shall be shed there in opposition to the laws of the United States, I will hang the first man I can lay my hand on engaged in such treasonable conduct, upon the first tree I can reach.
—Andrew Jackson

In the fall of 1832, the state of South Carolina passed an "Ordinance of Nullification" at a hastily convened convention of state lawmakers with the intent of nullifying—or making invalid—the federal tariffs on imported goods as outlined in the Tariff Act of

47

1832. The issue was not a new one: tariffs had been around for several decades and were the primary means of revenue generation for the federal government. Most of the Southern states—and in particular South Carolina—opposed the Tariff Act because, in their estimation, it had the effect of protecting Northern manufacturing interests at the expense of the Southern economy, which relied on raw materials from the North. The Southern congressional delegations had been fighting against tariffs for over a decade but were outmaneuvered at every turn by the Northern and Western factions. By 1832 the issue had reached a boiling point, and leaders in South Carolina decided the only recourse was to exercise their "right" to nullify the tariff altogether. It was a murky constitutional issue—lawmakers and scholars were divided over the legality of nullification—but one that could potentially have enormous implications for the Union. While lawmakers discussed and debated the issue, Andrew Jackson—a native of South Carolina and states' rights advocate—decided the matter for them.

* * *

The concept of nullification traces its roots back to the early years of the Republic and the presidency of John Adams. The central tenet of nullification theory held that the Constitution, in essence, was simply a "compact" among the sovereign states. Any powers not explicitly granted to the federal government belonged to the states, as provided by the Tenth Amendment. What this meant in practical terms, argued the nullifiers, is that the states had "veto power" (or the ability to nullify) any federal law or action that the states believed overstepped the federal government's limited authority.

Ironically, it was James Madison—the principal author of the Constitution—who first championed the idea in response to the Alien and Sedition Acts of 1798. Both Madison and Thomas Jefferson, who was serving as John Adams's vice president at the time, believed that the federal government had overstepped its authority in passing the Alien and Sedition Acts, a series of four laws that greatly restricted civil liberties, including the right to criticize the government. In response, the two men took to the pen, authoring the Virginia and Kentucky Resolutions, respectively, which held that the states—not the federal government—had the power to determine the constitutionality of a federal law. It's important to note, however, that this was prior to the Supreme Court's landmark decision, *Marbury v. Madison*, which in 1803 established that the

Supreme Court held the power of "judicial review"—or reviewing the constitutionality of federal laws. In their later years, both Madison and Jefferson would back away from the nullification views.

The Kentucky Resolution, which Jefferson authored, used the term *nullification*—a fact that would later be cited by Southern nullifiers and secessionists in the run-up to the Civil War.[1] His original draft of the resolution actually went further, citing secession as the logical remedy for nullification, but the passage was struck from the final version.[2] Both the Kentucky and Virginia legislatures passed the resolutions, though the concept didn't catch on with the other states. Nothing came of the controversy as the acts were repealed (and in some cases allowed to expire) by Jefferson when he became president a few years later. A potential crisis had passed.

Nonetheless, the advocates for nullification dusted off the language and logic in the Kentucky and Virginia Resolutions and used them as the cornerstone for their own case. If the authors of the Declaration of Independence and the Bill of Rights believed in nullification, then there must be something to it—or so they reasoned. Prior to taking office, Andrew Jackson's views on nullification were largely unknown. Most Southerners, and especially those from his native South Carolina, simply assumed that Jackson would be sympathetic to their plight. After all, he was born and raised in the South, considered Thomas Jefferson his political and philosophical role model, and had proudly championed states' rights issues in the past. It only stood to reason that Jackson would see the logic in nullification. As the nullifiers would come to learn, however, they had badly misjudged him.

Tariffs, Politics, and the South

Protective tariffs played a critical role in the financing of the federal government during the early years of the Republic. The second law passed by the first Congress of the United States, in fact, was a tariff designed to both raise revenues (to pay down the wartime debt) and protect fledgling US manufacturers from competing British goods. President Washington signed the tariff into law on July 4, 1789, and it was hailed by many as the "second American revolution."[3] In 1816 the tariff base was broadened and rates increased so as to protect American manufacturers from a glut of cheaply produced British goods that flooded the market following the end of the War of 1812. Like its predecessor, the Tariff of 1789, this tariff, too, received widespread support from all corners of the country, including Congressman John C. Calhoun of South Carolina. It would be the last time there was universal agreement on the subject.

The Tariff of 1824 was a different matter altogether. The brainchild of Speaker of the House Henry Clay, and supported by the leading nationalists of the day like John Quincy Adams and John Calhoun, the tariff was a complicated tapestry of sectional protections designed to insulate American business as well as raise revenue for internal improvements such as new and better roads, canals, bridges, and highways. Clay called these tariffs and improvements the "American System," and in many ways it was the embodiment of Alexander Hamilton's vision of a national economy of manufacturers, industrialists, and skilled tradesmen bound together by commerce and trade.

Not everyone saw it that way. Increasingly, leaders from the Southern states were beginning to view these tariffs as helpful to Northeastern manufacturing while harmful to Southern farming. And for the first time, the Southern faction couched their opposition in terms of the Constitution. Yes, the tariffs were harmful to the Southern way of life, they reasoned, but more importantly they were unconstitutional since the Constitution—in their estimation—only permitted tariffs, taxes, and imposts as a measure to raise revenue, not protect industries.

"I do not stop here," proclaimed Representative John Randolph of Virginia, one of the most vocal critics of the tariff, "to argue about the constitutionality of this bill; I consider the Constitution a dead letter; I consider it to consist, at this time, of the power of the General Government."[4] It was a myopic reading of the Constitution—one that ultimately failed—but foreshadowed future debates and events. The bill passed by a mere five votes in the House and even fewer in the Senate. Among the bill's fiercest opponents were two South Carolinians, Representative George McDuffie and Senator Robert Hayne, along with Randolph of Virginia—and by proxy the growing power of the federal government.[5]

Interestingly, while Southerners like Hayne and McDuffie were making the case against the tariff, Andrew Jackson, as a senator from

Tennessee, and John C. Calhoun, as secretary of war under President Monroe, were both supportive of the tariff, though not without some reservations. For reasons of political expediency, however, each went along with the measure—a decision both would come to regret.

The tariff was actually the second biggest development of 1824, the first being the disputed presidential election between John Quincy Adams and Andrew Jackson. Jackson actually bested Adams by ten percentage points in the popular vote and led in the Electoral College as well. The margin, however, fell short of a constitutionally required majority in the Electoral College, thanks to Henry Clay and William Crawford, who siphoned just enough votes to leave him shy of an outright victory. With that being the case, the decision was thrown to the House of Representatives (in accordance with the Twelfth Amendment), where Adams came out on top after receiving the support of Speaker Henry Clay, who detested Jackson.[6] Adams, in turn, appointed Clay as his secretary of state—which at the time was the most reliable stepping stone to the presidency—over the cries of foul play by Jackson and his supporters.[7] The presumed back-room deal between Adams and Clay so outraged Jackson's supporters—of which there were many—that it had the effect of virtually crippling Adams's presidency before it ever began. Sensing the opportunity for political gain, Jackson wisely positioned himself as something of a "president in exile." From that perch, he was given free rein to mount withering attacks against the "corrupt" Adams administration.

Jackson wasn't alone in his condemnation; the sinister deal also outraged Adams's own vice president, John C. Calhoun. Known for his principles and integrity, the corrupt bargain had left Calhoun bitter and critical of the president and his American System of tariffs and improvement (though as the sitting vice president, he was helpless to do anything about it publicly). The same wasn't true for his colleagues in South Carolina, and in 1825, the South Carolina legislature took the highly unusual step of condemning the Tariff of 1824 as unconstitutional on the grounds that "Congress does not possess the power under the Constitution to adopt a general system of internal improvement as a national measure . . . or to tax the citizen of one state to make roads and canals for the benefit of citizens of another state."[8] And while state officials didn't attempt to enforce their resolution, it signaled a new direction in the debate over tariffs—one that left John Calhoun uneasy and uncertain as to where to cast his lot.

It didn't take Calhoun long to sort the matter out. The vice president's sole remaining career ambition was to become president of the United States. His political instincts told him that he couldn't reach the summit without the unanimous and enthusiastic support of his home state. Calhoun had little choice but to disavow his nationalist policies and embrace sectional interests. Or as one historian described it, undergo a "breathtaking reinvention" of his political self.[9] It was only the beginning of his transformation from unionist to secessionist.

While Calhoun was undergoing his Road to Damascus conversion, Jackson resigned from the Senate in order to pursue his shadow administration contra Adams. As for his "platform," he made his displeasure over the "stolen" election of 1824 well known but offered little beyond that. On the subject of tariffs and the growing regional strife, Jackson said next to nothing for fear of alienating potential supporters and distracting from Adams's hemorrhaging presidency. He was simply biding his time for a chance to crush Adams in a rematch, and he wasn't about to let policy positions get in the way.

Calhoun, on the other hand, went public in a big way with his new-found antitariff position when he cast the tie-breaking vote in the Senate against a proposed tariff on wool in 1827.[10] By this time, conviction had all but given way to political expediency for Calhoun as Virginia, North Carolina, Georgia, and Alabama all passed resolutions that same year condemning the federal government's power to raise revenue through tariffs. Not to be outdone, lawmakers in South Carolina went even further than their Southern cohorts; it wasn't enough to simply rebuke the tariffs, or for that matter even declare them unconstitutional. On December 19, 1827, the state legislature passed a resolution declaring that the Constitution of the United States was nothing more than a mere *compact* between the "people of the different states with each other, as separate, independent sovereignties, and that for any violation of the letter or spirit of that compact by the Congress of the United States, it is not only the right of the people, but of the Legislature . . . to remonstrate against violations of the fundamental compact."[11] And with that, South Carolina had dramatically raised the stakes in the struggle over tariffs—

a fight that would push the Union to the brink of dissolution before it was said and done.

1828: The Year That Changed Everything

1828 is a year that stands out in American history. It's perhaps best remembered for Andrew Jackson's sweeping defeat of John Quincy Adams for the presidency, and rightfully so: Jackson's victory would mark a leap forward in the evolution and power of the office. But two other events—the "Tariff of Abominations" and the *South Carolina Exposition and Protest on the Subject of the Tariff*—played equally important roles in instigating an eventual showdown between Jackson and South Carolina.

Jackson's defeat of Adams was as close to a sure thing as existed in early American politics. Adams was horribly ineffective as president, and Jackson smartly avoided taking policy positions during the intervening four years, choosing instead to play victim of the "stolen" election of 1824. It came as little surprise when Jackson routed Adams; he won by 13 percentage points in the popular vote and swept most of the Electoral College, save New England.[12] With Jackson's victory also came a split in the reigning political party of the day. The Democratic-Republicans (of which Jackson and Adams were both members) morphed into the Democratic Party (headed by Jackson), while Adams and Henry Clay formed a new party, the Whigs, from the remnants of the Federalist Party. John C. Calhoun made the unusual move of bolting Adams's ticket to become Andrew Jackson's vice president—the last person to serve as vice president for two different administrations. The ever-opportunistic Calhoun knew that the winds of change favored Jackson, and his gut told him that the fastest route to the presidency was as Jackson's vice president. Time would prove him wrong.

It wasn't the only miscalculation that Calhoun would make in 1828. By this time, he was thoroughly and publicly antitariff, though his views on nullification weren't nearly as radical as those of his South Carolina brethren. Early in 1828 Congress began debating yet another increase to the existing tariff laws as cheap European goods continued to flood the market. Not wanting to disturb Jackson's broad coalition of support, yet desperate to kill any new tariffs in order to please his Southern base, Calhoun hatched an ingenious plan, or so he believed. He convinced his Southern colleagues in Congress not to oppose the bill outright, but rather lard it up with excessively high duties on the raw materials essential to Northern manufacturers so as to make it distasteful to them. This way, the northern members would reject the bill altogether, and with it own the blame for its defeat. Calhoun had all the angles figured except for one: a sizeable number of Northern senators and congressmen actually voted in favor of the tariffs in an effort to appeal to national unity. Despite fierce Southern opposition, the bill narrowly made it through Congress and a somewhat reluctant John Quincy Adams signed it into law. And so was born the "Tariff of Abominations," a series of broad-based tariffs that mostly protected Western and Northern industries while reducing overseas demand for Southern cotton (because it left British merchants with less money to purchase Southern goods since they couldn't sell as much material to the United States).[13]

Calhoun's plan had backfired, and the South was more enraged than ever over the punishing tariffs; it meant that trade with British merchants—whom Southern farmers depended on to purchase their cotton—would slow to a trickle now that the cost of entering the market had become exorbitantly high for foreigners.

With no other avenue of recourse remaining, state lawmakers in South Carolina borrowed a page from history and commissioned John Calhoun to write a formal document of protestation to be presented to the United States Senate for the following session. Like Thomas Jefferson three decades before him, the sitting vice president kept his authorship a secret for fear of alienating himself from the political establishment. He spent the summer of 1828 sequestered at his Fort Hill estate in South Carolina penning the *South Carolina Exposition*, which, after his authorship was revealed in 1832, would become known as "Calhoun's Exposition."

The document was startling for its tortured reading of the Constitution. The thrust of it held that protective tariffs violated the Constitution; that the states, not the federal government, reserved the right to determine the constitutionality of federal laws; that if a state declared a law unconstitutional it did not have to abide by it; and the proper remedy for the federal government was to amend the Constitution in order to make the "unconstitutional law" valid. And even then, Calhoun asserted, the state would still have the right to secede from the Union if it disagreed with the amended Constitution. "It would seem impossible to deny to the States the right of deciding on the infractions of their powers, and the proper remedy to be applied for their correction," Calhoun reasoned. "The right of judging, in such cases, is an essential attribute of sovereignty, of which the States cannot be divested without losing their sovereignty itself."[14]

The South Carolina legislature didn't act on the *Exposition*—that wasn't the purpose of it. Instead, they printed and distributed five thousand copies to political leaders throughout the country with the hope of gaining allies and seeding foment. In January of 1829, just months before Andrew Jackson's swearing in as president, the *Exposition* was formally presented to Congress by Senator William Smith of South Carolina, a radical secessionist. It was met with scant attention—the country was preoccupied with the upcoming inauguration—but it didn't go unnoticed by the president-elect. The nullifiers would revisit the document two years later.

"Our Union—it must be preserved."

A crowd of twenty thousand people converged on Washington, DC, to witness Andrew Jackson's oath of office in March of 1829. At the time, it was the largest gathering ever in the capital city. Jackson was a man of action more than words, and his inaugural address—one of the shortest in history—had little by way of soaring rhetoric or memorable flourishes. When it came to the combustible subject of tariffs, Jackson continued his practice of revealing almost nothing. "It would seem to me that the spirit of equity, caution, and compromise in which the Constitution was formed," he said plaintively, "requires that the great interests of agriculture, commerce, and manufactures should be equally favored, and that perhaps the only exception to this rule should consist in the peculiar encouragement of any products of either of them that may be found essential to our national independence." Nobody quite knew what it meant.[15]

Jackson managed to skirt the tariff debate for the entire legislative session of 1829 but decided to confront it in his Statement to Congress (what would now be considered the State of the Union address) in December of that year. It was his most pronounced recitation on the subject to date, and was motivated partly by a desire to lower tariffs in the upcoming Congress, something he hoped would appease Southern agitators and defuse the issue. But it was more than just political calculation at work. He felt strongly about the need to both preserve states' rights—he *was* a Southerner after all—as well as maintain the sanctity and preeminence of the Union. And he desperately wanted to do so *without* forcing a confrontation—an uncommon instinct for the normally volatile Jackson.

Jackson sympathized with the plight of the nullifiers and states' rights advocates, noting that "the great mass of legislation relating to our internal affairs was intended to be left where the Federal Convention found it—in the State governments." He went on to say that "nothing is clearer, in my view, than that we are chiefly indebted for the success of the Constitution under which we are now acting to the watchful and auxiliary operation of the State authorities. This is not the reflection of a day, but belongs to the most deeply rooted convictions of my mind." He concluded the sentiment with a stark admonition for his Unionist friends: "I cannot, therefore, too strongly or too earnestly, for my own sense of its importance, warn you against all encroachments upon the legitimate sphere of State sovereignty."

But Jackson didn't cast his lot entirely with the states' righters. He saved the most rousing passage for the cause of national unity, pleading that sectional difference be set aside for the good of the country. "In deliberating, therefore, on these interesting subjects [tariffs] local feelings and prejudices should be merged in the patriotic determination to promote the great interests of the whole. All attempts to connect them with the party conflicts of the day are necessarily injurious, and should be discountenanced . . . discarding all calculations of political ascendancy, the North, the South, the East, and the West should unite in diminishing any burthen of which either may justly complain."[16]

While both sides seemed comforted by Jackson's language, even his closest aides weren't entirely sure where he would land on the issue should it come to confrontation. Just weeks after his address to Congress, a heated debate broke out on the Senate floor—one of the most memorable in that body's history—between Robert Hayne of South Carolina and Daniel Webster of Massachusetts over the issue of nullification.[17] The thrust of Hayne's argument: the states, having predated the federal government, were the true repository and guardian of liberty, and as such had the intrinsic right to nullify any law or even secede from the Union. "As to the doctrine that the federal government is the exclusive judge of the extent as well as the limitations of its powers, it seems to me to be utterly subversive of the sovereignty and independence of the states," he concluded after two days of sparring with Webster. Responded Webster: "Sir, I do not desire to enlarge the powers of the government . . . but when it is believed that a power does exist, then it is, in my judgment, to be exercised for the general benefit of the whole."[18]

When Jackson inquired with a confidant about Webster's performance, the response was that "I'm afraid he's demolishing our friend Hayne." Replied Jackson: "I expected it."[19]

The debate between Hayne and Webster had gotten under Jackson's skin. In his mind, Hayne had gone too far—way too far. It was one thing to advocate for states' rights and limited federal government. That was well and good. Jackson, in fact, still considered himself a proponent of state sovereignty—as evidenced by his speech before Congress—and he had little reservation about vetoing expenditures that he believed served no national interest. It was something entirely different, however, to claim that states had the authority to unilaterally invalidate a federal law simply because they disagreed with it, or worse yet, to summarily pull out of the Union over something as fixable as tariffs. Jackson considered this distorted reading of the Constitution a treasonous assault on the Union and a recipe for anarchy. He could no longer stomach listening to it— politics be damned. At the end of the day, it was the vehemence and subversiveness of Hayne's position—there seemed to be no ameliorating the nullifier crowd—which convinced Jackson that confrontation might be the only resolution.[20]

Whatever confusion existed as to Jackson's true feelings on the subject were soon put to rest at the Democratic-Republican's annual Thomas Jefferson birthday celebration, which honored the founder of their party, who had recently passed away. The gala was the one night a year when party leaders came together for drink, food, and good company, and was usually capped with a series of rousing toasts from stalwarts. Fired up from the Hayne-Webster debate, Jackson thought it the perfect opportunity to let Hayne, Calhoun, and the other nullifiers know exactly how he felt. Why not shoot one across their bow at the social event of the season, he told nervous aides.

Hayne was the first to toast and predictably praised the states: "The Union of the States, and the sovereignty of the States." Jackson squirmed in his seat. He found Hayne's words revolting and abhorrent. When it was his turn, the president rose slowly and deliberately and glared at Calhoun. "Our Union—it must be preserved." A buzz enveloped the room as groans were heard from the Southerners. The battle had been joined. Calhoun returned volley: "The Union—next to our liberty the most dear."[21]

The evening settled little but revealed everything. Jackson had made unequivocal his intention to honor the Union before all else, and Calhoun dropped any remaining pretense about his allegiance to South Carolina. It was an irreparable breach between the president and vice president, and in some ways liberating to both men. Battle lines had been drawn. A showdown was becoming inevitable.

The Calm before the Storm

Andrew Jackson had a delicate problem. On the one hand, he was repulsed by nullification theory and everything it represented, and was growing more disillusioned by the day with its leading advocates, most notably John Calhoun and Robert Hayne. It was impossible to trust someone like Calhoun, he lamented, "an unprincipled man who would rather rule hell than subordinate in heaven."[22] Jackson believed with all his soul in the sanctity of the Union. On this issue, there simply could be no compromise. But he understood that a political solution was infinitely more desirable than a military one. For this to happen, there would need to be a bold reformation of the tariff laws; South Carolina had gone too far down the path of nullification to change course without a face-saving concession. He had to offer an olive branch without appearing to bend on principle.

His plan was a simple one: reduce the rates on the tariffs in question to 1824 levels, which would have the effect of undercutting the nullifiers' argument and isolating South Carolina from the rest of the South. If the nullifiers' thrust was that the constitutional process was inherently flawed because it failed to protect minority interests, then the act of sweeping tariff reform would reduce their theory to rubble since it did just that. And if they ignored the reduction and continued down that path anyway, they would go it alone because surely no other state would join such a reckless venture. "This will annihilate the nullifiers," he wrote Martin Van Buren of his plan, "as they will be left without any pretext of Complaint. And, if they attempt disunion, it must be because they wish it."[23]

For this to work, however, Jackson couldn't allow himself to be goaded into an impulsive or hasty military response to South Carolina's growing belligerence. To do so might offend states' rights advocates everywhere, especially those in his own party. Though the vast majority of people opposed nullification, they were equally uncomfortable with the notion of military force to suppress political discourse. In the minds of many patriots, there was a fine line between enforcing federal law and practicing tyranny. Jackson wanted to keep his distance from the latter.

The nullifiers knew this, too. Throughout the summer and fall of 1831, they continued to ramp up the rhetoric and act in defiance of the law with the intent of drawing a military response from the president. At the urging of the state leaders, two Charleston merchants refused to pay the government's tariff on commodities they had imported—perhaps it would incite a rash response from the administration. To his credit, Jackson didn't take the bait, choosing instead to order the US attorney to prosecute the men. Being a nullifier, the man refused and resigned. Jackson's instinct was to "impeach him for neglect of duty,"[24] but he thought better against it. He simply appointed a new attorney and had him prosecute the merchants, and later admonished Robert Hayne for taking his state down the path of "revolution with all its attendant evils."[25]

Later that summer, Calhoun made his most dramatic public statement to date on nullification with an opus that came to be known as the Fort Hill address. In it, he boldly declared that the practice of nullification was the only thing that could *keep* the Union together. As such, it was

high time that South Carolina—and all the other states for that matter—
began enforcing it. Until it was actually implemented, he correctly reasoned, the issue would not be resolved. It was up to the states to determine how best to "exercise this high power."[26]

Calhoun's Fort Hill address was a well-written, measured, and
somewhat persuasive document. To Jackson's chagrin, it found pockets
of sympathy outside of South Carolina and even outside the South. One
thing the president had counted on throughout the nullification conflict was the support of the people. He firmly believed that they didn't
want to see the Union held hostage by a single state, or worse, disbanded. With the Fort Hill address, he feared that Calhoun's eloquence
and passion could begin to win some converts, and he wasn't about to
let that happen. Jackson used his annual message to Congress to propose a deep reduction in the tariff; his hope was that it would blunt any
momentum the nullifiers had gained and put the matter to rest for
good.[27] Should they reject it, he told Martin Van Buren, it would be
unassailable evidence that they had been "indulging in their vitupera-
tions against the Tariff for the purpose of covertly accomplishing their
ends . . .disunion."[28]

"The eyes of all nations are fixed on our Republic"

Compromise and isolation were critical to Jackson's plan, which he set in
motion in the spring of 1832 with his tariff reform bill. It was met with
lukewarm support in Congress, but after some tinkering and horse-
trading, it passed the House and Senate by a comfortable margin.
Jackson didn't think it went far enough in lowering the objectionable tariffs, but believed the reductions in duties on imported coarse woolens,
blankets, sugar, and cotton products would be enough to mollify the nullifiers.[29] "You may expect to hear from South Carolina a great noise
stirred up by Calhoun and company," he wrote a friend shortly after
signing the bill, "but the good sense of the people will put it down."[30]

Jackson couldn't have been more wrong. Instead of defusing the
issue, the Tariff of 1832 seemed to fuel the nullifiers' rage. The *Charleston
Mercury*, the leading antitariff newspaper, complained that the "system
has been rendered more unequal and oppressive."[31] John Calhoun dis-

missed it entirely, noting that it would be impossible, and hypocritical, to endorse the nominal reductions after a decade of railing against the very principle. "The question is no longer one of free trade, but of liberty and despotism," he wrote a friend. After sitting through months of Senate debate, and watching the South come up short again, Calhoun was more convinced than ever that nullification—and perhaps secession—was the only acceptable solution. "The hope of the country," he warned ominously, "now rests on our gallant little state. Let every Carolinian do his duty."[32]

The reaction was not lost on Jackson. He was hoping that the people of South Carolina would "see that all their grievances [have been] removed, and oppression only exists in the distempered brains of disappointed ambitious men." He soon came to realize that wouldn't be the case.[33] Throughout the late summer and early fall, Jackson received a steady stream of dispatches from Unionists in South Carolina detailing the growing hostility and military posturing among the nullifiers. The American flag was seen flying upside down throughout the state on public buildings and steamboats, a provocative act of defiance. Meanwhile, a red flag with a black lone star became the ensign of volunteer regiments of nullifiers, which they proudly flew during drills. By all outward appearance, South Carolina was preparing for war, a fact that was confirmed by newly elected Governor Robert Hayne's appointment of a military aide-de-camp, who was "charged with the duty of raising, inspecting, and granting commissions to volunteer companies."[34] General Winfield Scott, the man in charge of the Union's military preparations, predicted that "blood would be shed and that he did not believe anything could prevent it."[35] Things did not look good.

If there was any doubt about the nullifiers' intentions, it was put to rest in November when the South Carolina state legislature passed an ordinance nullifying the Tariff Acts of 1828 and 1832. For the first time in the nation's history, a state made it illegal for its residents to obey a federal law—in this case, the collection of federal duties on South Carolina soil. The ordinance wouldn't take effect until February 1 of the following year, a proviso meant to give Jackson time to ponder his next move. It also stipulated that should Congress authorize the president to use force, it would be viewed as "inconsistent with the longer continuance of South Carolina in the Union."[36]

This was the point of no return for Andrew Jackson. For four years he had acted cautiously, judiciously, and mostly without prejudice to the parties involved. He had sought compromise, refrained from snap decisions, and assiduously avoided the hint of military aggression. He understood as well as anyone the delicate balance between majority rule and states' rights and used that knowledge to guide his decision making. As one historian put it, Jackson had come to embody statesmanship as the crisis dragged on.[37]

As far as Jackson was concerned, the ordinance was an act of war, and would be treated as such. He hoped that bloodshed could be avoided, but was preparing for the worst. He sent several undercover agents—spies essentially—to South Carolina to get a lay of the land. Could they count on any Union sympathizers? What type of troop strength and armaments did South Carolina have? What was the shape of the federal forts? Were there any traitors in the federal custom houses? The message back was that the federal forts were in poor shape, morale among the Unionists was shaky, and the custom houses were teeming with nullifiers.[38]

By this time, the old general and war hero in Jackson had kicked in. He directed Lewis Cass, the secretary of war, to gird for battle. "We must be prepared to act with promptness and crush the monster in its cradle before it matures to manhood," he counseled. When it came to troop movement and artillery deployment, Jackson gave specific instructions. "We will want three divisions of artillery, each composed of nines, twelves, and eighteen pounders, one for the east, one for the west, and one for the center divisions."[39] He insisted that the troops be ready to move within four days of receiving his order. No detail was too small for his attention.

Jackson hadn't given up on a peaceful solution; he was planning to introduce further tariff reductions when Congress reconvened in January. He knew from experience, however, that the most effective way to negotiate was from a position of strength. Mobilizing the troops sent an unmistakable signal to the nullifiers: You will be met with overwhelming force should the nullification ordinance be enforced.

To underscore that point, on December 11 Andrew Jackson issued his "Nullification Proclamation," an eight-thousand-word rebuttal to South Carolina's Nullification Ordinance. It was a masterful document—an intellectual tour de force—that combined soaring rhetoric with brute force and stark admonitions to devastating effect. In spots it was paternal: "let me use the influence that a father would over his children whom he saw rushing to certain ruin"; and cutting: "you are deluded by men who are either deceived themselves or wish to deceive you . . . to the brink of insurrection and treason"; and breathtaking: "I consider, then, the power to annul a law of the United States, assumed by one State, *incompatible with the existence of the Union, contradicted expressly by the letter of the Constitution, unauthorized by its spirit, inconsistent with every principle on which it was founded, and destructive of the great object for which it was formed.*"[40]

Jackson issued the Nullification Proclamation, in part, to stir up nationalist fervor and rally the public around the flag. Should it come to military intervention, the support of the people would be critical. On that score, the proclamation was more than equal to the task. It was met with acclaim and praise from all corners of the country, including the antitariff press. Cities erupted in spontaneous displays of unionism. Constitutional scholars and lawmakers declared it the most comprehensive and eloquent dissertation on the perpetual nature of the Union. Even some Southern towns commended Jackson for his firmness and dedication to holding the Republic together. In many ways, the proclamation marked Jackson's finest hour of the crisis and arguably his entire presidency. Wrote a leading biographer: "It is one of the most significant presidential documents in American history and has been frequently compared to Lincoln's inaugural address."[41]

With momentum on his side, Jackson quickly followed up with yet another tariff bill, one that dramatically lowered rates. It was a magnanimous gesture toward the nullifiers, a peace offering of sorts. In light of this pending legislation, the South Carolina state legislature temporarily suspended the February 1 nullification date as Congress debated the specifics. With the olive branch, however, also came a stick. Coupled with the tariff bill, Jackson sought congressional authorization to use military force in the event that South Carolina enforced its nullification ordinance. It was arguably unnecessary—the president probably had the power to unilaterally send in the troops to enforce the law—but Jackson understood the importance of political consensus for such a drastic step.

It was a brilliant tactical move that left the nullifiers with few options. With nationalism sweeping the country, tariff reform winding through Congress, and the president closing in on the sanctioning of force, the writing was on the wall for the nullifiers. They could either accept tariff reform and rescind nullification, or enforce it and incur the wrath of the Union. It was really no choice at all. On March 1, 1833, Congress passed both tariff reform and the Force Bill by wide margins; the following day the president signed both into law. To the nation's great relief, John Calhoun and his cohorts went along with it. Not long after, the South Carolina state legislature followed suit and rescinded the Nullification Ordinance.

After nearly a decade of debate, years of mounting tension, and months on the brink, disaster had been avoided. And Andrew Jackson was almost solely responsible. Congress played a role in the final compromise, and key confidants provided valuable counsel. But in the end, it was Jackson's astute leadership—the decisiveness, sense of purpose, ability to rouse the nation—that made the difference. He shouldered the burden adroitly and with clarity, never wavering from a single, simple truth: the Union was perpetual—it couldn't be dissolved. The Constitution reserved certain rights to the sovereign states, but that did not include the power to secede from the Union.

Jackson had come to understand that, in some respects, the United States was more than just a people, a nation. It was an idea, an experiment, a source of inspiration—and he took seriously his job to protect it. "The eyes of all nations are fixed on our Republic," he closed his second inaugural speech. "The event of the existing crisis will be decisive in the opinion of mankind of the practicability of our federal system of government. Great is the stake placed in our hands; great is the responsibility which must rest upon the people of the United States. Let us realize the importance of the attitude in which we stand before the world." Words that would guide another president some three decades later.[42]

* * *

The question is often asked: How would other presidents have handled the nullification crisis? Would they have been as decisive as Jackson? Unrelentingly "on message"? As committed to keeping the Union together?

Obviously, there is no way of knowing for sure. It's safe to say that Washington would have behaved similarly, just as he did during the

Whiskey Rebellion. There are many parallels, in fact, between the ways in which the two handled their respective insurrections. Both moved cautiously at first, preferring compromise and conciliation over hasty responses and military posturing. Each understood the delicate balance between federalism and states' rights and considered force an option of last resort. But they were also believers in the concept of "negotiation through strength," and didn't hesitate to flash the stick when necessary.

Jefferson and Madison may have approached it differently. It's hard to imagine that either would have been as forceful or single-minded in articulating and defending the notion of the "perpetual Union" as Jackson had. We know from the Kentucky and Virginia Resolutions that both men believed there was something to the idea of nullification. To be fair, they had come to recant—at least partially—their point of view on the topic years later. Even so, the notion of sending troops to enforce a polarizing federal law would have been difficult for them to swallow.

To borrow a cliché, Jackson was the right man at the right time to meet the challenge. Though philosophically he agreed with Jefferson and Madison on the issue of states' rights and limited government, it was tempered by his real-life experience as a warrior general who had gladly and successfully done battle for the Union to protect its interests and expand its territories. He may have been a Jeffersonian Democratic-Republican, but he was a Unionist first. And because of it, he had no reservations about expanding the power of the presidency and infringing on a state's will if it meant furthering the cause of unionism.

Jackson also had the perfect skills for the crisis, if not the demeanor. He was ruthlessly consistent with his rationale: the Union was formed by the people, not the states, and therefore could only be disbanded by the people through a Constitutional Convention, the way it was formed. He understood the importance of public support and was adept at rousing patriotism through his words and deeds. He wasn't afraid to be forceful when necessary, yet he tempered his natural impulsiveness because he knew it wouldn't serve him well. And he had the capacity to grow and learn, something that can't be said for every holder of the office.

In the end, Jackson did not prevent a civil war. He simply delayed it. He bought the country three more decades to peacefully reconcile the sticky issues of state sovereignty, slavery, and moral law—something it could not do. Some historians have speculated that South Carolina's reaction to the Tariff Acts of 1828 and 1832 was more about building a first line of defense for slavery than repealing the tariffs. There's probably something to that. Much of the intellectual framework for the South's defense of slavery was born during the nullification crisis. In a way, South Carolina had put the nation on notice: go after slavery, and it will be much worse than nullification. True enough.

Chapter 4

LINCOLN SIGNS THE EMANCIPATION PROCLAMATION

Courtesy of the Library of Congress Prints and Photographs Division, Washington, DC.

We think you are strangely and disastrously remiss in the discharge of your official and imperative duty with regard to the emancipating provisions of the new Confiscation Act. Those provisions were designed to fight Slavery with Liberty. They prescribe that men loyal to the Union, and willing to shed their blood in her behalf, shall no longer be held, with the Nation's consent, in bondage to persistent, malignant traitors, who for twenty years have been plotting and for sixteen months have been fighting to divide and destroy our country. Why these traitors should be treated with tenderness by you, to the prejudice of the dearest rights of loyal men, we cannot conceive.

—August 19, 1862, open letter from Horace Greeley,
publisher of the *New York Tribune*, to Lincoln

My paramount object in this struggle is to save the Union, and is not either to save or to destroy slavery. If I could save the Union without freeing any slave I would do it, and if I could save it by freeing all the slaves I would do it; and if I could save it by freeing some and leaving others alone I would also do that. What I do about slavery, and the colored race, I do because I

believe it helps to save the Union; and what I forbear, I forbear because I do not believe it would help to save the Union. I shall do less whenever I shall believe what I am doing hurts the cause, and I shall do more whenever I shall believe doing more will help the cause.
—Lincoln's public response to Greeley's open letter, August 22, 1862

And upon this act, sincerely believed to be an act of justice, warranted by the Constitution, upon military necessity, I invoke the considerate judgment of mankind, and the gracious favor of Almighty God.
—Emancipation Proclamation, January 1, 1863

On January 1, 1863, Abraham Lincoln signed an executive order which declared that all the slaves residing in the Confederate states were "forever free." Dubbed the Emancipation Proclamation, it was a bold and risky step for the embattled president, but a much-needed one. The war had been going badly for the North. The Confederate army was consistently outmaneuvering the Union army; Lincoln had become a highly polarizing and unpopular figure; and the outcome remained very much in doubt. Up to that point, Lincoln had been opposed to the idea of making the war a fight over slavery. In his mind, the struggle was about one thing only: preserving the Union. He had repeatedly rejected pleas from radical Republicans and abolitionists to recast it as a crusade for freedom because he believed he lacked the constitutional authority to free the slaves. He was also concerned about alienating the border states and possibly driving them into the Confederacy. But during the summer of 1862 Lincoln began to question his position. Desperate to alter the trajectory of the war, it became clear to him that emancipation was the best—and riskiest—option to turn the tide. With the stroke of the pen he freed more human beings than in all recorded history and committed the defining act of his or any presidency.

* * *

Slavery has been described as America's "original sin," an evil so thoroughly monstrous and abhorrent as to cast a permanent stain on the nation's soul. For the first nine decades of the United States' existence, it was the single dominant issue facing the country. Still, it wasn't much viewed a moral issue—very few thought about it as a transcendent evil—as it was a political one: Did it give unfair economic advantage to the South? Should it be expanded to the Western territories and how so? How should the law deal with runaways? and so on. While other issues came and went, slavery never strayed too far from the political discourse. It hung ominously over the nation like the sword of Damocles, threatening to slice America in half at a moment's notice.

It was an issue so complicated that few had the political or moral will to tackle it. The ethical considerations were largely cast aside save the most fanatical abolitionists, though it steadily grew in importance over time. There were all sorts of legal and constitutional uncertainties around the power to curb its expansion or eliminate it outright, which just added to the confusion. But perhaps the most intractable dimension was the economic and cultural one. Slavery *was* the driver of the Southern economy. It had helped fuel the nation's rapid economic growth, and after two centuries, had become a way of life in the Southern states. Very few slave owners were prepared to give it up. Proslavery politicians and business leaders considered its protection and continuation their single biggest priority; it shaped almost every decision of theirs. And it wasn't confined to just the South and West. Delaware and Maryland practiced legalized slavery, which would later prove enormously problematic to Lincoln during the Civil War.

The Founding Fathers found slavery just as vexing as their successors would, if not more so. Many of the great men who helped give birth to the nation, while slaveholders themselves, lamented its existence and knew, on some level, that its evil would be a blight on the cause of liberty for generations to come. "It is much to be wished that slavery may be abolished," wrote John Jay, for "the honour of the States, as well as justice and humanity, in my opinion, loudly call upon them to emancipate these unhappy people. To contend for our own liberty, and to deny that blessing to others, involves an inconsistency not to be excused."[1] Ben Franklin called it "an atrocious debasement of human nature, that its very extirpation, if not performed with solicitous care, may sometimes open a source of serious evils."[2] Virginian Patrick Henry, best remembered for his "give me liberty or give me death" speech, expressed hope as early as 1773 that slavery would someday be abolished. "I believe a time will come when an opportunity will be offered to abolish this lamentable evil. Everything we do is to improve it, if it happens in our day; if not, let us transmit to our descendants, together with our slaves, a pity for their unhappy lot and an abhorrence of slavery."[3] Even George Washington, who owned nearly three hundred slaves and was the largest landowner in the country, confessed his despair over slavery in a private correspondence to Marquis de Lafayette: "Your late purchase of an estate in the colony of Cayenne, with a view to emancipating the slaves on it, is a generous and noble proof of your humanity. Would to God a like spirit would diffuse itself generally into the minds of the people of this country; but I despair of seeing it."[4]

Be that as it was, the vast majority of men who gathered in Philadelphia during the summer of 1787 were more concerned about creating an enduring Constitution and Union than abolishing slavery. Noble sentiment and moral clarity gave way to political expedience and compromise with little discussion. On the issue of the proportional representation, slaves—or "other persons" as the Constitution euphemistically refers to them—were to be considered three-fifths of a white person for the purpose of the census. The Fugitive-Slave Clause of Article 4, Section 2, mandated that slaves who made their way to a free state or territory were to be returned to their master nonetheless. And the slave trade, which almost everyone except a few delegates from the South considered a breathtaking abomination, could not legally be abolished—per a clause in the new Constitution—until January 1, 1808.[5]

In essence, the Founding Fathers deferred to future generations a problem they could not themselves resolve (the start of a time-honored tradition in American politics, as it turned out). They may have genuinely believed that the issue of slavery would become less tractable over time, but the opposite turned out to be true. As each new state joined the Union, the slavery debate would resurface—only with more virulence. With tension mounting between the regional factions, Congress passed the so-called Missouri Compromise of 1820, which paired Missouri's entrance as a slave state with Maine's admittance as a free state, and banned slavery from extending north of the 36° 30' parallel. It was a temporary truce that pleased neither the abolitionists nor the advocates of slavery, but it was important in one regard: for the first time Congress had prohibited slavery in a new territory.[6] Writing to Maine senator John Holmes, Thomas Jefferson prophetically warned that the compromise was "a reprieve only, not a final sentence; a geographical line, coinciding with a marked principle, moral and political, once conceived and held up to the angry passions of men, will never be obliterated; and every new irritation will mark it deeper and deeper."[7]

Over the ensuing three decades, as settlers pushed farther west and more states were admitted to the Union, factional and geographic strife worsened, and the abolitionist and proslavery positions hardened. Congress narrowly averted civil war in 1850 with a complicated, patchwork-style compromise between free and slave states that provided just enough concessions for both sides to keep the Union together by a thread. Just four years later, however, this same Congress practically sowed the seeds of war with the passage of the controversial Kansas-Nebraska Act. Authored by Illinois senator Stephen Douglas, the highly polarizing law overturned the 1820 and 1850 compromises by declaring that only the territories and states themselves—*not* the federal government—could determine if they were to be free or slave. Douglas argued that it was done in the noble tradition of popular sovereignty, but Northerners cried foul over what they considered a huge concession to the South. Almost overnight, opposition coalesced to give birth to the Republican Party, whose raison d'être was to prevent the expansion of slavery into new states and territories, beginning with Kansas.

The Republican Party and the abolitionist cause were dealt an enormous setback in 1857 with the infamous *Dred Scott* Supreme Court case, widely considered the greatest miscarriage of justice in that body's history. The court ruled that black Americans (free and slave) were not citizens and therefore not afforded the protections of the Constitution. It further held that the Missouri Compromise of 1820 was unconstitutional because it violated the Fifth Amendment's due process provision against the deprivation of property. The court, in effect, had twisted the meaning of the Fifth Amendment in order to find constitutional protection for slaveholders against the taking of their property (in this case, slaves). In practical terms, it meant that Congress could no longer prohibit the expansion of slavery into any state or territory. Northerners were outraged by the court's ruling and flocked to the Republican Party. They feared that the decision would tip the balance of power in Congress to the slave states as new territories entered the Union. There was little doubt that the country was headed toward disunion.

* * *

No American figure has been more studied, written about, mythologized, and hailed as Abraham Lincoln. At last count, there are over ten thousand biographies of the sixteenth president, with scores of new additions every year. Some of our finest historians—Doris Kearns Goodwin, Harold Holzer, Allen Guelzo, and David Herbert Donald, to name a few—have dedicated the better part of their careers to dissecting and examining every aspect of his life. It has produced a treasure trove of literature well worth reading. Most historians (and Americans for that matter) consider Lincoln our greatest president, this author included.[8]

Isolating what many consider his signature decision—the signing of the Emancipation Proclamation—is fraught with peril. Entire books have been written on the subject, and even those seem only to skim the surface. A more complete understanding of his actions requires examination of the history of slavery, the framing of the Constitution, the growth of the Southern economy, the careers of dozens and dozens of legislators, western expansion, and the Civil War. In short, it is difficult to make sense of it all in a single chapter or even book.

As in the chapter on Jefferson, our approach here is to examine Lincoln's thinking decision mostly through his own words. Lincoln was one of the finest—and most prolific—writers of his or any generation. He labored over his correspondences, speeches, and official government documents with extraordinary care, refining and calibrating each word and phrase until it captured his intentions just right. To truly understand and appreciate the man requires a close inspection of his words.

Lincoln, Race, and Equality

Abraham Lincoln has often been described as a radical, an abolitionist, an egalitarian, a revolutionary in the spirit of the founders. However, at his core he was none of those. He was a Unionist. He believed in the institutions of government, adherence to the laws, and, above all, the sanctity of the Union. The first duty of any citizen, he told the Young Men's Lyceum of Springfield in 1838 in his first-known political speech, was "never [to] violate in the least particular, the laws of the country; and never to tolerate the violation by others . . . in short, let it become the political religion of the nation." That's not to say that he didn't find some laws objectionable, he told them, "but I do mean to say, that, although bad laws, if they exist, should be repealed as soon as possible, still while they continue in force, for the sake of example, they should be religiously observed."[9]

Lincoln would find those words difficult to live by some sixteen years later with the passage of the Kansas-Nebraska Act, a horrific law that he feared would lead to the spread of slavery to every corner of the land. As a candidate for the US Senate in the fall of 1854, Lincoln gave a rousing speech that revealed his beliefs on the pressing issues of the day—race, slavery, Unionism, liberty, and the Constitution—that would form the cornerstone of his thinking over the next decade. Of the spread of slavery, he thundered, "I cannot but hate. I hate it because of the monstrous injustice of slavery itself. I hate it because it deprives our republican example of its just influence in the world—enables the enemies of free institutions, with plausibility, to taunt us as hypocrites—causes the real friends of freedom to doubt our sincerity." Lincoln readily confessed, however, that if "all earthly power" was given to him tomorrow, he would not know what to do with the "existing institution." His first impulse, he said, "would be to free all the slaves, and send them to Liberia—to their own native land . . . we cannot make them equals." Lincoln would revisit this notion of recolonizing slaves (and free blacks) back to Africa time and again for the remainder of his life. He believed it was the only practical and fair solution for both blacks and whites since they were not "politically and socially our equals."[10]

Lincoln was at his most eloquent that day when he turned his attention to the Founding Fathers and their views on slavery. The true evil of the Kansas-Nebraska Act, thundered Lincoln, was that it provided a "moral right in the enslaving of one man by another," something the "fathers of the republic eschewed, and rejected." He went to great lengths to point out that the Founding Fathers' only excuse for not prohibiting slavery was one of "necessity"—an argument he understood and sympathized with. The British king, he lectured, was truly to blame for allowing the introduction of slavery in the colonies well before the Declaration of Independence and War for Independence. When given the chance, he noted, the founders outlawed slavery in the Northwest Territory a full year before the Constitutional Convention in Philadelphia—proof to Lincoln of their moral disdain for the practice.[11]

He closed his speech with a paragraph that would foreshadow many of the themes at Gettysburg some nine years later. He was still six years away from becoming president, but sensed that the nation would have to rediscover the definition of liberty in order to remain as one. "Our republican robe is soiled, and trailed in the dust. Let us repurify it. Let us turn and wash it white, in the spirit . . . of the Revolution. Let us turn slavery from its claim of 'moral right' back upon its existing legal rights and its arguments of 'necessity.' . . . Let us re-adopt the Declaration of Independence, and with it, the practices and policy, which harmonize with it. Let all lovers of liberty everywhere—join in the great and good work. If we do this, we shall not only have saved the Union, but we shall have so saved it, as to make, and keep it, forever worthy . . . that the succeeding millions of free happy people, the world over, shall rise up, and call us blessed."[12]

It's important to note that nowhere did Lincoln call for the outright abolition of slavery that day, a position he steadfastly held until the summer of 1862. Lincoln believed that immediate emancipation was neither practical—what would become of the freed slaves?—nor legal short of a constitutional amendment, which was out of the question. He was merely opposing the *expansion* of slavery. Like most abolitionists of the day, he was convinced that if slavery could be confined to the Southern states, it would gradually disappear as the balance of power in Congress shifted in favor of the antislavery states. And he was probably right. But with the passage of the Kansas-Nebraska Act, and later the *Dred Scott* case ruling, expansion became all but inevitable, and with it the likelihood of war.

The truth is that Lincoln was just as conflicted and confounded by slavery as the rest of the nation. His views were shaped by competing convictions that weighed equally on his conscience. He believed that nowhere in the Constitution did it provide for the abolition of slavery or the emancipation of the slaves. As much as he wished otherwise, it just wasn't there. Lincoln held the document with almost religious reverence; its word was scripture. He wasn't about to play fast and loose with its meaning to achieve a political goal, even one as noble as emancipation. To his close friend Joshua Speed, a slave owner who favored disunion over abolition, he assured him that "I am not aware that *any one* is bidding you to yield that right; certainly I am not . . . I acknowledge *your* rights and *my* obligations, under the constitution, in regard to your slaves." At the same time, on a personal level he was horrified to see the abuse and debasement that slaves suffered on a daily basis. It tormented him, he confided to Speed, to "see the poor creatures hunted down, and caught, and carried back to their stripes [whippings] and unrewarded toils."[13]

But Lincoln's greatest intellectual dilemma—the one that bothered him the most—was reconciling the meaning of the five noblest words of the Declaration of Independence—"all men are created equal"—with a Constitution that sanctioned slavery, a society that accepted it, and a nation that was being torn asunder by it. Unlike many Americans, Lincoln believed that the declaration's proviso applied to all people, including free blacks and slaves. Jefferson did not intend to "say all were equal in color, size, intellect, moral developments, or social capacity," asserted Lincoln in an 1857 speech shortly after the *Dred Scott* decision came out. "He meant simply to declare the *right*, so that the *enforcement* of it might follow as circumstances should permit." The distinction was important to Lincoln, for it allowed him to rationalize the seeming contradiction between the promise of the Declaration of Independence and the reality of slavery. The declaration, reasoned Lincoln, was "meant to set up a standard maxim for free society, which should be familiar to all, and revered by all; constantly looked to, constantly labored for, and even though never perfectly attained, constantly approximated, and thereby constantly spreading and deepening its influence, and augmenting the happiness and value of life to all people of all colors everywhere." Equality, in other words, was a goal to strive for—"placed in the Declaration for future use" as Lincoln would say—but not necessarily an immediate guarantee. This idea of gradually moving society closer to the declaration's ideals would form the foundation of Lincoln's strategy in the years ahead.[14]

Coming to Prominence:
The Lincoln-Douglas Debates

Having failed to win a Senate seat in 1854, Lincoln was back at it in 1858, challenging incumbent senator Stephen A. Douglas, a leading Democrat and proslavery sympathizer. Lincoln entered the race, in part, because

Douglas was the primary instigator behind the disastrous Kansas-Nebraska Act of 1854, a law that he believed recklessly put the nation on a path toward disunion. The *Dred Scott* decision only further convinced him that it was time to enter the fray.

At the state convention in Springfield that summer, Lincoln gave what would become known as his "house divided" speech in accepting the Republican nomination for the US Senate. It was jarring for its clairvoyance: "I believe this government cannot endure, permanently half slave and half free"; for its poetry: "a house divided against itself cannot stand"; and for its stark prediction: "Either the opponents of slavery will arrest the further spread of it, and place it where the public mind shall rest in the belief that it is in course ultimate extinction; or its advocates will push it forward, till it shall become alike lawful in all the States, old as well as new—North as well as South."[15]

The speech and ensuing debates (there were seven total) catapulted Lincoln to national prominence. He excited the Republican base—both in Illinois and across the country—with his rhetorical flourishes and soaring sentiment, his unyielding moral clarity and personal abhorrence of slavery, his reverence for the Constitution and defense of the Founding Fathers, and most of all his moderate (some abolitionists would call it limited) approach to defining and solving the slavery issue. There were other, more radical, and better-known Republicans exploring similar themes, but none had the combination of oratorical presence, sense of purpose, moral rectitude, and political instincts as Lincoln.

From his opening statement in their first debate, Lincoln made it clear that he had no intention of ending slavery where it lawfully existed, nor did he believe that the two races could live harmoniously together because of the physical differences. "I have no purpose directly or indirectly to interfere with the institution of slavery in the States where it existed," said Lincoln to applause. "I believe I have no lawful right to do so, and I have no inclination to do so." He went on to note that "there is a physical difference between the two, which in my judgment will probably forever forbid their living together upon the footing of perfect equality. . . . I am in favor of the race to which I belong, having the superior position."[16] At the time of the debates, Illinois had a law prohibiting blacks from entering the state.

Neither sentiment was particularly unusual. A majority of Americans, and a large percentage of Republicans, too, held similar beliefs. But he got his loudest applause for what followed. "Notwithstanding all this, there is no reason in the world why the negro is not entitled to all the natural rights enumerated in the Declaration of Independence, the right to life, liberty, and the pursuit of happiness. I hold that he is as much entitled to these as the white man." This was unusual; it was an argument that he had been developing for several years. Lincoln was fixated on the notion that the Declaration of Independence, while not legally superseding the Constitution and its tacit sanctioning of slavery, represented the Founding Fathers' true intentions—intentions not constrained by the compromises, deals, and accommodations required for crafting a constitution. Their true goal, he inferred with a minor leap in logic, was to provide equality for all men, including blacks. The Constitution might prohibit the eradication of slavery right now, but the Declaration gave license to form a more perfect union someday.[17]

That didn't mean that Lincoln was immune from pandering. Like every politician, he was stung by the criticism that came with the territory. Over the first several debates, Douglas hammered Lincoln and the "black Republican Party" for their belief "that the negro was made his equal, and hence is his brother."[18] In response, Lincoln assured voters during the fourth debate that "I have never had the least apprehension that I or my friends would marry negroes if there was no law to keep them from it. . . . I give the most solemn pledge that I will to the very last stand by the law of this State, which forbids the marrying of white people with negroes." He went on to add that he was not "in favor of negro citizenship" and would be "opposed to the exercise of it."[19]

But the criticism that hurt most was Douglas's contention that Lincoln had distorted the meaning of the Declaration of Independence in order to find equality for blacks. With each successive debate, Lincoln became more convinced—and vocal—that the equality described in the Declaration was indeed meant for all Americans. In their fifth debate, he delivered his most rousing defense to thunderous applause: "I believe the entire records of the world, from the date of the Declaration of Independence up to within three years ago, may be searched in vain for one single affirmation, from one single man, that the negro was not included in the Declaration of Independence. . . . Washington never said so . . . that any living man upon the whole earth ever said so, until the necessities of the present policy of the Democratic party had to invent that affirmation."[20]

By the seventh and final debate, Lincoln had come full circle. He had opened the first debate by declaring that he wasn't interested in abolishing slavery where lawfully enacted, and closed the final by recasting the struggle as a simple morality play, one between right and wrong, tyranny and freedom, war and peace. "The issue," he concluded, "is the eternal struggle between these two principles—right and wrong—throughout the world. . . . The one is the common right of humanity and the other the divine right of kings. It is the same principle in whatever shape it develops itself . . . whether from the mouth of a king who seeks to bestride the people of his own nation and live by the fruit of their labor, or from one race of men as an apology for enslaving another race, it is the same tyrannical principle. . . . This controversy will soon be settled."[21] Though he lost the Senate election, little could he know of the role he was about to play.

"The Union of these States is perpetual"

On November 6, 1860, Abraham Lincoln was elected the sixteenth president of the United States. He had won handily, with nearly 40 percent of the popular vote in a crowded four-candidate field, and his Republican Party commanded large majorities in the House and Senate.

A little over a month later, South Carolina became the first state to formally withdraw from the Union. In short order, Florida, Mississippi, Alabama, Georgia, Louisiana, and Texas had followed suit. In February, representatives from the rebel states met in Birmingham, Alabama, to write a constitution for the Confederate States of America. They appointed Jefferson Davis interim president.

Against this backdrop, Abraham Lincoln headed east for his inauguration. In his farewell address to Congress, outgoing president Buchanan implored Congress to work with the Southern states to craft a constitutional amendment that would prohibit Congress from abolishing slavery. Buchanan found the prospects of disunion dispiriting, but preferred to codify slavery into the Constitution—appease the South, essentially—rather than go to war.

Lincoln held the opposite view. He wasn't about to tamper with the Constitution just to mollify a handful of traitors, as he saw it. At noon on March 4, 1861, he stood on a platform erected on the east portico of the Capitol to deliver his inaugural address. He began by reassuring Southerners, as he had throughout the campaign, that he had no intention of abolishing slavery—the Constitution simply did not permit it. "The property, peace and security of no section are to be in any wise endangered by the now incoming Administration . . . consistent with the Constitution and the laws . . ." The Constitution also didn't permit disunion, however, a point he emphatically revisited throughout the address. "I hold, that in contemplation of universal law, and of the Constitution, the Union of these States is perpetual," said Lincoln. "Perpetuity is implied, if not expressed, in the fundamental law of all national governments. It is safe to assert that no government proper ever had a provision in its organic law for its own termination. Continue to execute all the express provisions of our national Constitution, and the Union will endure forever—it being impossible to destroy it, except by some action not provided for in the instrument itself." If civil war were to visit the land, he closed, it would come from "*your* hands, my dissatisfied fellow countrymen, and not in *mine*, is the momentous issue of civil war. The government will not assail *you*. You can have no conflict without being yourselves the aggressors."[22] Lincoln's admonition fell on deaf ears, and on April 12, 1861, South Carolina attacked the Union garrison at Fort Sumter. The war had begun.

From the onset of hostilities, the radical Republicans in Congress, as well as his own vice president, Hannibal Hamlin, prevailed on Lincoln to make the war a crusade to free the slaves. Unionism and freedom were synonymous, as they saw it, and now was the time do away with the horrible institution once and for all. Lincoln disagreed. From his standpoint, the war was not a conflict between two sovereign states, since the act of disunion was patently unconstitutional. Rather, it was an act of domestic insurrection by individuals in the Southern states. He steadfastly maintained that the Confederate states (a term he never used) were still part of the Union, and therefore the Constitution and the laws of the land still applied to them. This was an important distinction because it meant that he couldn't summarily abolish slavery without violating the Constitution, something he wasn't prepared to do.

On July 4, Lincoln addressed a joint session of Congress to outline his strategy for prosecuting the war and preserving the Union. What was extraordinary about the seven-thousand-word speech was that it never once mentioned slavery. Lincoln did this to appeal to pro-Union Southern sympathizers, who he hoped could act as a counterinsurgency and end the rebellion quickly. He was also fearful of driving the proslavery Union states, Delaware and Maryland, as well as the neutral border states—Missouri, Kentucky, and West Virginia—to the Confederacy. Should Maryland and Delaware secede, the capital would be surrounded by the rebel states. It would almost certainly mean the fall of Washington, DC, and possibly the Union. The war, he reassured them, was about preserving the Union, nothing more.

Like most Unionists, Lincoln anticipated that the insurrection would be turned back quickly and easily. He had initially requested seventy-five thousand militia, a sum he thought more than sufficient to do the job. His thinking changed, however, with the Union's resounding defeat at the Battle of Bull Run in July of 1861, the first major engagement of the war. Like most Northerners, Lincoln was stunned by the setback. It was expected that the troops would have an easy go of it. As the magnitude of the defeat sank in, Lincoln asked Congress for an additional five hundred thousand troops as he girded the nation for a much longer, bloodier, conflict. There would be no quick victory.

Lincoln's frustration mounted with each Union defeat. What little faith he had in his generals all but evaporated as the losses piled up. He found general in chief of the Union Army George McClellan's reluctance to pursue Robert E. Lee particularly maddening. He blamed McClellan's incompetence for the Union's struggles, and would ultimately fire him. Lincoln's popularity took a beating as things bogged down. By 1862, many Democrats in Congress, and even some conservative Republicans, began calling for an end to hostilities. Their rationale was simple: the war was going nowhere, casualties were mounting, and Northerners were losing confidence in Lincoln's ability to lead. Better to sue for peace with the Confederate states than let the bloody war drag on.[23]

The radical Republicans in Congress had lost patience with Lincoln, too, though for entirely different reasons. They had chosen Lincoln as their standard bearer because he had roused the nation to the moral failings of slavery, and articulated an intriguing theory of equality that sprang from the Declaration of Independence, thereby circumventing the shortcomings of the Constitution. But now he had gone silent on the subject. He was prosecuting a war to save the Union with nary a word about the injustice of slavery. Disappointed and confused, they decided to force the issue by passing the Confiscation Act of 1861, which held that slaves captured in battle belonged to the Union (up to that point, captured slaves were returned to their masters). Lincoln was reluctant to sign the bill. He thought it would offend the border states and cause more harm than good. He ultimately acquiesced to mounting Republican pressure but refused to enforce it. When one of his generals proclaimed that all slaves captured in his command were to be freed, Lincoln immediately rescinded the order. "No commanding General shall do such a thing . . . without consulting me."[24]

Lincoln was not oblivious to the pressure mounting from the radicals, nor had he abandoned the cause of freedom. He was simply preoccupied with turning the tide of the war. The Union was suffering defeat after defeat and there was little to be optimistic about. What good was emancipation, he reminded the cabinet, when physical liberation remained a distant possibility?

In the early months of 1862, Lincoln began quietly working on his own plan for emancipation. It didn't involve martial law, confiscation, or contraband theory—he believed those were all temporary solutions and possibly unconstitutional. He toiled in isolation, consulting with few about the details. On March 6, Lincoln sent a message to Congress requesting a Joint Resolution on Compensated Emancipation. His approach was simple: offer financial compensation to any state that voluntarily abolishes slavery. "The United States ought to cooperate with any state which may adopt gradual abolishment of slavery," he urged Congress, "giving to such state pecuniary aid, to be used by such state, in its discretion, to compensate for the inconveniences, public and private, produced by such change of system." The border states may not be ready to equate Unionism with freedom, he told the cabinet, but they should certainly understand financial gain.[25]

Lincoln's plan was met with resounding approval from the press. The editor of the *New York Times* called it "a master piece of practical wisdom and sound policy." The *New York Tribune* editorialized that it "had never printed a State paper with more satisfaction than we feel in giving to our readers the Special Message of President Lincoln to Congress yesterday," and thanked "God that Abraham Lincoln is President of the United States . . . and that we have at such a time so wise a ruler." According to the San Francisco *Daily Alta California*, it was "just the right thing, at the right time, and in the right place."[26]

The border states didn't greet it with nearly the same enthusiasm. Many from their delegations didn't trust Lincoln, and weren't convinced that Congress would actually appropriate the money. Lincoln tried to convince state leaders from Delaware, Maryland, Missouri, and Kentucky to accept the government's offer but to no avail. They found it impractical, borderline unconstitutional, and in some cases offensive. And with that, the plan for gradual, compensated emancipation quickly became a memory. It may have been a failure, but it was noteworthy in one regard: it was the first time a president had proposed any type of emancipation to Congress. And though the border states had rejected it, the public mostly supported it. Perhaps there was another way to go about it, Lincoln began to wonder.[27]

"I can only trust in God I have made no mistake"

The spring and early summer months of 1862 were a difficult time for Lincoln and the Union. The army had few successes to point to in the east and west; the best it could muster was a decisive victory in faraway Louisiana. Lincoln was constantly bickering with his generals and trusted none of them save Grant. The treasury was nearly bankrupt, and unemployment rampant. The European powers were close to recognizing the Confederacy as a legitimate government, a potentially crippling blow to the cause of union. They were disappointed that the Union had failed to emancipate the slaves. Lincoln's supporters in Congress had mostly turned against him, and the midterm elections for the Republicans looked grim. One respected magazine opined that "when the president leaves the White House, he will be no more regretted, though more respected, than Mr. Buchanan." Many agreed with that sentiment.[28]

The president had something to celebrate in April when Congress passed a law emancipating the slaves in the District of Columbia. Since it was a federal territory, it had the constitutional authority to free the nearly three thousand slaves that served in the capital, mostly as household butlers and maids. Over the objections of the local residents, Lincoln signed the bill in mid-April, though not without some trepidation. He was concerned that the provision for immediate emancipation of the slaves might overwhelm the capital's limited resources and infrastructure. "I'm a little uneasy about the abolishment of slavery in this District," he wrote Horace Greeley, "not but I would be glad to see it abolished, but as to the time and manner of doing it."[29] When told of the news, Frederick Douglass, the nation's most prominent black abolitionist, could hardly believe it was true. "I trust I am not dreaming but the events taking place seem like a dream."[30]

The district emancipation reenergized the Republican faithful in Congress and across the Union. They redoubled their pressure on Lincoln to enact universal emancipation. Lincoln, in turn, made one last desperate appeal to the border states to accept compensation for gradual emancipation. In early July he invited twenty-nine of their representatives and senators to the White House and made his pitch. "If you all had voted for the resolution in the gradual emancipation message of last March," he scolded them, "the war would now be substantially ended." Lincoln stressed that he wasn't seeking immediate emancipation, or even gradual emancipation for that matter, but simply a *declaration* of gradual emancipation. But he needed an immediate answer. If they didn't agree to it, he would be forced to seek another way, "an instance of it is known to you," Lincoln ominously warned. The border-state contingent was not impressed. Two days later they sent a testy letter to the president turning down his offer—again—and exhorting him to "confine yourself to your constitutional authority."[31]

This was the last straw for Lincoln. It was clear that the border states would not go along with any kind of emancipation. The Republicans in Congress took note, and shortly thereafter began debating a second Confiscation Act, one that would grant emancipation to slaves residing in Confederate states where the Union Army was in control. Lincoln wasn't enamored with this approach. He believed Congress lacked the authority to emancipate, and furthermore didn't believe it was their role. "It is startling to say that Congress can free a slave within a state," he observed.[32]

But he also understood that it was time to act. The war was going badly, army recruits had slowed to a trickle, the government was out of money, and enthusiasm to continue the fight was dangerously low. Once thought of as a risky proposition, emancipation was beginning to look like the surest—and maybe only—way to change the trajectory of the war. Lincoln had always believed that preserving the Union would provide all the inspiration needed to sustain the war effort. But it was turning out not to be the case. Northerners found nothing appealing about fighting and dying to save a country that had no intention of abandoning slavery. Many wanted it to be about something bigger than just the Union.

Lincoln finally made it about more than just holding the country together. He assembled his cabinet together in late July of 1862 to inform them of his intention. He had been toiling in private for several weeks writing a proclamation that would free the Confederate slaves. He wasn't looking for the cabinet's opinion, he warned at the outset of the meeting; he was simply seeking their reaction. His mind was made up: he was going to emancipate the slaves of the Confederate states on January 1, 1863, in accordance with his war powers. Lincoln read the draft in hushed silence. The cabinet realized they were witnessing a historic moment and provided little feedback. Lincoln told them that he would issue the Emancipation Proclamation after the next Union victory, which he hoped would be soon. He knew that battlefield momentum would be needed to give the proclamation legitimacy and impact.

Being a lawyer and constitutional expert, Lincoln made it clear that he was pursuing emancipation in his role as commander-in-chief in order to defeat the insurrection, that it applied only to Confederate slaves: "Now, therefore I, Abraham Lincoln, President of the United States, by virtue of the power in me vested as Commander-in-Chief, of the Army and Navy of the United States in time of actual armed rebellion against the authority and government of the United States, and as a fit and necessary war measure for suppressing said rebellion." He knew that under normal circumstances, the president didn't have the constitutional authority to interfere in a state's right to practice slavery. Under the loosely defined war powers provision in the Constitution, however, he probably did have the power to unilaterally emancipate the slaves, as long as it was to achieve a military objective. In this case, freeing the slaves would dramatically hinder the Confederate states' ability to wage war and surely hasten their demise. It was a murky constitutional point, but Lincoln sensed that Congress wouldn't object to it.

It would be two months before the Union army achieved another victory on the battlefield. It occurred in Maryland at Antietam, one of the bloodiest battles of the war. The army turned back General Lee's advance into the state, though a cautious General McClellan allowed the Confederate army to escape to Virginia largely intact. It was a missed opportunity more than a decisive win, but it was the first positive development for Union forces in months, and it gave Lincoln the opening he needed. After some tweaking and a final read-through for his cabinet, Abraham Lincoln issued the Emancipation Proclamation on September 22, 1862. "I could only trust in God I have made no mistake," he remarked to a joyful crowd that had gathered outside the White House upon learning the news.[33]

Reaction to the proclamation was varied and predictable. Abolitionists were overjoyed. The *Chicago Tribune* modestly called it "the grandest proclamation ever issued by man." The *New York Tribune* led with the headline "God bless Abraham Lincoln." Vice President Hamlin predicted that it would "stand as the great act of the age," and for Senator Charles Sumner of Massachusetts, it meant that "the skies are brighter and the air is purer, now that slavery has been handed over to judgment." Virtually every major city in the North celebrated the proclamation with rallies and parades, and the White House was flooded with thousands of letters in support of the decision.[34]

The border states had a different, though not entirely unexpected, take on emancipation. A "giant usurpation, unrelieved by the promise of a solitary advantage" was how the *Louisville Journal* described it. The Union Party in Tennessee completely disavowed the proclamation and Lincoln, calling it an "atrocity and act of barbarism" and nothing short of "treachery to the Union men of the South." Northern Democrats didn't think any better of it. "An act of Revolution," blared the *New York Evening Express*, while the *New York World* screeched that Lincoln was "adrift on a current of radical fanaticism." The *New York Journal of Commerce* starkly predicted that it would only serve to prolong the war.[35]

Lincoln was most puzzled by the foreign response. He had issued the proclamation, in part, to discourage France and Britain from recognizing the Confederate states, but they were unimpressed, at least initially. The

British foreign minister lamented that it lacked "no declaration of a principle adverse to slavery." The *London Spectator*, commenting on the fact that the border states were exempted, sniffed that "the principle asserted is not that a human being cannot justly own another, but that he cannot own him unless he is loyal to the United States." The *Times* of London served up the harshest criticism: "Where he has no power Mr. Lincoln will set the negroes free," it editorialized. "Where he regains power he will consider them as slaves."[36]

Lincoln made it official on January 1, 1863. When it came time to sign the document, he noticed that his right arm was trembling from all the handshaking he had been doing at a White House reception just minutes earlier. It was so cramped, in fact, that he had to back off from signing several times for fear of leaving an illegible mark. He joked to those around him that a shaky signature may be interpreted by future generations as doubt. "They will say, 'he had some compunctions,'" he said to laughs. He slowly and neatly applied his signature. "I never in my life felt more certain that I was doing right than I do in signing this paper."[37]

The emancipation of the slaves had a dramatic impact on the war and the country. For starters, it created a sorely needed influx in Union conscripts. Northerners, inspired by the new cause of freedom, enlisted in droves, while former Confederate slaves, as their first act of freedom, fought by their side in a cause they now shared. By the end of the war, there were 179,000 blacks—mostly former slaves—in the Union army. The infusion of men provided a decisive advantage to the North just when it needed it. Freedom also wreaked havoc on the Southern way of life. Lincoln's naval blockade of Southern ports, combined with the emancipation of the slaves, left their economy in shambles—and with it the ability to make war. And perhaps most important, emancipation made it clear to the world that the Union was on the side of good. It wasn't simply about holding the nation together by force. It had become a just and moral war, one for freedom and equality. In an instant it radically altered the nature of the struggle both at home and abroad.

Most of the border states voluntarily abolished slavery following the proclamation except, ironically enough, Lincoln's birth state of Kentucky. In that sense, emancipation wasn't fully realized until passage of the Thirteenth Amendment in December of 1865. Only then did Kentucky finally end the practice. Sadly, Lincoln wouldn't live to see the moment. He certainly would have relished it.

* * *

It has been speculated that one of the reasons for Abraham Lincoln's enduring popularity with the American people is that his views about freedom and slavery evolved over time. He grew in the office—something extremely rare in the presidency. True enough, external factors—an impatient Congress, a war locked in stalemate, foreign powers signaling their intention to get involved, a lack of conscripts—were the primary impetus for change, but Lincoln wisely and courageously accepted this reality and chartered a new course. It's possible he could have prosecuted the war to conclusion without emancipating the slaves, but it wouldn't have held the same meaning. He came to understand this in the spring and summer of 1862.

In some ways, a burden was lifted from Lincoln with the signing of the Emancipation Proclamation. For too long he had subordinated the ideal of universal freedom to the cause of union. In the years leading up to the war, and during his first year in office, he was determined to portray the conflict as one of union against disunion, nothing more. But with emancipation, there was a tacit admission that freedom had become a *means* to preserve the Union, that the two were inextricable—one not achievable without the other. Simply maintaining the Union wasn't enough for most Northerners if it didn't guarantee equality for everyone.

Lincoln would more eloquently make that point eleven months later at Gettysburg. By this time, his personal transformation and recasting of the war had been completed; freedom and union were now one in the same. "We here highly resolve that these dead shall not have died in vain; that this nation, under God, shall have a *new birth of freedom*; and that government of the people, by the people, for the people, shall not perish from the earth."

For all his fretting, consternation, and second-guessing over the Emancipation Proclamation, Lincoln was acutely aware of the historic nature of his actions. "I know very well that the name which is connected with this act will never be forgotten," he prophetically offered to Charles Sumner during the summer of 1862. To one friend, he called it "my greatest and most enduring contribution to the history of the war." To another, he wrote that it was "the central act of my administration, and the great event of the nineteenth century." He was wrong in one regard: it is arguably the defining action in American history.[38]

Chapter 5

TEDDY ROOSEVELT BUILDS THE PANAMA CANAL

Courtesy of the Theodore Roosevelt Collection, Harvard College Library.

I have had a most interesting time about Panama and Colombia. My experiences in all these matters give me an idea of the fearful times Lincoln must have had in dealing with the great crisis he had to face. When I see how panic-struck Senators, businessmen, and everybody else become from my little flurry of trouble, and the wild clamor they all raise for foolish or cowardly action, I get an idea of what he had to stand after Bull Run and again after McClellan's failures in '62 . . . however, I have kept things moving just right so far.

—Teddy Roosevelt to his son,
Theodore Roosevelt Jr., November 15, 1903

To my mind this building of the canal through Panama will rank in kind, though not of course in degree, with the Louisiana Purchase and the acquisition of Texas. I can say with entire conscientiousness that if in order to get the treaty through and start building the canal it were necessary for me forthwith to retire definitely from politics, I should be only too glad to make the arrangement accordingly; for it is the amount done in office, and not length of time in office, that makes worth having.
— Teddy Roosevelt in a letter dated December 29, 1903

It was a good thing for Egypt and the Sudan, and for the world, when England took Egypt and the Sudan. It is a good thing for India that England should control it. And so it is a good thing, a very good thing, for Cuba and for Panama and for the world that the United States has acted as it has actually done during the last six years. The people of the United States and the people of the Isthmus and the rest for mankind will all be the better because we dig the Panama Canal and keep order in its neighborhood.
— Teddy Roosevelt to Cecil Arthur Spring-Rice,
British Foreign Office, January 18, 1904

On November 18, 1903, the United States and the newly independent government of Panama signed a treaty that gave permission to the United States government to build, operate, and defend a forty-seven-mile canal through the isthmus that would eventually connect the Atlantic and Pacific oceans. The deal was the result of several years of negotiations, posturing, bullying, threats, clandestine communications, and ultimately a revolution in the former province of Colombia. The Panamanian government, in existence for less than two weeks, immediately ratified the agreement (no doubt persuaded by the $10 million payment and promise of military protection), and the United States Senate followed suit several months later. For Theodore Roosevelt, the treaty—and subsequent completion of the canal—was arguably the greatest, and most controversial, triumph of his political career. The single act captured the man and his presidency to near perfection: brash, unorthodox, path blazing, unrepentant, and resolute. No president, excluding Lincoln during the Civil War, had ever operated so boldly or unilaterally. In many ways, it marked the beginning of the modern presidency. The treaty was both celebrated and reviled at home and abroad, and represented the dawn of America's ascendancy as a world power, a process that wouldn't be completed until the conclusion of World War II.

* * *

In evolutionary biology, the theory of punctuated equilibrium suggests that evolution, rather than being a slow and incremental process, actually occurs during rapid bursts of speciation, or change. In some respects, the same could be said for the presidency. The growth in the office and its powers can be best measured by discrete moments and events instead of gradual transformation, as we've seen with the presidents we've discussed up to now—Lincoln being the most dramatic and obvious. But Lincoln was a unique circumstance. He certainly stretched the Constitution to its outer limit—finding powers where none had previously existed—but it was done in the name of preserving the Union. His actions were bold, imaginative, unilateral, and oftentimes temporary. The presidents that followed Lincoln, like many who had preceded him, were generally uncomfortable with exerting executive influence. Not all of them fall in the unfortunate category of "caretaker president." But many failed to think imaginatively about exploiting the inherent (and in some cases dormant) strengths of the office to achieve political and policy goals.

The same could not be said for Theodore Roosevelt. By personality, temperament, and approach, he stood in sharp contrast to those who preceded him, including Lincoln. And not surprisingly, his presidency resembles nothing that came before him. Few administrations have been as chronicled, studied, dissected, and interpreted as Roosevelt's, and rightly so: his tenure represents the most blatant and obvious example of punctuated equilibrium in the history of the office. And it wasn't confined to just one aspect of the presidency; his approach to regulation, big business, labor relations, conservation, foreign policy, and even politics drew on a playbook unique to him.

No moment illustrates that point as well as the Panama Canal treaty, where Roosevelt steamrolled Congress, bamboozled foreign countries, flaunted international law, embraced unsavory lobbyists, and repurposed the Monroe Doctrine, all for the "benefit of mankind," as he saw it.[1] It was certainly the most daring and outlandish act of his presidency, perhaps of any administration. But Roosevelt steadfastly believed that the ends justified the means. The canal would revolutionize global commerce and make the world a smaller place. And more importantly, he believed, it would give the United States unrivaled supremacy in the hemisphere, and later the world.

What is most compelling about the Panama Canal treaty, and by proxy the presidency of Theodore Roosevelt, is that a singular event accounted for two transformative moments in American history: the birth of the modern presidency and the emergence of the United States as a global power (and later superpower). These developments were far from mutually exclusive; in fact, the "American Century" could not have occurred without the dramatic expansion of the presidency. But to trace both their lineage to a single person and event is certainly remarkable. In the end, Teddy Roosevelt left the office much different than he found it, with future presidents—and arguably the nation—the beneficiaries.

De Lesseps's Folly

Ever since Vasco Núñez de Balboa became the first European to traverse the Isthmus of Panama in 1513, the idea of a man-made waterway connecting the Atlantic and Pacific oceans had intrigued heads of state, businessmen, and developers alike. As early as 1524, long before it was even technologically possible to move that much earth, Holy Roman Emperor Charles V ordered the first geographical studies to ascertain the feasibility of a canal, though his son Phillip II scuttled the plan upon Charles's death.[2] In 1811, the famous German explorer Alexander von Humboldt published the first quasi-scientific examination of the topography of the region, concluding that Nicaragua—not Panama—appeared to be "the most favorable for the formation of canals of a large dimension."[3] He emphasized that a crossing was "of the greatest interest for the balance of commerce, and the political preponderancy of nations."[4]

Evidently, Great Britain agreed with von Humboldt's assessment. In 1848, British gunboats seized several Nicaraguan port cities, including San Juan del Norte, in order to secure control over potential canal routes. The United States saw the action as a clear violation of the Monroe Doctrine, which held that the United States was the protectorate of the Western Hemisphere. Only last-minute diplomacy helped avert a war. To resolve the issue long term, a treaty was signed (Clayton-Bulwer), which committed the two nations to joint control of any future canal in Nicaragua or elsewhere in Latin America. Some in Congress believed that fusing US interests with Great Britain on this matter contradicted the spirit of the Monroe Doctrine, but the vast superiority of the British fleet persuaded a majority of lawmakers that the treaty was necessary, at least for the time being. It would, however, prove to be a hindrance to future development.

Spurred by the increase in traffic to California following the gold rush of 1849, the US government commissioned its first official study of an isthmus canal in 1855. Entitled the *Practicability and Importance of a Ship Canal to Connect the Atlantic and Pacific Oceans*, the report posited that a Panama crossing was both feasible and economically desirable. The authors estimated that a canal would shorten a typical voyage from New York to San Francisco (in which the ship had to sail around the tip of South America) by nine thousand nautical miles, cutting the amount of time at sea by two-thirds. This, in turn, would result in fewer shipwrecks, less cargo spoilage, reduced insurance costs, and a dramatic increase in the frequency of trips between the two coasts and Europe. By their estimation, the cost of construction would be a pittance compared to the revenue realized from a modest usage surcharge. "The convenience to the world of such a speedy transit from ocean to ocean," the report concluded, "can hardly be overstated."[5]

Several years prior to the study, the United States and New Granada (the predecessor of Colombia, which included the state of Panama) entered into the Mallarino-Bidlack Treaty. The pact gave the United States the right to use and safeguard any future route—whether American made or foreign, and whether canal or train—across the isthmus. In return, the United States guaranteed Colombia's sovereignty against foreign powers or insurrections.[6] Over the life of the treaty until 1903, there would be fourteen US military interventions. Most were done to protect American economic interests, but on several occasions it was at the behest of the Colombian government. Theodore Roosevelt would later cite the Mallarino-Bidlack Treaty as legal justification for his actions surrounding Panama's independence.

The treaty paved the way for the first "transcontinental" train crossing in 1855. Funded and owned by several American businessmen, the railroad covered forty-seven miles from Panama City to Colon and was an instant hit. Some four hundred thousand people used it in the first year alone, and it immediately became the preferred method of transportation for fortune seekers headed to California. Its success convinced leaders and businessmen from around the globe that a transoceanic canal was both technologically and financially feasible. It would be a race to see who could get it done.

For years it looked like a private French company under the direction of legendary diplomat and engineer Ferdinand de Lesseps would secure that honor. The aging developer had won global renown with the completion of the Suez Canal, and in 1880 he raised $60 million in a public stock offering—the largest of its kind—to undertake a Panamanian crossing. De Lesseps barnstormed across the United States in hopes of raising some of the money outside of France, but virtually no Americans invested in his venture.

Americans were wise to avoid the French project as it was beset with an assortment of problems from the moment it broke ground. The French team's poor understanding of the topography and failure to adequately survey the exact route caused de Lesseps to assume that a "sea-level" canal—like the one built at the Suez—would make more sense then a lock system, where the water would be raised and lowered to accommodate ships. But they neglected to calculate the twenty-foot difference in sea level between the two oceans in their plans. It wasn't until the undertaking was near ruin that de Lesseps finally conceded his error, but by then it was too late. And the working conditions were beyond appalling. A combination of suffocating heat and humidity, venomous insects and snakes, disease, unsanitary living quarters, and dangerous machinery took a staggering toll on the workforce. According to some estimates, over twenty thousand men perished during the ten years of the project, though several chroniclers put that number higher.[7] By 1889, de Lesseps had run out of money and credibility with little to show for it, and his dream of a canal was abandoned. An investigation by the French government would turn up all sorts of mismanagement, fraud, and criminal behavior with dozens, including de Lesseps and his son Charles, sentenced to prison.[8]

While the French were suffering their setback in the jungle, the United States continued to investigate a potential transoceanic crossing in both Panama and Nicaragua. With Nicaragua's stable government, and more hospitable climate and terrain, many in Congress actually preferred it over Panama, even though it was twice the distance from ocean to ocean. Southern officials in particular were enamored with Nicaragua for the simple reason that it was eight hundred miles closer to New Orleans than Panama, which meant that more commerce would flow through the port city. Study after study was commissioned throughout the 1890s as Congress kicked around the issue with no resolution in sight. President McKinley nominally favored a Nicaragua canal, but it wasn't a pressing concern for his administration. He had little interest in expending political capital to muscle the project to fruition. It would take a strong leader with a clear vision to make something happen.

Large Policy

Long before ascending to the presidency, Theodore Roosevelt firmly believed that the United States should build a canal in Latin America. Unlike Ferdinand de Lesseps, whose intent was to construct a "monument" to humanity and a "gift for civilization," Roosevelt was motivated by something entirely different: empire.

Since his time as a student at Harvard, he dreamed of the day when the United States would take its rightful place among the world's great powers. He would visit this theme time and again in his books, journal articles, speeches, and correspondence, the premise always the same: America's destiny lay on the open seas. "It is too much to hope that our political shortsightedness will ever enable us to have a navy that is first-class in point of size," he exasperatedly declared in his critically acclaimed 1882 book, *The Naval War of 1812*, "but there certainly seems no reason why what ships we have should not be of the very best quality."[9]

For Roosevelt, this notion wasn't merely an intellectual exercise; it fueled his ambition, oriented his policies and politics, and shaped his career in public service.[10] During a speech before the powerful Union League Club of New York in 1888, he scolded the businessmen and policy makers in attendance for their apparent indifference to upgrading America's navy. "It is a disgrace to us as a nation that we should have no warships worthy of the name, and that our rich sea-board cities should lie at the mercy of . . . a tenth-rate power like Chile."[11]

It wasn't until he read naval historian Alfred Thayer Mahan's highly regarded 1890 book, *The Influence of Sea Power*, however, that Roosevelt began to coalesce his ideas around sea dominance, the Monroe Doctrine, and empire building into a coherent philosophy about America's place in the world. Where most politicians regarded the two oceans as little more than protective barriers to the continental mainland, Roosevelt viewed them as an invitation to extend America's commercial and military reach to every corner of the globe. In the mid-1890s, he began collaborating with Mahan, Senator Henry Cabot Lodge of Massachusetts, future secretary of state John Hay, and others on a new, more muscular approach to America's foreign affairs. Dubbed the "Large Policy" by the group, it held that a first-rate navy was required to enforce hemispheric dominance consistent with the Monroe Doctrine's mandate. Anything less, and the European powers would take control of the region—and with it America's future. "I believe in ultimately driving every European power off this continent," Roosevelt wrote as early as 1893, "and I don't want to see our flag hauled down where it has been hauled up."[12] The Large Policy would eventually be realized as the Roosevelt Corollary to the Monroe Doctrine during his first term in office, and over time would come to define America's entire foreign policy.

Roosevelt felt strongly about this issue, and wasn't afraid to offer an opinion, even if unwelcome or unsolicited. His 1896 letter to the editor of the *Harvard Crimson* caused a minor stir with the press and the Cleveland administration for its strident tone and thinly veiled aggression aimed at allies. With Great Britain threatening to invade Venezuela to collect on defaulted loans, Roosevelt—then the police commissioner of New York—brazenly declared that "the Monroe Doctrine forbids us to acquiesce in any territorial aggrandizement by a European power on American soil at the expense of an American state. . . . If we permit a European nation in each case itself to decide whether or not the territory which it wishes to seize is its own, then the Monroe Doctrine has no real existence."[13]

His approach earned him few fans in the Cleveland White House, but did catch the notice of Cleveland's successor, William McKinley, who appointed him assistant secretary of the navy in 1897 (and would later make him his vice presidential running mate in 1900). It was the ideal job for Roosevelt, and he immediately set out to "build up our navy to its proper standing."[14] He lobbied Congress for funding for a dozen new battleships, six cruisers, and seventy-five torpedo boats; called for the annexation of Hawaii; declared the need for an isthmian canal to facilitate travel between the oceans—"we should build the Nicaragua canal at once"; and in a private letter to Alfred Mahan expressed concern about Spain's continued presence in Cuba: "Until we definitely turn Spain out of the island (and if I had my way that would be done tomorrow) we will always be menaced by trouble there."[15]

On more than one occasion, Roosevelt's bellicose enthusiasm landed him in hot water with Secretary of Navy John Long, Secretary of State Hay, and even the president himself. Following Japan's protestation that the United States' annexation of Hawaii would put the interests of twenty-five thousand of its residents in jeopardy, Roosevelt responded publicly that "the United States is not in a position which requires her to ask Japan, or any other foreign power, what territory it shall or shall not acquire." The occasional scolding notwithstanding, Roosevelt loved the job, and had more impact in his short tenure than any assistant (or secretary for that matter) in history. "I'm having immense fun running the Navy," he confessed to a friend.[16]

Roosevelt had considerably less fun as governor of New York following his triumphant return from Cuba, where his "Rough Riders" helped expel the Spanish from the island and the hemisphere. He found the position tedious and the task of governing unsatisfying, and time and again his attention wandered to foreign affairs. In the spring of 1899 he gave his famous "strenuous life" speech before a packed house at the Hamilton Club in Chicago, where he delivered a spellbinding and spirited defense of prosperity, expansion, and national greatness. "No country can long endure if its foundations are not laid deep in the material prosperity," he said unabashedly.

And how did he propose we get there? It was simple: build a canal and dominate the seas. "We cannot sit huddled within our own borders and avow ourselves merely an assemblage of well-to-do hucksters who care nothing for what happens beyond. Such a policy would defeat even its own end; for as the nations grow to have ever wider and wider interests, and are brought into closer and closer contact, if we are to hold our own in the struggle for naval and commercial supremacy, we must build up our power without our own borders. We must build the isthmian canal, and we must grasp the points of vantage which will enable us to have our say in deciding the destiny of the oceans of the East and the West."[17] Certainly not what de Lesseps had in mind some two decades earlier.

Roosevelt had profound respect for McKinley's secretary of state, John Hay, whom he considered among the finest to ever serve in that position. But even their friendship wasn't enough to keep his tongue in check when it came to disagreements concerning hemispheric supremacy and the canal. Hay was tasked with renegotiating the old Clayton-Bulwer Treaty with Great Britain, which had quietly served as a roadblock to any United States–led efforts to build an isthmian canal. Hay quickly worked out a deal with the British that would give the United States the right to construct and operate a canal on its own, but which prohibited its fortification. Hay and McKinley were pleased with the outcome, but Governor Roosevelt was not. And in short order his displeasure was splashed across the front page of all the New York newspapers.

Roosevelt's primary point of contention was that it defeated the purpose of a canal if it could not be fortified during times of war. "As you know, I am heartily friendly to England, but I cannot help feeling that the State Department has made a great error in the canal treaty," he wrote Alfred Mahan. "I do not see why we should dig the canal if we are not to fortify it so as to insure its being used for ourselves and against our foes in time of war." He went privately with his complaints to Hay, telling him that "we should consistently refuse to all European powers the right to control, in any shape, any territory in the Western Hemisphere which they do not already hold," and that the treaty was "fraught with very great mischief."[18] Stung by the criticism from Roosevelt in Albany and Lodge in the Senate, Hay offered his resignation to McKinley, who refused it. The Senate rejected the treaty, and Hay was forced to go back to the drawing board. Little could he know that Theodore Roosevelt was about to become his boss.

"Make Dirt Fly!"

In September of 1901, Theodore Roosevelt became the fifth vice president to ascend to the presidency upon the death of his predecessor.

William McKinley was assassinated while attending the Pan-American Exposition in Buffalo, New York. At forty-two, he was the youngest man to hold the office by far, though his age belied his vast experience in public life. He had done stints in the New York State Assembly and on the United States Civil Service Commission; served as police commissioner of New York and assistant secretary of the navy; commanded a regiment in Cuba during the Spanish-American War; served a term as governor of New York; and was elected vice president of the United States. All the while, he authored dozens of acclaimed books, gave thousands of speeches, wrote hundreds of magazine articles, and earned a reputation as one of the leading intellectuals of the era, a fact that is sometimes overlooked or forgotten.

What has not been overlooked is that, above all, he was a man of action. Unlike the other vice presidents who were unexpectedly thrust into the office, Roosevelt didn't view his job as merely advancing his predecessor's causes. He respected and admired McKinley, and generally agreed with his policies, but he had his own ideas, too. On a host of issues—trust busting, conservation, food safety—he unapologetically broke ranks with the McKinley administration. And when it came to hemispheric hegemony, global expansion, and the need for a two-ocean navy, Roosevelt's vision, approach, and commitment was completely novel. No other public figure of the day had given as much thought to "American Greatness," and now he was in the position to make things happen. If it took some creative action and bold maneuvering to bring it to life, so be it.

For Roosevelt, the linchpin to his foreign policy—his view of America's role in the world, in fact—was an isthmian canal. Building it would force much-needed investment in the naval fleet, secure unrivaled dominance in the hemisphere once and for all, and provide a springboard to becoming a leading world power. It was the key to his vision for America's future and became something of an obsession during his first years in office.

His first order of business was to encourage Secretary Hay to finalize a re-renegotiated treaty with Great Britain whereby the United States would have no encumbrances to building, operating, and fortifying its own isthmian canal. Hay wasted little time, and in November of 1901— just two months after Roosevelt took office—he presented the president with a new pact, one that met with his boss's approval. "Delighted!" was the response from the White House. The Senate found it much to their liking, too, and it was quickly ratified.[19]

With that out of the way, there was still the issue of location: Panama (which was a province of Colombia) or Nicaragua? Both routes had their supporters and detractors with their own vested interests. The Nicaraguan contingent was led by Senator John Morgan of Alabama, who, as the chairman of the powerful Committee on Interoceanic Canals, strongly favored a Nicaraguan canal because it was much closer to his beloved South than Panama and in his mind could better jumpstart their post-Reconstruction economy. Morgan emphatically opposed the Panama route, which he believed had been soiled "gangrene with corruption" from the "villainous" French.[20]

This could be a problem for Roosevelt, who favored Panama. Morgan had earned a reputation as a venomous bully, someone to be avoided if possible. His colleagues went to great lengths not to cross him for fear of disproportionate retribution, particularly on the issue of the canal. When it came to the Nicaraguan route, wrote his colleague Senator Shelby Cullom, himself chairman of the Foreign Relations Committee, Morgan "became almost vicious toward anyone who opposed him."[21]

Which meant little to Theodore Roosevelt. Notwithstanding that the Isthmian Canal Commission, which had been appointed by President McKinley to study the proposed routes, unanimously favored Nicaragua; that the House voted in favor of its findings, 308–2; and that Senator Morgan all but promised to railroad the commission's report through the Senate come springtime, Roosevelt was set on a Panama crossing, mostly because he thought it would be quicker to activate and complete. Time was of the essence. Roosevelt wanted to "make dirt fly" in time for the 1904 election, and Panama was his best shot.[22]

But it wasn't his only consideration. In the back of his mind, Roosevelt feared that a European power—perhaps Germany or Russia—would attempt to complete what the French had begun in the jungles of Panama. It would be prohibitively expensive and difficult for them to start from scratch in Nicaragua, but not so in Panama. He dreaded the idea of two competing canals in the region. It would undermine his plan for hemispheric hegemony and global expansion, which he couldn't countenance.

So what did he do? In typical Roosevelt fashion, he summoned the commissioners to the White House for a private session of arm-twisting and lecturing, and urged them to change their findings. It was highly unusual—some of the attendees didn't know what to make of the new president—but Roosevelt wouldn't ease up. He wanted a new report supportive of Panama. And for good measure, it had to be done unanimously. There could be no dissent.

Roosevelt got his way, much to the ire of Senator Morgan. The House quickly adopted the Panama route and the Senate followed suit, notwithstanding Morgan's impassioned plea to stick with Nicaragua. Attempting to negotiate with the corrupt and duplicitous regime in Colombia would frustrate Roosevelt and invariably lead to his taking of Panama by force someday, an infuriated Morgan brazenly predicted to his colleagues during a sweat-soaked three-hour speech on the Senate floor. This, he warned, would surely "poison the minds of people against us in every Spanish-American republic in the Western Hemisphere" and create a "most dangerous national pitfall into which we could plunge."[23] Morgan wasn't alone in his assessment. The *New York World* prophesied the same: "Talk about buying a lawsuit—the purchase of the Panama Canal would be buying a revolution."[24] Of course, Roosevelt saw it differently. He joyously predicted that the canal would be "the great bit of work of my administration, and from the material and construction standpoint one of the greatest bits of work that the twentieth century will see."[25]

Having secured congressional authorization to purchase the remnants of the French excavation and pursue a treaty with Colombia, all that was left was to ink a deal with the government in Bogotá. But negotiations that were expected to be completed in weeks dragged on for months. The Colombians haggled over everything—price, jurisdiction, sovereignty rights, duration—and shared little of Roosevelt's urgency. An impatient Roosevelt actually floated the idea of purchasing Panama outright from Colombia, quizzing Secretary Hay as to the possibility: "Why cannot we buy the Panama isthmus outright instead of leasing it from Colombia? I think they would change their constitution if offered enough."[26]

Fortunately it never came to that. After threatening to scuttle talks and begin negotiations with the Nicaraguan government, Secretary Hay finally convinced his Colombian counterpart to agree to terms. The Hay-Herran Treaty was signed on January 22, 1903, and within two months' time the US Senate had overwhelmingly ratified it. Roosevelt considered the $10 million lump-sum payment to the government in Bogotá plus annualized rent of $250,000 more than generous, but the Colombian congress felt differently. It was a pittance, in their estimation, for what was considered the "blood of Colombia" and their "cherished hope." But even more problematic was the perpetual lease term, which was angrily dismissed as wholly unacceptable, and the ambiguous language that supposedly safeguarded their sovereignty. "Without question public opinion is strongly against its ratification," the American minister in Bogotá informed Hay and Roosevelt. The Colombians, he warned, considered the entire document "favorable to the United States and detrimental to Colombia."[27]

Just as the Colombian minister to the United States had adopted a leisurely pace to the treaty negotiations, so, too, did the Colombian Congress in ratifying it. Months after the US Senate had approved the deal, its Colombian counterpart hadn't even begun deliberations. But even more worrisome, there were ominous reports coming from Bogotá that it could be years, not months, before the Congress would eventually get around to it, something Hay and Roosevelt found unfathomable. In early June, Hay decided to force the issue. At Roosevelt's urging, he fired off a tersely worded cable to the US minister in Bogotá with instructions to warn the Colombian government that should they "reject the treaty or unduly delay its ratification, the friendly understanding between the two countries would be so seriously compromised that action might be taken by the Congress next winter which every friend of Colombia might regret."[28]

The "action" that Hay referred to was never specified, though the following day the *New York World* hinted at it with a blockbuster exclusive: "The State of Panama ready to secede if the treaty is rejected by the Colombian Congress," screamed the headline, "Roosevelt is said to encourage the idea." Among other things, the anonymously authored story stated that the president had no intention of beginning negotiations with Nicaragua—he was determined "to have the Panama canal route"; predicted that the "State of Panama, which embraced all the proposed Canal Zone, stands ready to secede from Colombia and enter into a canal treaty with the United States"; declared that the United States would "promptly recognize the new government" and "at once appoint a minister to negotiate and sign a canal treaty"; and concluded that his cabinet and the Senate supported this approach.[29] To the surprise of many close observers, the White House issued no denials after its publication. Of course, there was no reason to: Roosevelt had leaked the piece through a lobbyist intermediary.

Revolution

On August 12, 1903, the Colombian congress rejected the canal treaty by unanimous vote. It hardly came as a shock; both Roosevelt and Hay had been expecting the worst. The president learned the news while vacationing at Sagamore Hill, his Long Island estate. Just days before, Senator Shelby Cullom, chairman of the Committee on Foreign Relations, happened to be visiting with Roosevelt. After finishing lunch with the president, the senator held an impromptu press conference with several reporters from the New York newspapers. By this time, speculation was rampant that the treaty would be rejected, to which a reporter asked what would become of the canal should that occur. "We might make another treaty," replied Cullom, "not with Colombia, but with Panama." When another pointed out that Panama wasn't a sovereign state, Cullom responded that there was "great discontent on the Isthmus over the action of the Congress of the central government, and Panama might break away and set up a government which we could treat with." Only after being pushed by a third reporter over whether the United States would actually support a Panamanian revolution did Cullom inch back a little. "No, I suppose not. But this country wants to build that canal and build it now."[30]

It might as well have been Roosevelt answering those questions, for he had no intention of abandoning the Panamanian location. "We may have to give a lesson to those jack rabbits," he wrote Hay, as they "should not be allowed permanently to bar one of the future highways of civilization. . . . What we do now will be of consequence, not merely decades, but centuries hence."[31] Toward the end of August, Hay visited with Roosevelt at Sagamore Hill to review their options. Roosevelt had recently gotten his hands on a provocative memo from John Bassett Moore, the leading international law scholar of the day. It made a strong case that the United States was perfectly within its rights to begin construction of a Panamanian canal under the terms of the nearly forgotten Mallarino-Bidlack Treaty of 1846. Moore's thesis was simple: according to article 35 of the treaty, it guaranteed "a free and open transit not only for the citizens but also for the 'Government' of the United States. This means for the use of the government itself," and included "any modes of communication that now exist, or that may hereafter be constructed."[32]

In light of Moore's memo, Roosevelt and Hay settled on three potential courses: begin construction of the canal under the Mallarino-Bidlack Treaty and risk war with Colombia (which both thought would be quick and inexpensive); begin negotiations with Nicaragua in order to apply pressure on Colombia; or delay construction until "something transpires to make Colombia see the light"—namely, a revolution. Though Roosevelt wholeheartedly agreed with Moore's opinion—"I feel we are certainly justified in morals, and therefore justified in law, under the treaty of 1846, in interfering summarily and saying that the canal is to be built and that they must not stop it," he wrote Senator Mark Hanna—his preference was to "interfere when it becomes necessary so as to secure the Panama route without further dealing with the foolish and homicidal corruptions in Bogotá." Or as he told Albert Shaw, editor of the *Review of Reviews* magazine in a private correspondence, "I freely say to you that I should be delighted if Panama were an independent state, or if it made itself so at this moment; but for me to say so publicly would amount to an instigation of a revolt, and therefore I cannot say it."[33]

Roosevelt was correct: He couldn't publicly encourage a revolution. But that didn't mean he would wait passively for one to come about. It wasn't in his nature to sit idly while events conspired around him, especially not for something as important as an isthmian canal. But the truth was that revolution was already afoot in Panama, the consequences of which were not lost on the Colombians. "President Roosevelt is a decided partisan of the Panama route," the Colombian minister in Washington relayed back to Bogotá, "and hopes to begin excavation of the canal during his administration. Your excellency already knows the impetuous and vehement character of the president, and you are aware of the persistence and decision for which he pursues anything to which he may be committed."[34]

As Roosevelt would point out years later in his autobiography, the province had a history of rebellion. According to his count, there had been at least fifty-three disturbances, riots, uprisings, insurrections, and outright revolutions over the preceding half century, many of which were quelled by the US military at Colombia's request. "Had it not been for the exercise of the United States of the police power in her interest, her interest with the isthmus would have been sundered long before it was," he wrote in defense of his policies.[35]

It has long been debated as to what role the Roosevelt administration played in privately instigating the Panamanian revolution. Publicly, Roosevelt remained silent on the topic throughout the late summer and fall. His instincts told him that even the slightest utterance favoring an independent Panama would tarnish any uprising and be used against him by political opponents. Privately, however, was a different story. He made no secret in his correspondences that he fully expected Panama to secede from Colombia, and that it would be recognized immediately. On two occasions, Roosevelt met with lobbyists representing the defunct French company that had previously failed in Panama, but which stood to gain handsomely since the United States had agreed to purchase its assets for $40 million. All that was required to secure their payout was a signed treaty, and both men pressed Roosevelt for a commitment to support a Panamanian uprising, should one occur. One of the lobbyists, a Frenchman named Philippe Bunau-Varilla, had been consulting with Panamanian leaders—one of whom actually traveled to New York in October to seek his guidance—on how to pull off a successful revolution. As one historian put it, Bunau-Varilla created something of a "revolution kit" for the skittish Panamanian leaders, which included a prewritten declaration of independence and constitution, a military plan to defend Colon, a canal treaty with the United States, and even a flag for the new country (which his wife had sewn).[36]

While Roosevelt was scrupulous in avoiding using specific language that would indicate support for a revolution, he left a clear impression with Bunau-Varilla that he was in favor of it. "I have no use for a government [Colombia] that would do what that government has done," he told the Frenchman in their October 10 meeting. Roosevelt would later write about the meeting that he had "no doubt that Bunau-Varilla was able to make a very accurate guess, and to advise his people accordingly. In fact, he would have been a very dull man had he been unable to make such a guess."[37]

Bunau-Varilla wasn't a dim man, but he was a nervous one. He wanted stronger reassurances that the United States was on board before directing the Panamanians to proceed with the uprising. Several days after his White House meeting with Roosevelt, he had a final, private encounter with Secretary of State John Hay at Hay's home. The two chatted for a while about the events that led to the current situation, both agreeing that it would likely result in a revolution. Should this happen, Hay told him, the United States would "not be caught napping. Orders have been given to naval forces on the Pacific to sail toward the Isthmus." It was just the confirmation Bunau-Varilla was seeking, and he quickly passed the news along to the revolutionaries.[38]

With that, the revolution was set in motion. On November 4, the insurgents seized control of Panama City and Colon and declared the isthmus an independent country. Two days prior, Roosevelt had ordered the US fleet in the area to "maintain free and uninterrupted transit" for the isthmian railroad in the event that it was threatened by "an army force with hostile intent." The naval commanders knew exactly what Roosevelt meant. The directive's intention was to block the Colombian military from landing its men in Colon and Panama and squashing the rebellion. Unable to dispatch its forces on its own soil, the Colombian government gave up without a fight.[39] Panama was an independent country, and Roosevelt could finally build his canal.

* * *

At 12:51 on November 6, 1903, less than three days after the uprising, the United States government formally recognized the Republic of Panama. The press reaction was split. The conservative papers praised Roosevelt, including the *Pittsburgh Times* ("Colombia got what she deserved"), the *Chicago Tribune* ("It was the only course he could have taken in compliance with our treaty rights"), the *Baltimore Sun* ("[It was] to the advantage of the world"), and the *Buffalo Express* ("Even if the United States fomented the revolution, it acted in the interests of the governed"). A majority of the international press felt similarly. The *Chilean Times* welcomed the revolution "no matter how it has been brought about." According to the *Times* of London, Roosevelt's actions had been "studiously correct." Even *El Relator*, a leading newspaper in Bogotá, couldn't help but blame its own government for the insurrection. "We have cut their rights and suppressed all their liberties. We have robbed them of the most precious faculty of free people."[40]

Roosevelt had his critics, too, and the chorus of naysayers grew stronger as the details became public over the weeks and months ahead. The *New York Times* called it an "act of sordid conquest," while the *Evening Post* described it as Roosevelt and Hay's "vulgar and mercenary adventure," one that had "committed the country to a policy which is ignoble beyond words."[41] Referring to it as a "national bank robbery," William Henry Thorpe of the *Globe* compared it to the worst conquests of Nero and Alexander the Great. The *New York American* cartoonist Homer Davenport may have captured it best with his sketch of a soaring eagle clutching an isthmus-shaped animal in its claw.[42]

Press reaction notwithstanding, Secretary Hay wasted no time in ironing out a canal treaty with the infant country, which had appointed the French provocateur Bunau-Varilla as their ambassador to the United States. On November 18, the two countries signed a deal that transferred sovereignty rights for a ten-mile strip of land across the isthmus to the United States government in exchange for $10 million and a $250,000 annual fee—the same terms that the Colombians had turned down. It was a kingly sum for the two-week-old country, but over time it would become a point of discontent between the two countries.

Roosevelt vociferously defended his actions before a joint session of Congress in early December, and again in his State of the Union address a month later. Had he not recognized the breakaway republic and quickly hammered out a treaty, he lectured Congress, "the Government of the United States would have been guilty of folly and weakness, amounting in their sum to a crime against the Nation."[43]

Could Roosevelt have gone about creating an isthmian canal another way? Certainly. Eventually he would have reached an acceptable deal with the Colombian government had he sweetened the pot and acceded to a few of their demands. But the process might have dragged on for years, something Roosevelt couldn't stomach. Or he could have gone to

Nicaragua, which would have happily obliged his one-sided terms and meant fewer lives lost during construction. But like the negotiations with Colombia, it would have delayed groundbreaking and prolonged completion. In the end, Roosevelt did what he always did: followed the path of least temporal resistance. If taking the land from Colombia was the fastest and most favorable solution, then it was the only option as far as he was concerned.

* * *

It is easy to pass stern judgment on Roosevelt's behavior using today's ethics as a filter. Inciting and abetting a revolution in order to acquire valuable foreign real estate for the purpose of building a self-serving edifice would be wholly unthinkable in our modern world. It would violate too many tenets of the presidency itself, global citizenship, and the American public's sense of fair play and decency to stand a chance of succeeding. A hundred years ago was a different story. Imperialism, colonialism, and racial subjugation still ruled the day. There was no League of Nations to mediate disputes. The "world community," for all intents and purposes, did not exist. And it would take two world wars before something resembling global policing would emerge.

Theodore Roosevelt would revisit the topic of the Panama Canal time and again throughout his postpresidency to defend his actions. He considered its construction the crowning achievement of his administration, and believed it would be regarded as one of the greatest of the century, if not all time. "I have always felt the one thing for which I deserve most credit in my entire administration was my action in seizing the psychological moment to get complete control of Panama," he wrote his successor, William Howard Taft. In that regard, he was probably right; the canal did more to usher in the modern, global economy and propel the United States to world power status than any single event in the twentieth century. There's little doubt that it would have taken years longer, if not decades, to build had Roosevelt not seized the initiative at the turn of the century. And it's quite possible that it would have been located in Nicaragua, which most legislators favored, leaving the partially completed Panamanian route free for European powers to build a competing canal. Had this occurred, it would have dramatically altered

America's hemispheric dominance and likely stunted its development as a global power.[44]

But Roosevelt could never understand the criticism. It genuinely baffled him that some in the press and in Washington would so strongly condemn his behavior in securing the canal treaty and joining the oceans. He was simply acting in America's best interest, and to the benefit of all humanity, he would tell anyone interested in listening. He never considered it anything but perfectly legal, justified, and proper: no treaties or agreements were violated; nobody died during the Panamanian uprising; and if he had so chosen, he could have legally built the canal pursuant to the old 1846 treaty with Colombia, irrespective of an uprising. If some feathers were ruffled or shortcuts taken along the way, so be it. That was the price for ushering in modernity by creating a spectacular monument to mankind.

Even so, Roosevelt could be his own worst enemy at times. The condemnation grew louder and broader following his 1911 boast during a speech in Berkeley that he "took the canal zone" instead of submitting a "dignified state paper" to Congress because he knew that "Congress would debate and while the debate goes on, the canal does too."[45] Right around the time the canal was set to open, things got so heated that Woodrow Wilson lobbied the Senate to ratify a new treaty with Colombia that included a formal apology, $25 million in indemnity, and granted special rights in the Canal Zone, but Roosevelt's allies in the Senate filibustered the bill and it died.[46]

If the recriminations and lingering controversy chastened Roosevelt, he never let on. In a speech before the National Press Club in January of 1918, just a year before his death, Roosevelt gave what may be the most honest—and revealing—explanation for his motives in the fall of 1903: "Panama declared itself independent and wanted to complete the Panama Canal, and opened negotiations with us. I had two courses open. I might have taken the matter under advisement and put it before the Senate, in which case we should have had a number of most able speeches on the subject. We would have had a number of profound discussions, and they would still be going on now, and the Panama Canal would be in the dim future yet. We would have had a half century of discussion, and perhaps the Panama Canal. I preferred we should have the Panama Canal first and the half century of discussion afterward."[47] The sentiment perfectly captures Roosevelt and his presidency.

Chapter 6

WOODROW WILSON AND THE LEAGUE OF NATIONS

Courtesy of the Woodrow Wilson Presidential Library, Staunton, Virginia.

The terms of the immediate peace agreed upon will determine whether it is a peace for which such a guarantee can be secured. The question upon which the whole future peace and policy of the world depends is this: Is the present war a struggle for a just and secure peace, or only for a new balance of power? If it be only a struggle for a new balance of power, who will guarantee, who can guarantee the stable equilibrium of the new arrangement? Only a tranquil Europe can be a stable Europe. There must be not a balance of power but a community power; not organized rivalries but an organized, common peace.

—Woodrow Wilson, "Peace without Victory" speech, January 22, 1917

Shall we or any other free people hesitate to accept this great duty? Dare we reject it and break the heart of the world?

—Woodrow Wilson, 1919

This league is altogether too much like a political alliance to make me feel
that it is likely to be either enduring or successful.
                                        —Senator Henry Cabot Lodge, 1919

*On January 22, 1917, Woodrow Wilson delivered his famous "Peace without
Victory" speech before the United States Senate with the hopes of convincing the
belligerent nations to pursue a compromise settlement that avoided the notion of
winners and losers. At this point, the United States had not entered the war, and
Wilson desperately wanted to keep it that way. During the address, he vaguely
referenced a new form of collective security that would replace the system of
"entangling alliances"—a foreshadowing of the League of Nations. The idea
was not quite fully formed, but in due time would become the cornerstone of
Wilson's vision for a new world order. With Germany's declaration of unrestricted submarine warfare shortly thereafter, Wilson was left no choice but to
enter the conflict later that spring. Over the course of the next year and a half,
he would further develop this idea of a collective body—the League of Nations—
as a way to prevent regional wars and global conflicts in the future. For Wilson,
the formation of the league had become the primary goal of an Allied victory—
not the excessive punishment of the Central Powers. While Britain and France
sought—and won—a more severe settlement than Wilson had recommended,
they, along with forty other countries, agreed to join Wilson's League of Nations.
The only question: could Wilson convince his own country to do the same?*

* * *

Woodrow Wilson was something of an accidental president.
His victory in 1912 would not have been possible but for
Theodore Roosevelt's decision to come out of retirement
and challenge his protégé, President William Howard Taft, for the
Republican nomination. When he failed to dislodge Taft at the Republican convention, Roosevelt bolted the GOP and launched a third-party
candidacy under his hastily formed Bull Moose Progressives banner. The
two former friends, now bitter enemies, campaigned relentlessly against
each other. They effectively split the Republican vote, which allowed
Wilson to capture the White House with only 41 percent of the popular
tally—one of the lowest totals for a winning president in history. His victory snapped a streak of four consecutive Republican administrations,

and his narrow reelection in 1916 would make him the first Democrat since Andrew Jackson to win consecutive terms.[1]

Which is not to say that Woodrow Wilson governed like someone who had slipped into office through the back door. As a professor of political science and later president of Princeton University, Wilson had spent much of his career examining the institutions of government—in particular the relationship between the executive and legislative branches of government. Among his many observations was that the modern presidency—the one that Theodore Roosevelt had helped create—would someday become "as big and influential as the man who occupies it."[2] He had studied Roosevelt's activist approach to the presidency and somewhat begrudgingly admired the way he transformed the office in such a short period of time, even if he disagreed with many of his policies.

Their biggest disagreement came in the area of foreign policy. Whereas Roosevelt had championed rigorous enforcement of the Monroe Doctrine and bold expansion of America's might and influence around the globe, Wilson approached it much differently. Like Roosevelt, he believed the United States should play a greater role on the world stage. Being a leader in the world community meant having an active voice in the great issues of the day. What it did not mean, however, was adopting a militant "America First" tact to global relations. Wilson deplored this approach. He viewed it as a form of imperialism that would alienate natural allies and enrage natural foes. It's what led the European and Asian powers to become embroiled in the Great War, and was the motivation for trying to keep the United States out of the conflict.[3] If Roosevelt's motto was "Speak softly and carry a big stick," then Wilson's could easily have been described as "Lead boldly but share an equal voice."

Wilson spent much of his first term focused on domestic policy, enacting his New Freedom platform of banking reform, tariff reductions, antitrust modification, and labor regulations, among other things. At the time, it was easily the most activist domestic agenda of any president in history, and still ranks second only to Franklin Roosevelt's first term in legislative accomplishments. His foreign policy consisted of little more than maintaining neutrality in the Great War. On several occasions he tried to mediate a settlement among the warring powers, but his overtures were never taken seriously. On the strength of his domestic achievements, a strong economy, and continued neutrality in the war, Wilson narrowly won reelection in 1916, upping his popular vote total from 41 to 50 percent in the intervening four years.

Woodrow Wilson's second term was almost the complete reversal of his first. He spent little time on domestic matters as the war in Europe grew bloodier and more disruptive to the world economy. In late 1916, he again tried to mediate a truce and settlement, and was again rebuffed. The Allied Powers informed him of their intention to prosecute the war until victory, while Germany responded by reinstituting its policy of unlimited naval warfare. With the specter of German U-boats indiscriminately sinking merchant vessels in the waters around the British Isles, Wilson knew that it was only a matter of time before the United States would be drawn into the conflict. His fears were confirmed when the British government decoded a German cable intended for the president of Mexico that promised his country assistance in reclaiming Texas, Arizona, and New Mexico should Mexico declare war on the United States. The British code-breakers wisely leaked the cable to the press, which served to inflame American passions against Germany. Neutrality was no longer an option.

On April 2, 1917, Woodrow Wilson reluctantly went before a joint session of Congress to ask for a declaration of war against Germany. "With a profound sense of the solemn and even tragical character of the step I am taking," he intoned, "I advise that the Congress declare the recent course of the Imperial German Government to be in fact nothing less than war against the government and people of the United States." He reiterated that the United States had no imperialist designs on Germany or its territories and no quarrel with its citizens—that wasn't the purpose of entering the war. Rather, it was "to vindicate the principles of peace and justice in the life of the world as against selfish and autocratic powers," for in Wilson's opinion, the world was "at the beginning of an age in which it will be insisted that the same standards of conduct and of responsibility for wrong done shall be observed among nations and their governments." He concluded, as he had a few months earlier in his "Peace without Victory" speech, by hinting at the need for a new world body, one that would collectively maintain the peace for generations to come. "A steadfast concert for peace can never be maintained except by a partnership of democratic nations. No autocratic government could be trusted to keep faith within it or observe its covenants. It must be a league of honor, a partnership of opinion."[4] He would spend the remainder of his presidency trying to make this vision a reality.

Fourteen Points

At times during his presidency, Woodrow Wilson was mistakenly labeled a pacifist by both friends and detractors. However, unlike his first secretary of state, William Jennings Bryan, who actually *was* a pacifist, Wilson was not opposed to the concept of war. He was simply opposed—repulsed really—to the "mechanical slaughter" of men that had come to symbolize this particular war.[5] At the heart of it, he couldn't understand what the belligerents were fighting over. Sure, there were territorial gains to be made and colonies to be had, but did it justify the ritual sacrifice of millions of combatants and civilians? The war, Wilson believed, had resulted from nothing more than a confusing web of ill-conceived treaties and alliances quilted together by a bunch of out-of-touch ruling autocrats. There was nothing noble about it—certainly no righteous cause or high-minded principle that would warrant sending American boys to a certain death. Try as he might, however, Woodrow Wilson couldn't keep the United States out of the conflict forever. Germany's unrestricted U-boat campaign—"the military masters of Germany denied us the right to be neutral," claimed Wilson—made that an impossibility.[6] Still, it was a difficult decision—one that he stewed over for months and months—for it required of him to find meaning and purpose where none seemed apparent.

In short order, Woodrow Wilson would divine that greater meaning. From the onset of America's involvement in the war, his higher calling became a lasting peace, one that would endure for generations. This war was different from all the others because the goal, as he saw it, was a structural change in the way nations related to one another. Collective security would someday replace unilateral aggression, at least as far as Wilson was concerned. He didn't seek a punitive settlement like the other Allied Powers because he didn't believe that vengeance and territorial concessions would make for a permanent peace. He understood

France and Britain's desire for total victory and harsh terms, but with America's involvement came American idealism, something Wilson had in spades. "This is a People's War," he exclaimed during a Flag Day speech in June of 1917. "A war for freedom and justice and self-government amongst all the nations of the world, a war to make the world safe for the peoples who live upon it."[7] Wilson made it his mission to convince the Allied Powers that any peace must be tethered to this greater purpose, and he used every opportunity to reiterate that message. "We are seeking a permanent, not temporary, foundation for the peace of the world," he stated a few months later during his State of the Union address, "and we must seek it candidly and fearlessly." If that wasn't the case, he reminded the American people, then the entire war effort was for naught.[8]

Wilson's strategy for conducting the war was simple: supply the Allies with food, money, munitions, and other aid as quickly as possible while taking longer to send servicemen overseas. He was in no rush to resupply the front with fresh American troops. His earnest hope was that the war would wind down, and a peace settled upon, without the need for a heavy dose of American soldiers. But that wasn't to be the case. The fall of 1917 saw the Bolsheviks seize power in Russia, the Allied debacle at the battle of Caporetto in Italy, mutinies on the Western front, and the continued havoc of German U-boats on Allied merchant vessels in the North Atlantic. Toward the end of the year, British prime minister Lloyd George convinced the Allied Powers, which now included the United States, to form a supreme war council that would be responsible for unified command on the Western front.[9] It was done, in measure, to accelerate the deployment of American troops to the most pressing hot spots in Europe. All told, over six hundred thousand American troops would see action on the Western front by war's end.

Unlike Franklin Roosevelt, who was intimately involved in the military strategy during World War II, Woodrow Wilson would mostly leave the battlefield decisions to the British and French leaders. Troop movements, campaign tactics, weaponry technology, and the like were neither his interest nor strong suit. Peace was. Even at the height of the fighting, Wilson was consumed by a single thought: what would the world look like *after* the Great War, and how could another one be prevented? The British and French could prosecute the war to conclusion; his focus was the aftermath. And he approached it with a missionary's zeal.

On January 8, 1918, Wilson took a big step toward that vision with his Fourteen Points address before a joint session of Congress. He had been working for weeks in isolation on the speech, showing drafts only to his wife, Edith, and close advisor Edward "Colonel" House. The purpose was twofold: outline a future settlement consistent with his "Peace without Victory" approach, and introduce the concept of a collective peace organization, or as he stated in point fourteen, "a general association of nations must be formed under specific covenants for the purpose of affording mutual guarantees of political independence and territorial integrity to great and small states alike."[10] Wilson closed by expressing his solemn hope that his vision for the peace—and in particular the notion of collective security—would transform the Great War into "the final war for human liberty."[11]

Did Wilson achieve his goals with the speech? In some respects, for as one historian put it, he had finally "put flesh on the skeleton of peace without victory, inviting both friend and foe to accept a liberal, non-punitive settlement."[12] But while it galvanized liberals in the United States and around the globe, it didn't mean that the Allied leaders necessarily agreed with all (or even most) of the points. They didn't. As Wilson and the world would come to learn, Britain and France still harbored a strong desire to inflict the most punitive terms possible on the Central Powers, which included Germany, Austria, and the Ottoman Empire. The part of the speech that resonated most, and what it has become known for, was the introduction of the concept of the League of Nations. It was here that Wilson made his greatest impact, for he again fused the terms for a nonpunitive settlement with the need for a future collective organization that he believed would put an end to naked aggression and global wars. He knew there would be a give and take on the settlement terms—he wasn't so naïve to think the Allies would rubber-stamp it—but collective security was not negotiable. As he would tell the world a few weeks later in a follow-up address to Congress, "We believe that our own desire for a new international order under which reason and justice and the common interest of mankind shall prevail is the desire of enlightened men everywhere."[13]

A League of Its Own

For all his vague talk about the need for a peacekeeping organization to help usher in this new world order, Wilson struggled with getting it past the conceptual stage. On some level, he was concerned that a premature unveiling of this collective body would spook Republicans in the Senate, particularly the isolationists, who tended to look askance at international alliances of any kind. He knew there would be resistance—strong resistance—from conservatives, but he was hoping that the horrors of war would soften their opposition over time. To former president William Howard Taft, who was himself a strong advocate for a peacekeeping league and who lobbied the president to be more declarative on the subject, Wilson "gave it as his opinion that the Senate of the United States would be unwilling to enter into an agreement by which a majority of other nations could tell the United States when they must go to war." On another occasion he told advisors that public discussion about a league would only draw sharp rebukes from congressional Republicans, most notably the leading isolationist Senator Henry Cabot Lodge, who in Wilson's opinion "would cry that he had gone too far in committing the United States to a utopian scheme."[14] His words would be eerily prophetic.

As spring turned to summer, however, and the prospects of an Allied victory grew increasingly likely, Wilson recognized the need to make a stronger public case for a postwar governing body. At a Fourth of July address at George Washington's Mount Vernon estate, he insisted that any peace settlement must include the "establishment of an organization of peace which shall make it certain that the combined power of free nations will check every invasion of right and serve to make peace and justice the more secure by affording a definite tribunal of opinion to which all must submit." On this point, he told the gathering, there could be no compromise, for what was needed was "the reign of law, based upon the consent of the governed, and sustained by the organized opinion of mankind." It was the closest he had come to making a full-throated endorsement of the league concept, though the details were still a work in progress.[15]

With the conclusion of the war just months away, Wilson gave his most expansive remarks about the league in late September before a gathering at the Metropolitan Opera House in New York. The occasion was supposed to kick off yet another war bond drive, but he instead used it to offer the most detailed sketch of what he envisioned for this global organization, which he formally referred to as the League of Nations for one of the first times. Calling it an "indispensable instrumentality formed under covenants that will be efficacious," Wilson insisted that the "constitution of the League of Nations" should be considered the most "essential part of the peace settlement itself." It couldn't be formed now, he explained to the surely puzzled audience, because if done so "it would be merely a new alliance confined to the nations associated against a common enemy." He acknowledged the need for more specifics so that it would "sound less like a thesis and more like a practical program," and proceeded to enumerate a few, including the desire to mete out justice equally, the power to sanction economic boycotts on recalcitrant nations, and the elimination of secret treaties and alliances among league nations.[16]

Wilson had upped the rhetoric for a just peace and an organization to enforce it, in part, because he was troubled by the "intolerant and revengeful" tone being used by some politicians at home and Allied leaders abroad as the end drew near. His greatest fear had always been that a "nonhealing peace"—one that emphasized reparations, territorial gains, and subjugation above all else—would do nothing but fuel hatred and revenge and sow the seeds for future conflicts. He believed that a wisely adjudicated peace—*his peace*—was the only way to break the cycle of retribution and retaliatory wars, for which the League of Nations was a big part.[17]

The beginning of November saw frantic negotiations between the Allied and Central Powers. By this time, the war was essentially over; all that remained was an agreement for preliminary armistice terms. Wilson kept one eye on negotiations, and the other on the congressional elections, which, as it turned out, occurred a week before the armistice was signed. Wilson felt uneasy heading into the midterm contests because he knew it would serve as a referendum of sorts on his "Peace without Victory" approach, and to a lesser extent, on his plan for the League of Nations. He had good reason to be nervous: the Republicans picked up twenty-five seats in the House and seven in the Senate to seize control in both chambers. Not surprisingly, they interpreted the results as a vote of no confidence for Wilson and his policies, a view that Theodore Roosevelt—who more and more was beginning to look like the Republican nominee in 1920—gleefully shared with Britain's foreign secretary: "In any free country, except the United States, the result of the Congressional elections on November 5th would have meant Mr. Wilson's retirement from office and return to private life," said Roosevelt.[18]

As it turned out, the loss of Congress would be a devastating blow to Wilson and the League of Nations. For one thing, it emboldened the Republicans to publicly savage the president and his new world order, which they did relentlessly. For another, it encouraged Allied leaders to demand a more severe peace—something Wilson adamantly opposed. But worst of all, it gave the chairmanship of the critically important Senate Foreign Relations committee to Henry Cabot Lodge, an avowed isolationist and staunch league opponent. Wilson couldn't know it at the time, but as Congress went, so did his prospects for the Leagues of Nations.

On the morning of November 11, 1918, World War I officially came to an end. Four and half years of fighting had resulted in nearly 16 million deaths—7 million of which were civilians—and 21 million wounded. Great Britain lost over a million lives. France suffered 1.7 million deaths, or approximately 4 percent of its total population. Germany lost 2.5 million, with another 4 million wounded. The United States escaped relatively unscathed, losing "only" 113,000 men, or about a tenth of 1 percent of its population. It was the lowest percentage by far among the combatant countries. British prime minister Lloyd George spoke for the world when he told the House of Commons that the armistice, he hoped, would bring "to an end all wars."[19]

Defeat

The next year would produce one of the fiercest political debates in American history. It would pit the president of the United States against a rabid band of isolationist senators. At stake was whether the United States would join the League of Nations—an intergovernmental peacekeeping organization that the president himself had conceived, nurtured, and championed for the better part of three years. Wilson believed that nothing less than the future of civilization teetered in the balance. He would, quite literally, give his life to the cause.

The plan was to travel to Paris in early 1919 for the Peace Conference, where he would draft and unveil the charter for the League of Nations. Wilson firmly believed that the league was the most important aspect of the peace process. Should the Allied Powers insist on imposing harsh settlement terms, at least it would be mitigated by the peace-keeping body.

Wilson's first order of business was to select representatives to attend the Paris conference to negotiate on behalf of the United States. This was no ceremonial appointment. It's important to keep in mind that transoceanic communication was still in its infancy. To some extent, the negotiators would be on their own with wide latitude to shape the discussion—and possibly the outcome—at their discretion. Picking the right team would be critically important to success.

Wilson never imagined for a second that he wouldn't personally lead the delegation. The league was his baby, too important to be entrusted to others. Not everyone around the president agreed with his participation, however. Trusted advisor Colonel House gently counseled him that some were of the opinion that his presence "would involve a loss of dignity and your commanding position." Secretary of State Robert Lansing bluntly told Wilson that it was a bad idea. Wilson's only response, Lansing would record in his diary, was a "harsh, obstinate expression which indicates resentment at unacceptable advice. He said nothing but looked volumes."[20] Senate Democrats were evenly split on the matter; some preferred he keep away while others thought it made perfect sense for the president to spearhead the negotiations. As for the Allied leaders, both Britain's Lloyd George and France's George Clemenceau suggested to Wilson that he appear at the opening of the conference but keep distant from the actual negotiations—an approach that Wilson angrily dismissed. Underlying all the reticence was an unspoken fear that Wilson would be too domineering and inflexible to allow for a collaborative shaping of the peace and the league. It was a reasonable concern.

But even more troubling than his decision to lead the American contingent was his choice for the other delegates. The smart move would have been to select several sitting senators, then preferably one from each party, as a way to grease the skids for eventual Senate ratification. It was just plain common sense and good politics, and those around the president urged him to include a couple of heavyweights from that body. For reasons not altogether clear, Wilson ignored the counsel, choosing instead to appoint an unimpressive quartet that included House, Lansing, and two other minor players, or as House described it to a British colleague, a collection of "mouthpieces for the president."[21] Most notable for their absence were any Republicans *or* senators. It was an appalling mistake that would come back to haunt him.

In mid-December, Wilson arrived in Europe to great acclaim. He was greeted by the joyous masses as a conquering hero of sorts in his visits to London, Rome, Milan, and other stops before reaching Paris. He had arranged with the presiding leaders that the League of Nations would be the first order of business taken up at the conference and began the new year by writing a first draft of the charter. Pulling an all-nighter with House, the president, working on his favorite typewriter from home, personally tapped out the twenty-two-page initial draft, drawing liberally from some other plans that were making the rounds. He made some minor tweaks to the document after soliciting feedback from the American delegation, and submitted it to the League of Nations Commission, which he had helped to set up and would come to dominate. There, it underwent another round of revisions, though it mostly remained the guts of Wilson's draft. On February 14, little more than a month after putting ink to paper, Woodrow Wilson presented the League of Nations charter to the full conference. As one attendee put it, it amounted to nothing less than a "new declaration of independence, of the world's national independence . . . the (creation) of a super nation." He departed Paris that evening content that he had created a "constitution of peace" that would serve as a "guarantee by word against aggression."[22]

The Draft Covenant, as it became known, was met with mixed reaction back home. Support mostly fell along party lines, with the Democrats behind it and Republicans against it. Opposition generally fell into two camps: those who disagreed with even the *concept* of a league of nations—a faction led by radical isolationist Senator William Borah, who without having seen Wilson's handiwork declared that "if the Savior of mankind should revisit the earth and declare for a League of Nations, I would be opposed to it"[23]—and those who had reservations about some of the language in the Draft Covenant. For the "reservationist" Republicans, the big issue was article 10, which held that in the case of aggression against a league member, the "council shall advise upon the means by which this obligation shall be fulfilled." In their estimation, this violated the spirit of the Monroe Doctrine, and, more worrisome, bound the United States to enter foreign conflicts against its better judgment. Some went as far to say that it threatened the nation's sovereignty.

With the Republicans in control of the Senate, Wilson had his work cut out to obtain the two-thirds approval needed for ratification. Senator Henry Cabot Lodge, chairman of the Foreign Relations Committee, used a little-known parliamentary maneuver called the "round-robin" to put the president on notice that that passage would be impossible without some kind of alteration to article 10. In early March, Wilson headed back to Europe (for what turned out to be a four-month stay, the longest stretch that a sitting president has been out of the country) to participate in the peace settlement negotiations. Advisors urged him to assuage the Republicans' primary concern by amending article 10, but Wilson wouldn't hear of it. Exempting the Monroe Doctrine and specifying a withdrawal process was fine, but that's where he drew the line. Altering the collective security provision of article 10 or watering down its commitment, he believed, would effectively gut the league. On this issue, he would not back down. It would be his downfall.

The final peace settlement—the Treaty of Versailles—was signed on June 28, 1919, five years to the day of Archduke Franz Ferdinand's assassination, which had triggered the war. Wilson wasn't thrilled with the terms—he thought it was too harsh on Germany—but, as always, considered it secondary to the League of Nations. The treaty, in his view, would be long remembered for establishing this new global organization rather than the excessive punishment meted out on the losers.

Wilson returned to the United States in early July to find that nothing had really changed. During the intervening four months, opposition to the league had simply hardened and coalesced. The modest modifications to the covenant did little to alter minds or opinions, particularly in the Senate. Wilson knew he was in for an uphill fight. According to one newspaper tally, 43 senators favored the treaty, 51 opposed it, and 4 remained undecided.[24] The president would have to flip those numbers, and then some, in order to achieve ratification.

At this point, Wilson had a strategic decision to make: stay in Washington and lobby opponents one at a time, or hit the road and take his case directly to the people. Though he found the prospect of endless groveling to people whom he quietly despised unappealing, he gave it a shot, meeting with twenty-two Republicans and a handful of Democrats during the final weeks of July. By all accounts the meetings were cordial but did nothing to win any converts. The Republicans left the president with a simple warning: without modifications to article 10 (through a process known as "reservations") the treaty would fail. One senator confided to a friend that Wilson had left him with "the impression of a spoiled society belle, who considered herself irresistible to men."[25]

To the chagrin of his closest advisors, Wilson refused to consider reservations to article 10. Whether it was stubborn pride, failing health (by this time he was suffering debilitating headaches and severe fatigue), or just plain principle, he wouldn't budge on the Republicans' request. Wilson dismissed Secretary of State Lansing's suggestion of compromising on the reservation issue by shooting him an "expression which comes whenever anyone tells him a fact which interferes with his plans."[26] Had Wilson adopted even mild reservations to the treaty, he would have surely driven a wedge among the Republican holdouts and forced them to defend their position. As it stood, his unwillingness to bend on the matter only served to unify the opposition and strengthen their resolve.

Having failed to win any votes through direct lobbying, in late August the president—against the wishes of his wife and doctor—decided to embark on a month-long whistle-stop tour to whip up support for the treaty. It was a desperate move, but the president had few remaining options at this point. It kicked off on September 4 in Columbus, Ohio, where he characterized the Republican position as a "radical misunderstanding" of the League of Nations, to the delight of four thousand people. In Indianapolis he spent much of his time defending article 10 to the crowd of sixteen thousand people, encouraging them to "tell that to Harry New and Jim Watson," the state's two senators. And so it went. The first week alone saw stops in Missouri, Iowa, Nebraska, South Dakota, and Minnesota, where the president would give two speeches a day, sometimes more. In Omaha he prophetically warned that "within another generation there will be another world war if the nations of the world—the League of Nations—does not prevent it by concerted action." In Kansas City he spoke of fighting for something "as great as the cause of mankind."[27]

As the tour rambled through the plains states and across the Rocky Mountains, the cumulative effect of the stress, oppressive summer heat, and thin air began to wear on Wilson. He complained of severe headaches that would last for days, and frequently found himself short of breath. He told his physician that he had trouble sleeping. Always a powerful extemporaneous speaker, he struggled to get through his speeches, even when reading from prepared text. There was some talk of forgoing the West Coast swing and heading home, but Wilson overruled the suggestion. In Oakland, he warned the parents at a rally that without article 10, "there will be another and final war just about the time these children come to maturity." In San Diego the rhetoric got even more heated. Speaking again about "the children," he morbidly predicted that should we "not win this great fight for the League of Nations, it would mean their death warrant."[28]

By the end of the September, the whistle-stop tour had pivoted back toward the east. He gave one of his worst speeches in Salt Lake City before fifteen thousand people at the Mormon Tabernacle, where he lashed out in anger at the audience for their applause of a proposed Republican reservation. In Denver, he referenced the "next war" and its advanced weaponry, which by comparison would make those of the last war seem like "toys." On September 25 he gave his best speech of the tour—some have called it the finest of his presidency—at the Colorado state fairgrounds in Pueblo. "We have accepted that truth [of liberty and peace]," he closed, "and we're going to be led by it, and it is going to lead us, and, through us, the world out into the pastures of quietness and peace such as the world has never dreamed of before." As it turned out, those would be the last words of the last speech that he delivered as president.[29]

Following the Pueblo address, Wilson's health took a turn for the worse. We now know that he suffered a series of mini-strokes on the train as it raced back to Washington. Upon returning to the White House, he was ordered to bed rest by his physician. He seemed to be doing better when, on October 1, he suffered a massive stroke. It would leave Wilson a semi-invalid and effectively ended his presidency, though the public would never know the full extent of his incapacitation.

It also killed any chance for ratification of the treaty. With the president all but out of the picture, Senator Lodge and the Republicans were left unchecked to characterize the treaty as an assault on American sovereignty. Ratification was always a long shot, but without the president's unrelenting campaigning, vociferous defense, and skilled maneuvering, it stood no chance. On November 19, Lodge brought the treaty to a floor vote, where it was rejected overwhelmingly. He held a second vote, this time with Republican reservations, and that, too, was defeated handily. Four months later, the Democrats would force a third vote on the treaty, and again it failed. And with that, the United States would be the only major power to reject the treaty and refuse to join the League of Nations. It would sign a separate peace treaty with Germany in 1921 to officially end the war.

* * *

It has often been asked: how could something as seemingly benign as a League of Nations, whose primary purpose was to arbitrate disputes between nations, ignite such a towering firestorm of controversy in the United States—such a backlash, in fact, that it was ultimately rejected by the United States Senate?

There is no simple explanation. Some of it had to do with the political climate: Republicans had taken control of the Senate and were determined to give the president a rough go of it no matter what. Isolationism ran strong and deep in the nation's psyche; most Americans, in fact, still subscribed to George Washington's admonition in his farewell address to avoid foreign entanglements (though few would be able to cite Washington as the originator of it). Wilson's tactical blunders in writing the league charter and selling it to the American people certainly played a role. His stubbornness and refusal to compromise didn't help matters. And, of course, his failing health delivered a crippling blow from which he couldn't recover.

It certainly wasn't from lack of trying—or leadership. It's hard to think of another president—Lincoln and the cause of union being the obvious exception—more committed to an issue, an ideal, a program than Wilson was to the League of Nations. He pursued it virtually to the exclusion of all else. His entire second term was a singular campaign for peace without victory and for the league. He threw everything he had into it, and then some. It simply was an idea ahead of its time.

One could only speculate how history would have unfolded had the

United States been an active participant in the League of Nations. Maybe it would have forced Coolidge, Hoover, and Roosevelt to get more involved in European affairs in the mid-1920s and 1930s, perhaps stemming the rise of fascism. It probably would have aligned the United States with the Allied nations much sooner. Would this have discouraged Hitler from his latent territorial expansion in the late 1930s? Possibly. A unified Allied front with the United States leading the way may have given the madman pause. At the end of the day, it's impossible to predict how things might have turned out differently.

There's no doubt that failure to join the league is a stain on Wilson's legacy. Had he convinced Senate Republicans to ratify the treaty, it would be hard to deny his inclusion among the greatest presidents. As it stands, few presidents have achieved more domestic and legislative accomplishments than Wilson. Franklin and Theodore Roosevelt come to mind, maybe Lyndon Johnson. It's a short list. He deserves credit for keeping the United States clear of the carnage of Europe for as long as he did, though some would argue that it wasn't long enough. He did everything in his power to steer Allied leaders away from a vindictive peace, which in hindsight looks prophetic. And while he came up short in the league debate, it wasn't because the idea lacked merit. It was just two decades too soon.

Chapter 7

FRANKLIN ROOSEVELT AND THE LEND-LEASE PROGRAM

Courtesy of the Franklin D. Roosevelt Presidential Library and Museum.

The moment approaches when we shall no longer be able to pay cash for shipping and other supplies.
—Letter from Winston Churchill to Franklin Roosevelt, December 1940

Personally, I do not believe that England is in a position to win the war. If she does not win, or unless our aid is used in negotiating a better peace than could be otherwise obtained, we will be responsible for futilely prolonging the war and adding to the bloodshed and devastation of Europe.
—Charles Lindbergh's testimony before Congress against Lend-Lease, January 1941

On June 22, 1940, the French government signed an armistice with Nazi Germany to end hostilities between the two countries after little more than a month of fighting. It was a devastating blow to the Anglo-French alliance as it left Hitler in total control of continental Europe. Some in the British government favored a negotiated settlement with Germany that would consolidate Hitler's gains but leave England intact. Their newly installed prime minister, however, vehemently opposed that approach. On the eve of the epic Battle of Britain, Winston Churchill roused his nation to "defend our island whatever the cost may be" while putting its citizens on notice that if they should fail, in "God's good time the New World with all its power and might" would set forth with the "liberation and rescue of the Old." It was a plea for help as much as a promise to his people. At the time, the American public—and many in its government—overwhelmingly supported continued neutrality in the "European conflict," even as things grew bleaker for England. Fortunately for Churchill, Franklin Roosevelt did not share that sentiment. He saw England's survival as essential to protecting America's liberty and was determined to help the broke, demoralized country stay in the fight. It would result in the strongest military alliance between two countries in history and quite possibly saved the world from Nazi rule.

* * *

Few topics arouse more interest, study, and opinion than the origins, prosecution, and aftermath of World War II. It is endlessly fascinating on many levels. The accumulated literature on the topic is staggering and still growing. Measured that way, it has likely been the most chronicled event in human history.

Here we look at a narrow slice of the period—Franklin Roosevelt's Lend-Lease program, which provided critical armaments and supplies to Britain during its hour of greatest need. Of all the decisions related to World War II, why focus on Lend-Lease? For starters, it was something that Roosevelt personally struggled with and settled. As a consequence, few episodes are more illustrative of his leadership style and ingenuity. Moreover, it was neither popular nor easy. To the contrary, most Americans were opposed to supplying munitions to Great Britain, at least initially. And of course, the ramifications were enormous. Among other things, it provided an immediate life preserver for Britain during their greatest hour of need; brought the two countries into an unprecedented military alliance (which remains to this day); gave birth to the military-industrial complex that would transform America into the "arsenal for democracy" for the duration of the war and beyond; and, in some ways, marked the final break from the nation's isolationist past. Somehow Roosevelt managed to win congressional authorization for the program, rally the American people to support it, and all the while quietly bring the country into the war without creating a major uproar. It required brilliant maneuvering by the president and his advisors and merits a closer examination.

Roosevelt and Isolationism

According to British prime minister Lloyd George, the Great War was supposed to be the "war to end all wars." But just as Woodrow Wilson had predicted, the harsh settlement terms created the conditions that would ultimately give rise to Adolph Hitler and fascism. Without American involvement, the League of Nations turned out to be ineffective as a peacekeeping body. And for reasons too long to recite, the European powers did nothing to prevent Germany's remilitarization and subsequent aggression against its neighboring countries. At some point in the late 1930s, as a result of flawed logic, myopic analysis, and plain naiveté, an avoidable war became inevitable.

Preoccupied with the Great Depression, most Americans paid scant attention to the rising tension in Europe. For much of the decade, the overwhelming sentiment had been to steer clear of Europe's problems. A sizable segment of the population, in fact, believed that the country had been "duped" into World War I by greedy industrialists and bankers looking to profit from American entry. They also believed that Woodrow Wilson expedited US involvement by overstepping his presidential authority. Measures were taken to prevent this from happening again, including the Johnson Act of 1934, which prohibited Americans from making loans to any government in default on their World War I debt. The banned list included most of the European powers except Finland, which continued to make payments.[1] The following year, Congress passed the first in a series of Neutrality Acts that outlawed the trade of arms and munitions with countries at war, and restricted presidential discretion in this area. The Neutrality Act of 1936 extended the embargo to include all loans and credit to belligerent nations. Though he disagreed with this approach, Roosevelt—not wanting to alienate his Democratic base during an election year—went along with the laws, even though it limited his ability to aid friendly countries.[2] "History is filled with unforeseeable situations that call for some flexibility of action," said a reluctant Roosevelt at the first bill-signing ceremony in 1935. "In other words, the inflexible provisions might drag us into war instead of keeping us out."[3]

Notwithstanding the isolationist mood of the country and the restrictive Neutrality Acts, Roosevelt sought ways to defuse the escalating hostilities across the ocean, particularly following his reelection in 1936. He was troubled by Italy's invasion of defenseless Ethiopia in the fall of 1935 and even more troubled by the League of Nations' refusal to do anything about it. He was also concerned about Japan's growing militarism. Roosevelt privately encouraged leaders in Germany and Italy to consider disarmament of all nondefensive weapons, but the suggestion went ignored. Meetings at the White House with European leaders like British prime minister Neville Chamberlain and Belgian prime minister Paul van Zeeland to discuss steps that could be taken "to establish more healthy conditions in the world" amounted to little.[4] He even sent an emissary to Russia to "win the confidence of Stalin." The result was a fresh round of Soviet propaganda.[5] "European leaders," said an exasperated Roosevelt at a July 1937 press conference, were looking for someone to come forward "with a hat and a rabbit in it." Well, he said to laughs, "I haven't got a hat and I haven't got a rabbit in it."[6]

For his part, Roosevelt was doing everything within reason to prepare the United States for the potential of war. When he put forward an unprecedented $1.1 billion defense budget in 1935, it was met with large antiwar protests in Washington and "peace rallies" on college campuses around the country. "We are rapidly sinking to the levels of Hitler and Mussolini" is how the normally pro-Roosevelt *Nation* magazine described the peacetime budget.[7] But Roosevelt didn't believe appeasement would mollify Hitler one bit. It would simply fuel his hunger for more territory. In the face of this challenge, isolationism made no sense. Pretending that the problem didn't exist, Roosevelt believed, would only make it worse. And unlike many politicians and a sizeable chunk of the population, he clearly supported the Allied Powers against Germany; he saw no moral equivalency between Hitler's Germany and Britain and France. In that sense, he was never neutral. "Roosevelt knew from the start," writes one historian of the era, "and before Hitler himself did, that Hitler was a menace to him. Roosevelt knew that the world's democracy could never be safe nor America unambiguously the world's most important country while Hitler reigned and Hitlerism flourished."[8]

To that end, Roosevelt won an important concession in the 1937 Neutrality Act with the "cash-and-carry" provision, which allowed for the sale of munitions and supplies to belligerent nations as long as it was paid in cash and transported on their own ships. Roosevelt insisted on the policy because he knew that should war break out between Germany and the Allied Powers, the only nations to benefit would be Britain and France since they controlled the seas; it would be impossible for the Axis Powers to send merchant vessels to purchase and pick up the supplies. Isolationists in the Senate cried foul over the provision but lacked the numbers to prevent it. Their leader, Senator Hiram Johnson, vowed to stop FDR's "sinister grasp of . . . the war making powers" at all costs.[9]

Roosevelt further incensed the isolationist crowd with his famous "quarantine speech" in October 1937, where he outlined a more interventionist and muscular approach to thwarting the expansionist desires of Germany, Italy, and Japan. Without naming the countries, he spoke of the innocent peoples and nations that were "being cruelly sacrificed to a greed for power and supremacy which is devoid of all sense of justice and humane considerations." He warned that if those things could "come to pass in other parts of the world, let no one imagine that America will escape, that America may expect mercy, that this Western Hemisphere will not be attacked." Part of the problem, he explained, was that for too long America had its head in the sand. "There is no escape through mere isolation or neutrality," he thundered. "Peace-loving nations must make a concerted effort in opposition to those violations of treaties. . . . There must be a recognition of the fact that national morality is as vital as private morality." Roosevelt lamented that the "epidemic of world lawlessness is spreading," and noted that "when an epidemic of physical disease starts to spread, the community approves and joins in a quarantine of the patients in order to protect the health of the community against the spread of the disease." He reiterated that the United States was "determined to keep out of war," yet conceded that "we are adopting such measures as will minimize our risk of involvement" since there could be no "complete protection in a world of disorder in which confidence and security have broken down." He concluded with a simple call to action: "Peace-loving nations must express themselves to the end that nations that may be tempted to violate their agreements and the rights of others will desist from such a course. There must be positive endeavors to preserve peace."[10]

Roosevelt was out in front of public opinion, and he knew it. It was by far his most public utterance denouncing isolationism. Not surprisingly, the reaction was swift and severe. Respected Yale professor Edwin Borchard credited Roosevelt with putting America's foreign policy "under as complete a dictatorship as Germany or Italy." Alf Landon, the former Republican presidential nominee whom Roosevelt had vanquished a year earlier, warned that "collective action through a quarantine means economic sanctions—meaning a blockade if it is to be successful—which means war." For Senator Gerald Nye of North Dakota, striving to bring peace to the world was well and good, so long as it didn't drag "130 million people into another world death march." Not to be outdone, Senator Hiram Johnson blamed the speech on Roosevelt's "delusions of grandeur" that he was "the savior of mankind." A former undersecretary of state modestly predicted that Roosevelt's approach would "inevitably lead us into war."[11] How bad did it get? A proposed constitutional amendment requiring congressional declarations of war to be approved by a majority of the American people through a referendum was only narrowly defeated in the House of Representatives in the months following the speech.

The isolationists were correct in one sense: Roosevelt's quarantine theory would probably lead to military intervention at some point—it was simply a matter of when. But to allow Hitler and imperial Japan to go unchecked in their territorial conquests wasn't a strategy for peace; it was simply forestalling the inevitable day of reckoning, reasoned Roosevelt. He was convinced that isolationism, neutrality, and nonaction wouldn't satiate the world's bullies in the slightest. It would only embolden them.

Roosevelt shared those thoughts with the Allied leaders during the ensuing Czechoslovakia crisis, which came to a head in the summer of 1938 after Czech leaders refused Hitler's demands to turn over the heavily German-populated Sudetenland region to his control. He thought that the continued appeasement of Hitler was a mistake, and told the British consulate as much in a private meeting just two weeks before the Munich Conference. He went so far as to outline for the ambassador a secret plan to aid Britain and France in the event that war broke out—a plan, Roosevelt warned him, that could result in his impeachment should it "be known to anyone that he has even breathed a suggestion."[12] His hope was that this promise of solidarity would stiffen the Allies to Hitler's outlandish requests. Luckily for Roosevelt, word of the meeting never leaked out. The Czechs, however, were less fortunate. On September 29 at the Munich Conference, France and Britain—ignoring Roosevelt's prior counsel—handed Germany half of Czechoslovakia's land and 70 percent of its industrial, defense, and manufacturing capacity, making it all but certain that Hitler would quickly swallow the other half. And while Neville Chamberlain was busy proclaiming that he had achieved "peace in our time," Hitler set his gaze on other territorial conquests.[13]

Appeasement Fails

The policy of appeasement came to an ignominious end on March 15, 1939, as German tanks rolled through what remained of Czechoslovakia. Neville Chamberlain reluctantly learned what Roosevelt had known for a while: Adolph Hitler was a lying madman intent on conquering Europe. What particularly concerned Roosevelt was the growing gap in air superiority between Germany and Britain and France. Roosevelt's ambassador to France reported that the French air fleet was much older and about a tenth the size of the German Luftwaffe. The Germans "would be able to bomb Paris at will," he warned Roosevelt, and inflict destruction that "would pass all imagination."[14]

Roosevelt had little doubt that Hitler's next target would be Poland. Following the fall of Czechoslovakia, the leaders in Britain and France came to the same conclusion, and reminiscent of World War I, offered unqualified support for Poland should Germany invade it. Roosevelt considered it a foregone conclusion that Europe would be engulfed in war before year's end. "If the Rhine frontiers are threatened the rest of the world is, too," he lectured a group of senators in a private meeting at the White House. "Once they have fallen before Hitler, the German sphere of action will be unlimited."[15] He told them bluntly that he would do everything possible to help France and Britain thwart Hitler's advances. "It is to our interest, quite frankly, to do what we can, absolutely as a matter of peace, peace of the world, to help the French and British maintain their independence. . . . Their independence is threatened today."[16]

To make matters worse, Congress—over FDR's objections—allowed the "cash-and-carry" provision of the Neutrality Law to expire, which meant that Britain and France could no longer purchase munitions and supplies from the United States should war break out. It couldn't have come at a worse time. Roosevelt feared that Hitler and Mussolini would interpret it as a sign of America's desire to remain isolated from European conflicts. To counter that impression, he made a series of speeches and public remarks in the spring and early summer of 1939 that he hoped would give pause to Hitler, as well as spur Congress to revise the Neutrality Law. In late March while vacationing in Warm Springs, Georgia, he told the traveling press corps that the goal of the Nazis was to "attain world dominance, and make subject to them a great many other nations and races. That is what is giving the world concern today." He reminded the reporters that his remarks weren't for attribution and they were "not to bring me into" the story.[17] A week later he had another "swell story," again not for attribution (he advised the reporters to quote "sources close to the White House") that hinted at the dire economic consequences of German domination. "One of the results of successful military aggression . . . is the control of commerce, not only within their own territory but in other territories." He warned that nations like the United States, which "pay better wages and work shorter hours," would be forced to either lower their standard of living or massively subsidize their exports in order to compete against the militarized economies. This would be the new economic reality should Germany conquer Europe.[18]

Roosevelt was even more pointed in his remarks on April 14 to the governing board of the Pan-American Union. He dismissed Mussolini's recent diatribe about being a "prisoner in the Mediterranean" and Hitler's complaint that Britain was "encircling" Germany by creating an alliance with France and Poland as plain silly. "There is no such thing as encircling or threatening, or imprisoning any peaceful Nation by other peaceful nations. We have reason to know that in our own experience." Referring to their dreams of conquest as "ridiculous as they are criminal," he lamented that Germany and Italy could "find no better methods of realizing their destinies than those which were used by the Huns and the Vandals fifteen hundred years ago." Roosevelt was speaking to the fascists overseas and the isolationists in Congress when he unambiguously declared that "we have an interest, wider than that of the mere defense of our sea-ringed continent." For in the end, "we know that for the development of the next generation will so narrow the oceans separating us from the Old World, that our customs and our actions are necessarily involved with hers, whether we like it or not."[19]

Roosevelt followed up the speech with diplomatic letters to both Hitler and Mussolini seeking written assurances that their "armed forces will not attack or invade the territory or possessions" of thirty-one specific nations (which he listed). In return, Roosevelt offered to participate in a trade and disarmament conference to resolve any lingering issues. What he hoped to accomplish from the gesture is not entirely clear, but to no surprise, Hitler and Mussolini derisively rejected the overture. Il Duce publicly called it an "absurd" and "Messiah-like message," while Hitler, in a speech before the Reichstag, essentially told the president to mind his own business. Equally not surprising, the isolationists in America found comfort in Hitler's response. "Roosevelt put his chin out and got a resounding whack," mused Hiram Johnson. "I have reached the conclusion that there will be no war." It was nothing more than a Roosevelt ploy to "knock down two dictators in Europe so that one may be firmly implanted in America," Johnson groused.[20]

Roosevelt spent the better part of the spring and summer lobbying Congress to revise the Neutrality Act to include the cash-and-carry provision again. Without it, the United States would be hamstrung from helping the Allies combat Hitler and Mussolini in the event of war. In late June, the House delivered a setback to the president when it defeated the bill by a slim four votes. Hoping to find better luck in the Senate, Roosevelt was met with more bad news when the bill was killed in committee. FDR fumed to his secretary of the treasury that there would "be great rejoicing in the Italian and German camps" when they learned what had happened. He acidly proposed that statues of Republican Senators Bob Taft, Warren Austin, Henry Cabot Lodge, and Arthur Vandenberg be erected in Berlin with a "swastika on them."[21] For the time being, neutrality reform was dead.

Cash and Carry

On the morning of September 1, 1939, at 2:50 a.m., President Roosevelt was awakened by a frantic phone call from his ambassador to Paris, William Bullitt. He was informed that Germany had just invaded Poland. The president made a few phone calls and calmly went back to sleep. World War II had begun. "It's the end of the world, the end of everything," remarked a despondent Ambassador Joe Kennedy from his official residence in Great Britain.[22]

The news came as little surprise. Just a week earlier, Hitler and Stalin had stunned the world with the news of a nonaggression pact between their two countries. To many observers, this unholy alliance was a clear indication that Poland was about to be overrun. Roosevelt took to the radio airwaves a few days later for one of his Fireside Chats. He reassured the American people that his goal was to keep out of the war. Curiously, he added that while "the nation will remain neutral," he could not "ask that every American remain neutral in thought as well. Even a neutral has a right to take account of facts." It was his way of subtly implying that Germany was at fault.

With defenseless Poland under siege and France and Britain officially at war with Germany, Roosevelt redoubled his efforts to push neutrality reform through Congress. The time had come to reinsert the cash-and-carry provision so that Britain and France could purchase munitions as Hitler amassed his force on the Western front. Public opinion seemed to be moving in FDR's direction. Several new Gallup polls showed that over half the country now supported arms sales to the two countries. Roosevelt felt sure enough on the matter to tell Neville Chamberlain that the arms embargo would be "repealed within a month."[23]

This time around, Roosevelt would leave nothing to chance. On September 13, he asked Congress to convene a special session to take up the legislation immediately. He followed it with a speech to that body in which he insisted that, contrary to what the isolationists had been preaching, aid to Britain and France would help to keep the nation out of war, not drag it in. "I give to you my deep and unalterable conviction," he told the assembled, "based on years of experience as a worker in the field of international peace that by the repeal of the embargo the United States will more probably remain at peace than if the law remains as it stands today."[24] Roosevelt wisely invited prominent Republicans like former secretary of war Henry Stimson, 1936 Republican nominee Alf Landon, and Frank Knox, publisher of the rabidly pro-Republican *Chicago Daily News*, to the White House for special briefings on the matter. He persuaded them to speak publicly in support of the cash-and-carry provision. It was a brilliant strategic move that helped neutralize the isolationists' thrust. By the time Congress put it to a vote in late October, the rout was on, and both chambers passed it by a wide margin. Roosevelt would call it one of his most satisfying legislative victories. In England, Neville Chamberlain breathed a sigh of relief and sent Roosevelt a note of thanks for his "profound moral encouragement."[25] It was the last good news the Allies would receive for quite some time.

As the calendar changed from 1939 to 1940, continental Europe went eerily quiet. With Germany and the Allied Powers technically at war, some in the press dubbed it the "Phony War" in light of the lack of hostilities and battles. During his State of the Union address, Franklin Roosevelt remained hopeful—and cautiously optimistic—that the United States could keep out of the conflict. "I can understand the feelings of those who warn the nation that they will never again consent to the sending of American youth to fight on the soil of Europe," he told Congress. "But," he reminded them, "nobody has asked them to consent—for nobody expects such an undertaking." He pointed out that there was a vast difference between "keeping out of war" and pretending that it was "none of our business." Of course, he couldn't let the moment pass without taking a dig at Hitler and Mussolini: "It becomes clearer and clearer that the future world will be a shabby and dangerous place to live in—yes, even for Americans to live in—if it is ruled by force in the hands of a few."[26]

The "Phony War" came to an end on May 10, 1940, as Hitler's army tore through the Low Countries—Holland, Belgium, Luxembourg—in a matter of days, and was deep into France within weeks. The rapidity and ferocity of the attack stunned the world. The French premier described their defenses against this German onslaught as "walls of sand that a child puts up against waves on the seashore."[27] In a little over a month's time, the Axis Powers had taken control of most of continental Europe, including France, which formally surrendered on June 22, 1940. The only impediments that stood between Hitler and total domination of Western Europe were the English Channel, Winston Churchill, and Franklin Roosevelt.

Winston and Franklin

It would be overly simplistic to analyze the United States' aid to Great Britain during 1940, culminating with the Lend-Lease program in early 1941, solely through the lens of the relationship between Winston Churchill and Franklin Roosevelt. Events of this magnitude are more complicated and nuanced than just two individuals, and reducing history to a few personalities is fraught with peril.

But in the context of understanding Franklin Roosevelt's decision making, it makes quite a bit of sense. Their partnership was so unique, so unprecedented, so well documented, that it would be remiss *not* to use it as the primary filter for understanding how the United States came to assist Great Britain during its darkest hour. There's little doubt that Churchill was the dominant influence on Roosevelt as he grappled with the thorny issue of supplying beleaguered England with the munitions it needed to fend off Hitler while at the same time maintaining full neutrality.

In many ways, Churchill viewed this partnership—or more specifically, getting the United States off the sidelines—as his primary responsibility when he promised the British people his "blood, sweat, and tears" upon taking over as prime minister in May of 1940. In his very first correspondence to Franklin Roosevelt as Britain's wartime leader, he painted a dark portrait of the European landscape. The small countries had been "smashed up like matchwood," he told Roosevelt shortly before the fall of France, and he fully expected England to be next on Hitler's wish list. He reassured the president that they were prepared to "continue the war alone," but warned that the "voice and force of the United States may count for nothing if they are withheld too long." It was an astonishing admission for someone tasked with stopping the Nazi war machine. He closed with a remarkably blunt request: "All I ask now is that you should proclaim non-belligerency, which would mean that you would help us with everything short of actually engaging armed forces."[28]

Churchill's plea revealed a certain naiveté and ignorance about Roosevelt's predicament. The president had spent the better part of the past year trying to convince the American people and Congress that the cash-and-carry concept wouldn't disturb American neutrality; that private companies, in effect, should be allowed to sell munitions to countries with both the hard cash and transport capabilities to pick it up. But to have the United States *government* sell directly to England surplus ships, planes, guns, and ammunition, as Churchill had pleaded, was out of the question. Congress would never go along with it. Neither would the American public. It would virtually make the United States an enemy combatant against Germany. There were already fears in some quarters that Roosevelt aspired to be an "American dictator." This type of move would only inflame those sentiments—in an election year, no less. Roosevelt politely told Churchill that it probably wasn't wise for "that type of suggestion to be made to the Congress at this moment" and thought that would be the end of it.[29]

But Churchill wouldn't let it go. To his great credit, he kept after Roosevelt—a trait that would come to define their relationship over the next five years. "I do not need to tell you about the gravity of what has happened," he responded to Roosevelt. "If American assistance is to play any part, it must be available soon." Churchill was determined to get Roosevelt to break with neutrality. "I shall drag the United States in," he bragged to his son.[30]

Roosevelt was not oblivious to Churchill's plight. He knew full well the stakes and consequences should England also fall. On May 16 he went before Congress to ask for dramatic increases in defense spending and munitions capacity, equipment modernization, and a larger army. He reminded the nation that the two oceans no longer provided a natural barrier to the dangers that lurked, that attack is no longer "so unlikely or impossible that it may be ignored." But the real purpose of the speech was to begin to redefine—in a way broaden—the concept of a first line of defense. "The clear fact is that the American people must recast their thinking about national defense."[31] He wanted to implant the idea that arming Britain was, in fact, a smart way to protect the American homeland.

In some ways, Roosevelt's dilemma was greater than just congressional intransigence and the deep isolationist streak that ran through the country. It was one of priorities. In the spring of 1940, America's own military preparedness was pitiful at best. With 245,000 men in active duty, the army ranked twentieth in the world, just after the Dutch. Even more disconcerting, it had only 5 mechanized divisions compared to Germany's 141 on the Western front alone. Most of the rifles and munitions dated back to World War I, as did much of the naval fleet. The air force was a fraction the size of the German Luftwaffe; so small, in fact, that there weren't enough planes to train new pilots. Roosevelt rightly pressed Congress to convert America's industrial economy into a military one, but that was going to take time—something Britain didn't have.[32]

Confronted with this reality, Roosevelt had a strategic choice to make. He could either stockpile armaments, munitions, equipment, and supplies for America's defenses or provide them to Britain immediately. It was a wrenching decision because it would leave America vulnerable should Germany overrun Britain, too—a very real possibility. But Roosevelt firmly believed that the best way to protect America was to keep Britain in the war. If Hitler could be contained to continental Europe, it would only be a matter of time before the United States and Britain eventually overwhelmed him. But if England fell, Germany would control the Atlantic and ultimately threaten South America, Greenland, and perhaps even Canada. At some point, the war would come to America's shores. "If Great Britain goes down," reflected Roosevelt, "all of us in the Americas would be living at the point of a gun."[33]

To make matters worse for the president, his top military advisors—and many in the cabinet—disagreed with his approach. Army Chief of Staff George Marshall noted to Roosevelt that the "War Department would naturally and rightfully be subject to the most serious adverse criticism" should the country be dragged into the war without adequate supplies to wage battle. Ambassador Joe Kennedy pessimistically counseled that since France and Britain were a lost cause, it would be "better to fight in our own backyard." His own secretary of war "absolutely disapproved of the sale of any US military property" to Britain. Roosevelt knew it was a huge gamble. "If I should guess wrong," he confided to Secretary of the Interior Harold Ickes, "the results might be serious."[34]

As Churchill braced England for what would be the epic Battle of Britain, the country faced a calamitous shortage of guns and munitions. Most of it had been left on the beaches of Dunkirk in France after their narrow escape from the Nazi army. According to one estimate, there were six hundred thousand rifles in the entire nation and only five hundred cannons, many of which were lifted from museums. "Never has a nation been so naked before her foes," shuddered Churchill. He kept on Roosevelt for assistance. "Our intention is, whatever happens, to fight on to the end in this island," he wrote him. "Members of the present administration would likely go down during this process should it result adversely, but in no conceivable circumstance will we consent to surrender. . . . Excuse me, Mr. President, for putting this nightmare so bluntly."[35]

Churchill's hectoring paid off. While he didn't get the 50 surplus destroyers that were sitting in dry dock, he got just about everything else, including 500,000 rifles, 93 bomber planes, 184 tanks, 76,000 machine guns, and 100 million rounds of ammunition to go with it. It took twelve ships to transport the equipment—worth about $300 million—to England. Roosevelt got around congressional scrutiny by classifying the military supplies (somewhat deceptively) as "surplus materials," which meant that they could be sold to a private company, which in turn could sell them to the British government under the cash-and-carry provision of the Neutrality Act. It was brilliant maneuvering on Roosevelt's part, and wouldn't be the last time he resorted to sleight of hand to help his friend overseas.[36]

In the greater scheme of things, the munitions would be a pittance compared to what the United States would ultimately provide Great Britain and the other Allies throughout the duration of the war. But at the time it was enormous. And, perhaps more importantly, it was a clear sign that Roosevelt was intellectually and emotionally committed to doing everything short of declaring war to help Britain stave off defeat. Churchill took great comfort in this. There would be yet even darker days ahead, but the partnership had turned a corner.

"This is a thing to do now"

The darkest days would constitute the Battle of Britain, which began in July of 1940 and lasted through the autumn of that year. Hitler's plan was to exploit German air superiority and bombard the island nation for months, followed by a massive sea invasion. He was convinced that an unrelenting terror campaign from above would soften their defenses and break their spirit, paving the way for German occupation.

Churchill would later say of the British people that the Battle of Britain represented "their finest hour." The same could be said of Churchill himself. Rarely has a leader so rallied the spirit of a nation through words and sheer force of will as Churchill that summer. Day after day his majestic oratory provided sustenance to a beleaguered people, his elocution serving as a last line of defense against nightly raids that couldn't be thwarted. Never was he better than on June 4, when speaking before the House of Commons he thundered that "we shall go on to the end. We shall fight in France, we shall fight on the seas and oceans, we shall fight with growing confidence and growing strength in the air, we shall defend our island, whatever the cost may be. We shall fight on the beaches, we shall fight on the landing grounds, we shall fight in the fields and in the streets, we shall fight in the hills, we shall never surrender."[37]

The British people weren't the only ones to take comfort in Churchill's speeches and determination. So did Franklin Roosevelt and millions of American citizens. It may not have been Churchill's intention, but they couldn't help but be affected by his stirring imagery and unflinching confidence in the face of terrible odds. Less than a week later, partly in response to Churchill's moving rhetoric and desperate plight, Franklin Roosevelt gave a full-throated endorsement of the Allied Powers, telling the graduating class at the University of Virginia Law School (where his son was getting a degree), that "in our American unity, we will pursue two obvious and simultaneous courses: we will extend to the opponents of force the material resources of this nation; and, at the same time, we will harness and speed up the use of those resources in order that we ourselves in the Americas may have equipment and training equal to the task of any emergency and every defense . . . full speed ahead."[38] Roosevelt was well on his way to ending American neutrality in this great struggle against tyranny.

Roosevelt followed up his heated performance at the University of Virginia by reorganizing his cabinet to do away with the isolationists and defeatists. He fired the secretary of war and the secretary of the navy, both of whom favored neutrality, and replaced them with two staunch Republican interventionists, Henry Stimson and Frank Knox, respectively. It was a bold and brilliant move, one of the best personnel decisions of his presidency. Stimson, who had formerly served in the same post under William Howard Taft some three decades earlier, was highly regarded by members of both parties and an outspoken supporter of the Allies. He would become one of Roosevelt's closest advisors over the next five years. Knox, who had actually run against Roosevelt as Alf Landon's ticket-mate in 1936, was a particular favorite among the far right. Both men would play decisive roles in selling the president's agenda and preparing the country for war.

By late summer, things were not looking good for Great Britain, and Churchill was again pleading to Roosevelt for the fifty US destroyers that were sitting in mothballs. "The Germans have the whole French coastline from which to launch U-boat and dive-bomber attacks upon our trade and food," he starkly wrote Roosevelt. "We must be constantly prepared to repel by sea action threatened invasion in the narrow waters." Churchill wanted to position the destroyers, many of which were relics from World War I, in the English Channel to help thwart a potential amphibious assault on the island. "The whole fate of the war may be decided by this minor and easily remediable factor," he practically begged Roosevelt. "I cannot understand why, with the position as it is, you do not send me at least 50 or 60 of your oldest destroyers . . . *in the long history of the world this is a thing to do now.*"[39]

It wasn't quite that simple. Roosevelt was more than happy to give the destroyers to Britain. He knew they had much greater value defending the British Isles than sitting idly in the United States. That wasn't the problem. Congress was. Roosevelt had little confidence that he could win their approval in a reasonable amount of time. With that being the case, Roosevelt went about it another way. What if he structured the transfer so that the United States got something of tremendous value in return—so great, in fact, that he could simply bypass Congress altogether using his commander-in-chief powers? Few would cry foul if it was a lopsided deal for the United States. In return for the destroyers, Roosevelt asked Churchill for ninety-nine-year naval leases on eight of Britain's Western Atlantic colonies, including Bermuda, Newfoundland, Trinidad, and British Guiana—something that would have been unthinkable even a few months earlier. But desperate times called for desperate deals. Churchill knew he was getting the short end of the stick, but so be it. He needed the destroyers. Roosevelt wisely consummated the deal first, *then* informed Congress. His attorney general argued that the transfer didn't require congressional approval because it amounted to a *net increase* in the nation's national security. It was a flimsy legal argument, but Congress didn't much object. Even the most devout isolationists could find little to fault with the result, the means notwithstanding. Roosevelt modestly called it the most important land acquisition since the Louisiana Purchase, a sentiment echoed by many of the leading newspapers.[40]

As usual, Churchill captured the moment best, telling the House of Commons that from this point forward, the two countries would be "somewhat mixed together," the strength and momentum from which would resemble that of the mighty Mississippi. Like the great river, the partnership will "keep rolling along. Let it roll. Let it roll on full flood, inexorable, irresistible, benignant, to broader lands and better days."[41] Churchill would later call it "a decidedly un-neutral act by the United States" that would have "justified the German government in declaring war upon them."[42] He was right on both counts.

"Arsenal of Democracy"

Since the mid-1930s, Franklin Roosevelt had slowly been preparing the United States for the possibility of war. He had done it in spite of a mostly hostile Congress (on this issue), a public that desperately wanted to stay removed from world affairs, and members of his administration who believed that neutrality and isolation was the best policy. At times he was straightforward and persuasive; other times manipulative and cunning; and still other times outright duplicitous. But he understood the stakes as well as anyone, perhaps more so. He had believed all along that Hitler's goal was world domination, nothing less. The United States needed to be equal to the task.

In the early part of 1940, Roosevelt began whispering to close confidants that he didn't want to seek a historic third term. He would much rather go back to Hyde Park and write his memoirs than face the rigors of another campaign. But the fall of France, the Battle of Britain, and the prospect of Hitler controlling the Atlantic changed all that. The American people had (mostly) come to terms with the fact that the United States would have to stand shoulder to shoulder with its closest ally during its hour of greatest need, and Roosevelt wanted to see it through.

Nobody was happier with this decision than Winston Churchill. The prospects of fighting Hitler alone terrified the prime minister. His relief was palpable upon learning the news that Roosevelt had defeated his Republican opponent, Wendell Willkie. "I did not think it right for me as a foreigner to express my opinion upon American politics while the election was on, but now I feel you will not mind me saying that I prayed for your success and I am truly thankful for it," he cabled Roosevelt the day after the election. "Things are afoot which will be remembered as long as the English language is spoken in any quarter of the globe, and in expressing the comfort I feel that the people of the United States have once again cast these great burdens upon you, I must avow my sure faith that the lights by which we steer will bring us all safely to anchor."[43]

Churchill was relieved, in part, because he had another request of the president. Britain was rapidly going bankrupt. It had exhausted virtually all of its cash buying munitions from the United States. With the German war machine cranking at full capacity across continental Europe, Britain had no way to keep pace except to purchase supplies from the United States. Without the cash to do so anymore, the war could be lost in a matter of months.

Churchill's plea came in the form of a seven-thousand-word letter delivered to Roosevelt by sea plane while he was yachting in the Bahamas during the first week of December. It was one of the most carefully composed documents of Churchill's career—and among the most important. He labored over several drafts and solicited feedback from his circle of advisors, a rarity for the leader. "The result," writes one historian, "was classic Churchill—long, well argued, and passionate yet practical."

It was also blunt and direct. He requested US convoys and patrols in the Atlantic; an endless list of armaments, munitions, and advanced weaponry; and raw materials and domestic supplies to feed the starving nation. And there was a catch: he couldn't pay for it. "The moment shall approach where we shall no longer be able to pay cash for shipping and other supplies," concluded the letter. "While we will do our utmost and shrink from no proper sacrifices to make payments across the exchange, I believe you will agree that it would be wrong in principle and mutually disadvantageous in effect if, at the height of this struggle, Great Britain were to be divested of all saleable assets so that after the victory was won with our blood, civilization saved and the time gained for the United States to be fully armed against all eventualities, we should stand stripped to the bone. Such a course would not be in the moral or economist interest of either of our countries."[44]

By all accounts, the president was deeply moved by the letter. He absorbed the full meaning of it while rejuvenating his spirits in the Bahamas. In retrospect, there's no doubt that the Lend-Lease program was born directly of this missive. If the president couldn't find a creative way to provide cost-free munitions and supplies to England, the war in Europe would be over. And the war for the Americas would be next.

His solution was pure genius. Instead of lending money or selling munitions to Great Britain, the United States would form a gentlemen's agreement of sorts whereby it would loan supplies in return for "repayment in kind" after the war. If England couldn't repay in kind then it would provide cash equivalents—after the war. This, reasoned Roosevelt, would get around the Johnson Act, which prohibited loans to countries that had forfeited on their World War I debt, and the Neutrality Acts, which authorized cash purchases only, since it was a temporary loan of products, not money. Of course, there was little expectation that the "equipment" would be returned someday.

How, exactly, he came up with the specific idea of Lend-Lease is a bit of a mystery. His closest advisor, Harry Hopkins, later told Churchill that FDR "brooded silently" over the letter for two days while aboard the *Tuscaloosa*, never sharing his thoughts with him or anyone else.[45] Roosevelt's secretary of labor, Frances Perkins, observed that Lend-Lease came to him as a "flash of almost clairvoyant knowledge and understanding." She described the process as similar to a composer when he hears "the structure of an entire symphony or opera."[46]

The campaign to sell it to the American people and Congress was equally as brilliant as the plan itself. In a press conference on December

16, Roosevelt used a simple analogy to explain how the program would work. "Suppose my neighbor's home catches on fire," he nonchalantly told the assembled press corps, "and I have a length of garden hose four or five hundred feet away. If he can take my garden hose and connect it up with his hydrant, I may help to put out his fire. Now what do I do? I don't say to him before that operation, 'Neighbor, my garden hose cost me $15; you have to pay me $15 for it.' What is the transaction that goes on? I don't want $15—I want my garden hose back after the fire is over. All right. If it goes through the fire all right, intact, without any damage to it, he gives it back to me and thanks me very much for the use of it." And should it be damaged or destroyed, Roosevelt explained, he could simply replace it or give money for it. "What I'm trying to do," he emphasized, "is to eliminate the dollar sign. That is something brand new in the thoughts of practically everybody in this room, I think—get rid of the silly, foolish dollar sign."[47]

Roosevelt continued his public relations assault a week later with perhaps his most famous Fireside Chat—what would become known as the "Arsenal of Democracy" speech. By this time, Roosevelt had become a committed partisan to defeating Nazi Germany. The only thing that was missing was a formal declaration of war. "The Nazi masters of Germany have made it clear," he solemnly opened the radio broadcast, "that they intend not only to dominate all life and thought in their own country, but also enslave the whole of Europe, and then to use the resources of Europe to dominate the rest of the world." It was a stark description of where the world was headed in language more severe than the American people had ever heard from Roosevelt. As for arming and supplying Great Britain to the hilt, Roosevelt made the choice seem simple. "Does anyone seriously believe that we need to fear attack anywhere in the Americas while a free Britain remains our most powerful naval neighbor in the Atlantic? And does anyone seriously believe, on the other hand, that we could rest easy if the Axis Powers were our neighbors there?"

If Hitler defeated England, Roosevelt warned, then "the Axis powers will control the continents of Europe, Asia, Africa, Australia, and the high seas—and they will be in a position to bring enormous military and naval resources against this hemisphere. It is no exaggeration to say that all of us, in all the Americas, would be living at the point of a gun—a gun loaded with explosive bullets, economic as well as military." In other words, "Great Britain and the British Empire are today the spearhead of resistance to world conquest. And they are putting up a fight which will live forever in the story of human gallantry."

He urged private business to continue making the "planes and ships and guns and shells" as quickly as possible, reassuring them that "your government, with its defense experts, can then determine how best to use them to defend this hemisphere . . . how much shall be sent abroad and how much shall remain at home." He closed with one last thought: "We must be the great arsenal for democracy."[48]

On the day Roosevelt addressed the nation, London was hit with its heaviest aerial bombing yet from the Luftwaffe. Thousands of civilians were killed and major sections of the city lay in ruins. Nonetheless, the "spirit of Londoners," Churchill wrote Roosevelt, "was as high as in the first days of the indiscriminate bombing . . . months ago. I thank you for testifying before all the world that the future safety and greatness of the American Union are intimately concerned with the upholding and the effective arming of that indomitable spirit."[49]

President Roosevelt formally introduced the Lend-Lease bill (H.R. 1776—a nice touch by the House parliamentarian) to Congress on January 6, 1940, the day of his State of the Union address. He spent most of the speech reiterating the critical importance of keeping Britain in the fight, which Lend-Lease would make possible. "I ask Congress for authority and for funds sufficient to manufacture additional munitions and war supplies of many kinds, to be turned over to those nations which are now in actual war with aggressor nations," said Roosevelt. "Our most useful and immediate role is to act as an arsenal for them as well as for ourselves. They do not need manpower, but they do need billions of dollars' worth of the weapons of defense." He reminded Congress that Britain was out of money, but vowed that we "will not tell that they must surrender merely because of present inability to pay for the weapons which now they must have."[50]

It was the president's third major discussion of Lend-Lease in a little more than two weeks, with good cause: the country remained evenly split on the issue of aid to Britain. To be sure, the mood of the nation had shifted noticeably since the bombing of Britain commenced. The concept of Lend-Lease would have been unthinkable only six months earlier.

Even so, it wasn't a sure thing that Congress would pass the bill. There remained a large contingent of devout isolationists, particularly in the Senate, where all it takes is one to gum up the works. Roosevelt knew it would require intense lobbying of Congress and the American public on his part to make it law.

Congressional hearings for H.R. 1776 kicked off in mid-January. The House Foreign Relations Committee stacked the witness list with a bunch of heavyweight isolationists, including Charles Lindbergh ("An English victory would necessitate years of war and invasion on the continent of Europe") and Joseph P. Kennedy, FDR's former ambassador to England. The White House countered with its own secret weapon, Wendell Willkie, whom Roosevelt just defeated just months earlier. He had recently returned from England, where he witnessed up close Britain's lonely struggle against Hitler. Before a standing-room-only crowd, Willkie warned his fellow Republicans that "if the Republican party makes a blind opposition to the bill and allows itself to be presented to the American people as the isolationist party, it will never again gain control of the American government."[51]

Though opposition to Lend-Lease was intense, it ultimately proved to be narrow.[52] Willkie's powerful testimony, along with that of Harry Hopkins, Secretary of War Henry Stimson, and Navy Secretary Frank Knox helped tip debate in favor of the bill. Like a prize fight that fails to live up to the hype, the final vote was a bit anticlimactic as the measure passed both chambers easily. On March 11, 1940, President Roosevelt signed Lend-Lease into law. An overjoyed Churchill proclaimed to Parliament that "the most powerful democracy has, in effect, declared in a solemn state that they will devote their overwhelming industrial and financial strength to insuring the defeat of Nazism."[53] Within hours of the ink drying, the navy began transferring thousands of naval guns, millions of rounds of ammunition, and two dozen PT boats to Britain. At long last the war had been joined.

* * *

Winston Churchill would call the passage of Lend-Lease the most "unsordid act in the whole of recorded history." From his perspective, the statement is understandable. Had President Roosevelt not devised a scheme to essentially give Great Britain munitions, equipment, and other supplies at no cost, the war may have been over by the middle of 1941. No other country had the wealth, industrial capacity, or inclination to attempt something similar. And no other leader except Franklin Roosevelt had the creativity, vision, popularity, and confidence to pull it off.

The Lend-Lease program remained in effect until the spring of 1945. All told, the United States gave away over $50 billion (equivalent to $800 billion today) worth of equipment, munitions, raw materials, and food supplies. England was the largest recipient with $31.4 billion, followed by the Soviet Union at $11.3 billion, and France and China with several billion each. As for repayment, the vast majority of the $50 billion was never collected. Great Britain was held accountable for only $600 million of their $30 billion tally, and the Soviets even less. On December 31, 2006, England made its last debt payment—$83 million—to the United States government. "In a nutshell, everything we got from America in World War II was free," said economic historian Mark Harrison of Warwick University in England.[54]

As for shaping the "American Century," Lend-Lease is right up there with the Panama Canal in transforming America's role in the world. Gone for good were the days of isolationism and protectionism; never again would the United States play the role of global recluse. Roosevelt's "Arsenal of Democracy" would quickly morph into the "world's policeman" as the Cold War settled in. With Western Europe in ruins, Eastern Europe behind the Iron Curtain, and China about to fall to communism, the United States had no choice but to step up as global protectorate of freedom and capitalism. In that respect, the Marshall Plan—the $25 billion recapitalization of Western Europe—can be viewed as an extension of the Lend-Lease program. Harry Truman recognized the importance of getting the European economy back on its feet in order to stave off the spread of communism, and took a page from Roosevelt's playbook. Of course, all this largesse made it easier for the United States to open the Western European markets to trade, which greatly benefited American companies.

Among Franklin Roosevelt's long list of achievements and triumphs, the Lend-Lease program is rarely mentioned. The New Deal, bringing the nation out of the Depression, and prosecution of the two-front war typically receive the accolades, and little else. But that thinking is a bit shortsighted. One can only imagine how the war would have turned out had Roosevelt not come up with Lend-Lease.

Chapter 8

Truman Drops the Bomb

Printed with permission of the US Army Signal Corps.

He asked me to speak of a most urgent matter. Stimson told me that he wanted me to know about an immense project that was under way—a project looking to the development of a new explosive of almost unbelievable power. That was all he felt free to say at the time, and the statement left me puzzled.

> —Harry Truman, writing in his memoirs
> about his first encounter with Secretary of Defense
> Henry Stimson shortly after Truman was sworn in as president

Now I am become death, the destroyer of worlds.

> —J. Robert Oppenheimer, quoting the Hindu Scripture,
> the *Bhagavad-Gita,* after the successful test of the first atomic bomb

This is the greatest news in history.

> —Harry Truman's first words after learning about the
> successful bombing of Hiroshima

On July 16 at 5:29 a.m., deep in the New Mexican desert, the first atomic bomb was successfully detonated. It was the culmination of years of toil by the world's leading physicists on behalf of the United States government at a total cost exceeding $2 billion as part of the super-secretive "Manhattan Project." The scientists and civilians working on the project had a vague understanding of how this new weapon would be deployed. Among the military and government administrators of the program, however, there was little doubt that the bomb would be used on Japan as quickly as possible to bring the war to an end. For Harry Truman, the presidency was coming at him fast and furious. Having been on the job for only three months, he was still getting up to speed on many aspects of the war, including the bomb. Never before had a newly elevated president been confronted with such a momentous decision. For better or worse, it would come to define his presidency and, in some ways, the twentieth century.

* * *

The bomb. There are few phrases as evocative, descriptive, and universally recognized as those two words. It's arguably the best-known decision in the history of the American presidency, one for which everyone has an opinion. It's also a convenient point of demarcation for the twentieth century—a singular moment that brought an end to the global war, marked the beginning of the atomic age, and solidified America's undisputed position as a world superpower. In that sense, the dropping of the bomb is an event with virtually no parallels in history.

It would be impossible to write a book about presidential leadership without including a chapter on Truman and the bomb. For most Americans, it's the personification of the extraordinary pressure that comes with the modern presidency. What could be more contentious, wrenching, and complicated than the debate and discussion surrounding the use of an atomic weapon on a civilian population? Nothing, it would seem. There were layers of consideration. Was it morally justifiable? Would it even work? Could it be deployed in a way that wouldn't kill civilians? Would it force the Japanese into submission? Was there a risk in setting off an "arms race" with the Soviet Union? The list of factors was almost endless.

And yet what's most intriguing about the topic isn't how and why Truman, and those around him, ultimately decided to drop the bomb.

Rather, it's the lack of reflection, introspection, and even discussion that went into it. On the face of it, of all our discussions of presidents, this one might seem to have the strongest narrative, require the deepest analysis, provide the most vivid insight into the essence—"the moment of truth" as it were—of presidential decision making. It would appear to be the perfect case study on the subject. That's certainly what this author expected to find in tackling the subject.

But for many reasons, as we'll see, that's not really the case. At the same time, however, it elucidates other aspects of the presidency—institutional continuity, succession, the civilian-military relationship—more so than we've previously seen.

The Manhattan Project

On August 9, 1939, less than a month before Germany's invasion of Poland, Albert Einstein, the world's most renowned and celebrated physicist, sent a two-page letter to President Franklin Roosevelt. Written with the help of fellow physicists Leo Szilard, Edward Teller, and Eugene Wigner, and delivered by his friend, Wall Street economist (and informal Roosevelt advisor) Alexander Sachs, it informed the president that recent discoveries in nuclear fission made it probable that a new type of weapon—something unlike anything the world had ever seen—would someday soon be constructed. "A single bomb of this type," he warned the president, could be "carried by boat and exploded in a port" and might very well "destroy the whole port together with some of the surrounding territory." Einstein was concerned that Germany, with its access to the large uranium mines in Czechoslovakia and some of the world's leading physicists in Berlin, could be well on its way to acquiring such a weapon. He urged the administration to do everything in its power to secure its own stockpile of uranium ore, the largest-known quantities of which existed in the Belgian Congo, and to "speed up the experimental work" that was currently taking place at university laboratories across the country by providing funds and other resources.[1] Years later, Einstein would express regret for his role in sending the letter, as it began the chain of events that led to the creation and use of the atomic bomb.

Roosevelt took the matter seriously. Though preoccupied with Hitler's blitzkrieg of Poland and the imminent threat that it posed to Western Europe, he nonetheless ordered the formation of an Advisory Committee on Uranium to look into the potential for atomic weapons. The committee's first report, issued at the beginning of November, recommended that the government procure fifty tons of uranium ore and immediately begin funding fission research and experiments.[2] The following June, Roosevelt reorganized the Uranium Committee into the National Defense Research Committee, which was broadened to include military personnel, scientists, and business leaders and whose funding came directly from the federal government, not the military. This was important because the administration needed to cloak its activities so as not to arouse scrutiny from discerning politicians and the press.[3]

Some in the scientific community, including notable physicists like Edward Teller and J. Robert Oppenheimer, who would later lead the testing at Los Alamos, felt uneasy about collaborating with the government to create a weapon of infinite destruction. These were career academics, not inventors. Most had never worked outside a university setting, and few among them were militarists. The vast majority, in fact, were left-leaning pacifists, something that wasn't lost on Roosevelt. Speaking before the Pan-American Scientific Congress just weeks before the fall of France, he seemed to offer absolution to those scientists struggling with the moral aspects of weapons making. "You who are scientists," he assured the audience of mostly scientists, "may have been told that you are in part responsible for the debacle of today . . . but I assure you that it is not the scientists of the world who are responsible. . . . What has come about has been caused solely by those who would use, and are using, the progress that you have made along lines of peace in an entirely different case." Today Hitler dominates continental Europe, warned Roosevelt, but "we know down in our hearts" his goal is to "encompass every human being and every mile of the earth's surface."[4]

Though the administration was funding scientific research to decode the mystery of atomic fission, Roosevelt had not committed to pursuing the bomb—yet. He wanted to see more progress before mobilizing the billions of dollars it would require to make it happen. Just weeks before the attack on Pearl Harbor, he was given a report that showed conclusively that an atomic bomb was achievable, perhaps within two years.

Roosevelt didn't get around to reading it until January of 1941, by which time the country was at war and his mood had darkened considerably. He returned the document to its author with a simple notation: "Ok . . . I think you had best keep this in your own safe. FDR." And with that the Manhattan Project was born.[5]

For Roosevelt, formal pursuit of the bomb was not an intellectual or academic endeavor. And it wasn't meant as a defensive measure, either. Hitler controlled continental Europe and was threatening to topple Moscow. Japan ruled the oceans stretching from Pearl Harbor to India and was brutalizing everyone in its path. While the Manhattan Project would soon encompass tens of thousands of scientists and other civilians around the country—and would eventually top over one hundred thousand people—Roosevelt kept counsel with only a handful of advisors, most notably Secretary of War Henry Stimson and Army Chief of Staff George Marshall, on the broader implications of using such a horrific weapon. It was his prerogative—and his alone—as commander in chief to determine if, when, and how the bomb would be used. According to all contemporary accounts, remembrances, and secondary sources, Roosevelt had always intended to use the bomb as soon as it was available. He admitted as much during a Fireside Chat just days following the attack on Pearl Harbor. "We must face the fact that modern warfare as conducted in the Nazi manner is a dirty business. We don't like it—we didn't want to get in it—but we are in it and we're going to fight it with everything we've got."[6] Years later, William Leahy, Roosevelt's wartime chief of staff, remarked that he knew "FDR would have used it in a minute to prove that he hadn't wasted two billion dollars."[7]

What's remarkable is how little thought he gave to the bomb, other than an occasional update from Stimson on its progress and a reminder to the secretary to speed it along. Just months after authorizing the Manhattan Project, he told Vannevar Bush, the top civilian administrator, that the "whole thing should be pushed not only in regard to development, but also with due regard to time. This is very much of the essence."[8] Roosevelt saw to it that money was never an impediment. By the end of 1942, the president had committed nearly $500 million toward its development, with another $1.5 billion to be spent before all was said and done. He was motivated, in part, by an acute fear that Hitler would get there first—an unspeakable horror. But the savage combat in the Pacific islands factored into his thinking, too. The fighting was more brutal and slow going than anyone had anticipated. As the war in Europe began winding down, it became increasingly likely that the bomb wouldn't be available—or required—to bring it to conclusion. Convincing the military rulers of Japan to accept unconditional surrender, however, would be a different matter altogether.

"I felt like the moon, the stars, and all the planets had fallen on me"

On April 12, 1945, Vice President Harry Truman was having a late afternoon drink with House Speaker Sam Rayburn and a few others in the Speaker's hideaway office on Capitol Hill when he received an urgent message to call the White House. On the other line was Roosevelt's press secretary, Steve Early, who told him to return as "quickly and as quietly" as possible to the White House. He was to enter through the side entrance to avoid the press. "Jesus Christ and General Jackson," muttered Truman as he put down the phone.[9]

When he got to the White House, Truman was greeted by Early, Eleanor Roosevelt, daughter Anna, and her husband John Boettiger, a presidential aide. "The president is dead," Eleanor plaintively told Truman. After a long pause, Truman asked Eleanor if there was "anything I can do for you?" Eleanor stopped him. "Is there anything *we* can do for *you?*" she responded to the still-stunned Truman, "for you are the one in trouble now."[10] Truman would later tell the press that he felt as if the "moon, the stars, and all the planets" had crashed upon him.[11]

Of course, Eleanor was right—Truman was the one in trouble. On the job for less than three months, he had been kept in the dark on virtually everything, including the atomic bomb. In fact, Truman had only met with the president twice since being sworn in, both times for little more than small talk. It was no secret that the two weren't particularly close. When Roosevelt decided to dump then vice president Henry Wallace from the 1944 ticket (he thought he was too liberal, too bombastic to be president should anything happen to him), Truman wasn't the first or second choice to replace him. For his part, Truman wasn't interested in the position. "The Vice President," he told a friend, "simply presides over the Senate and sits around hoping for a funeral. It is a very high office which consists entirely of honor, and I don't have any ambition to hold an office like that." But when no consensus emerged after the first ballot at the Democratic convention in Chicago, the moderate senator from Missouri was put forward as a compromise candidate and reluctantly agreed to the nomination. His acceptance speech, short and garbled, inspired little confidence among the delegates. The *New Republic* summed up what many were thinking, noting that "Truman is a nice man, an honest man, a good Senator, a man of great humility, and a man of great courage. He will make a passable vice president. But Truman as president of the United States in times like these?"[12]

It was still a fair question in April of 1945, too. Though he was the sixth vice president to be elevated to president, none—perhaps with the exception of Andrew Johnson—had as much on their plate from day one as Truman. Or bigger shoes to fill. An entire generation of Americans had known only one president their entire lives. For them—and many others—Franklin Roosevelt *was* the federal government. He had steered the country through the Great Depression; successfully prosecuted a two-theater war to near completion; and was in the process of sketching the postwar map and future alliances with Allied leaders when he died. "It's needless to say that President Truman comes into this gigantic assignment under a handicap," asserted the *Washington Post* in an editorial. "He must pick up the work of a world-renowned statesman who had had more than 12 years of experience in the White House." It was impossible to ignore, opined the *Post*, "the great disparity between Mr. Truman's experience and the responsibilities that have been thrust upon him." The paper spoke for many that day. It was difficult to imagine anyone other than Roosevelt running the country.[13]

Most Americans had only a vague awareness of Harry Truman when he was suddenly thrust into the Oval Office. He had achieved a bit of notoriety for his work in the Senate to uncover fraud and mismanagement of military contracts, and some had heard rumblings about his being the product of a political machine in Kansas City.[14] But beyond that, he was a blank slate. Many in Roosevelt's inner circle were unsure of what to make of Truman; some were downright despondent. "What a great, great tragedy. God help us all," remarked David Lilienthal, the powerful head of the Tennessee Valley Authority. "The Country and the world don't deserve to be left this way." The elite American generals in Europe were similarly circumspect of their new commander in chief. "From a distance Truman did not appear at all qualified to fill Roosevelt's large shoes," observed Omar Bradley. Never one to mince words, George Patton could barely conceal his contempt. "It seems very unfortunate that in order to secure political preference, people are made vice president who are never intended, neither by Party nor by the Lord to be presidents."[15]

Secretary of War Henry Stimson wasted little time in getting acquainted with the new president. Minutes after Truman's impromptu swearing-in, he took the president aside and informed him about a top-secret project that was looking into the "development of a new explosive of almost unbelievable power." Stimson didn't share any details beyond that, a fact that left Truman a bit baffled.[16]

Stimson, the new secretary of state Jimmy Byrnes, his undersecretary Dean Acheson, and other remnants from the Roosevelt old guard embarked on something of a crash course to get Truman up to speed on military operations, classified intelligence, postwar planning, the Russian threat, and even the personalities he would be dealing with. They took it for granted that Roosevelt was on a first-name basis with everyone on the planet worth knowing. Truman had never met Churchill, Stalin, or many of his top officials, for that matter. The learning curve was steep.[17]

On Truman's twelfth day in office, Stimson decided it was time for a comprehensive briefing on the bomb. In a letter to the president requesting a confidential meeting, he reminded him of their brief conversation following his swearing-in, and explained that he had not "urged" the matter "on account of the pressure you have been under." But he couldn't delay any further, since "it has a bearing on our present foreign relations and has such an important effect upon all my thinking in this field."[18] He met with Truman alone in the Oval Office, and sat patiently while the president read a three-page memo that Stimson had prepared himself. "Within four months," it began starkly, "we shall in all probability have completed the most terrible weapon ever known in human history, one bomb which can destroy a whole city." Curiously, the memo was less about the prospects of using the bomb to shorten the war in the Pacific than it was an analysis of its impact on future diplomacy.

"Since segments of its production and discovery are widely known among scientists in many countries," it was highly probable that "the future may see a time when such a weapon may be constructed in secret and used suddenly and effectively with devastating power by a willful nation." Stimson accurately forecasted that the "only nation which could enter production within the next few years is Russia." Should that happen, and given the state of "moral advancement" around the globe, "modern civilization might be completely destroyed."[19] It closed with a recommendation—which Truman accepted—to establish a special select committee (entirely civilian) that would further examine the use and postwar implications of this terrible weapon, as well as advise the War Department on any actions "prior to that time." Truman would write years later in his memoirs that Stimson "seemed at least as much concerned with the role of the atomic bomb in the shaping of history as in its capacity to shorten the war."[20]

It was an astute observation. There was virtually no discussion that day about whether to use the weapon against Japan. Was that because the issue had already been decided, or was Stimson giving Truman time to digest everything before pressing the matter? Perhaps a little of both.

"It seems to be the most terrible thing ever discovered, but it can be made the most useful"

It's been called the most second-guessed decision in the history of the presidency. That may well be correct. Few presidential actions are as easily understandable, relatable, and debatable as the one to drop the atomic bomb on Hiroshima and Nagasaki. It was a binary proposition: use it or don't use it. Sure, there were shades of grey—there always are—but at its core was a simple question of action or inaction. In that sense, it was a fairly straightforward matter.

And for the most part, it was treated that way by Truman, Roosevelt before him, and their closest advisors who had been working on the project from its inception. It was viewed solely through a military prism: would the bomb help bring the war to an end? Aside from some hand wringing and last-minute jitters by a few of the scientists who had been involved in the project, very little consideration was given to the moral aspects of using such a heinous weapon. The country was at total war. Any and every weapon in the arsenal was considered fair game. Unconditional surrender was the goal. That was the backdrop in the summer of 1945.

Truman wisely consented to Stimson's suggestion to form a civilian committee to explore the various considerations for deploying the bomb. Of course, knowing so little about the Manhattan Project at the time of Roosevelt's death, the new president probably didn't have much choice in the matter. It would have been nearly impossible for him to make an informed decision without robust guidance from the panel. Would Roosevelt have required similar outside counsel? Most likely not. He was well versed on all the considerations and undeniably comfortable making tactical military decisions. Beyond that, it simply wasn't his leadership style to defer decisions to others. Roosevelt was at his best when pulling bits and pieces of information from multiple sources and forming his own conclusions. "Never let your left hand know what your right hand is doing," he liked to joke with his aides about his penchant for secrecy and manipulation.[21]

The committee—known as the Interim Committee on S-1—was comprised of eight members: three scientists, two undersecretaries, an outside businessman, Secretary of State Jimmy Byrnes, and Stimson. They convened four times in May to, in Stimson's words, "recommend action that may turn the course of civilization." The final session, a two-day affair that would conclude with specific recommendations for the president, was joined by Army Chief of Staff George Marshall, who represented the military, as well as four outside scientists, including the eminent Italian physicist Enrico Fermi and J. Robert Oppenheimer, who flew in from Los Alamos. The committee made three specific directives: The weapon should be used as quickly as possible, against Japan (without warning), and on a city that had been relatively unscathed by the relentless traditional bombings so as to make "a profound psychological impression on as many inhabitants as possible."[22] Byrnes took the recommendations directly to Truman who, according to a later account by Byrnes, agreed "with reluctance. . . . He could think of no alternative."[23]

To their credit, the committee considered ways to showcase the enormous power of the bomb without actually inflicting it on a city. One suggestion was to show Japanese military leaders a demonstration in a remote area where few lives would be jeopardized. The scientists, in particular, pushed for this approach. To them, this was Hitler's bomb. They hadn't foreseen its use against Japan. Ultimately, the committee decided against it, citing concerns that the bomb might not work, or worse yet, the Japanese would plant American POWs in the vicinity or shoot down the plane. And that's to say nothing of losing the inherent shock value of the bomb, which many considered its biggest asset.

As May became June, and with testing of the bomb still a month away, Truman struggled with the best way to bring the war to an end. "I have to decide Japanese strategy," he reflected in his diary. "Shall we invade Japan proper or shall we bomb and blockade? That is my hardest decision to date." Nowhere did he mention the atomic bomb.[24]

There were two schools of thought on this issue. Some believed that a "bomb and blockade" approach made the most sense because it would slowly suffocate Japan's ability to make war and eventually force surrender. It could very well take years to bring about victory, but it would be dramatically less bloody than an assault of the main islands. Others held that an invasion was the only practical solution, that the Japanese would continue to wage war so long as the homeland remained unoccupied. Truman asked George Marshall to design an invasion plan for his review. Presented on June 18 at a White House meeting, it called for a two-phase assault, the first commencing in the fall of 1945 and the second in the spring of 1946. The amphibious landing would be larger than that of Normandy, Marshall warned, and the fighting more brutal than that in Okinawa, where 12,000 Americans had been killed and triple that number wounded. But that was a guess. Nobody was sure about casualties. Marshall predicted 30,000 losses in the first thirty days alone; Admiral King had the number at 41,000; Admiral Nimitz said closer to 49,000; and MacArthur thought it would top 50,000. The Pentagon estimated that American casualties could reach a quarter million when it was all said and done, with the Japanese total topping four times that. For the remainder of his life, Truman would cite a quarter-million casualties—a number he claimed to have received from Marshall at the Potsdam Conference.[25] While there was little agreement on estimated casualties, there was unanimity on one point: the fighting would be savage beyond comprehension, more ghastly than Iwo Jima, Saipan, and Okinawa combined. The military brass was convinced that the Japanese army, as well as most civilians, would rather fight to the death than surrender their homeland to the invaders. How difficult did the Pentagon expect it to be? One memo estimated that "more bombs will be dropped on Japan than were delivered against Germany during the entire European war."[26] As the meeting broke, Truman told Marshall to begin preparing for the invasion.

This was the plan as Truman headed to Potsdam to discuss postwar Germany with Churchill and Stalin. On the eve of the conference, after returning from a tour of the smoking rubble that was left of Berlin, the president was handed a note from Secretary Stimson. The message came from New Mexico via Washington: "Operated on this morning. Diagnosis not yet complete but results seem satisfactory and already exceeded expectations." The bomb was a success. A relieved Stimson joked with a friend that since he was responsible "for spending two billion dollars on this atomic venture," now that it is "successful I shall not be sent to prison in Fort Leavenworth."[27]

The test results seemed to change the president's thinking, as well as his demeanor at the conference. "It was apparent that something happened," observed an aide to General Eisenhower of Truman's disposition. Churchill, too, saw a noticeable difference in the president, and later learned why. "This atomic bomb is the Second Coming in Wrath," he exclaimed to Stimson.[28] The bomb was no longer an abstraction—it was real. Truman was positive, he wrote in his diary from Potsdam, that the "Japs will fold up . . . when Manhattan [the bomb] appears over their homeland."[29] The question now was whether to give the Japanese some kind of warning of the terrible destruction that was about to be inflicted on them. Most everyone in Truman's inner circle agreed that a final ultimatum made sense, in part because it would preserve the "moral high ground" and perhaps bring about surrender. It came in the form of the Potsdam Declaration, which was jointly issued by the United States, Great Britain, and Nationalist China at the conclusion of the conference. "We call upon the government of Japan to proclaim now the unconditional surrender of all Japanese armed forces," it demanded, "and to provide proper and adequate assurances of their good faith in such action. The alternative for Japan is prompt and utter destruction." Nobody was surprised when the Japanese prime minister contemptuously dismissed it and vowed to "resolutely fight for the successful conclusion of the war." For Truman, and those around him, Japan had been fairly warned.

As Truman biographer David McCullough points out, there was no single "moment" when Truman decided to use the atomic bomb on Japan. In fact, it was just the opposite. "Most likely," writes McCullough, "he never seriously considered not using the bomb. Indeed, to have said no at this point and called everything off would have been so drastic a break with the whole history of the project, not to say the terrific momentum of events that summer, as to have been almost inconceivable."[30] Truman aide George Elsey echoed conventional wisdom with his observation that "Truman made no decision because there was no decision to be made. He could no more have stopped it than a train moving down a track."[31] For his part, Truman never indicated the precise moment when he made up his mind, probably because there wasn't one. The closest he came was a diary entry on July 25: "We have discovered the most terrible bomb in the history of the world. . . . This weapon," he writes matter-of-factly, "is to be used against Japan between now and August 10. I have told the secretary of war, Mr. Stimson, to use it so that military objectives and soldiers and sailors are the target and not women and children. Even if the Japs are savages, ruthless, merciless and fanatic, we as the leader of the world for the common welfare cannot drop this terrible bomb on the old capital or the new. . . . The target will be a purely military one and we will issue a warning statement asking the Japs to surrender and save lives. . . . It is certainly a good thing for the world that Hitler's crowd or Stalin's did not discover this atomic bomb. It seems to be the most terrible thing ever discovered, but it can be made the most useful."[32]

On the same day as Truman's diary entry, a military directive—reviewed and approved by Stimson and Marshall but not the president—was issued to the Air Force commander assigned to the mission. It detailed the potential targets (Hiroshima, Kokura, Niigata, and Nagasaki), the timing ("after about August 3rd"), and the protocol for disseminating information after the fact (the president and the secretary of defense would do all the speaking). The feeling among the military brass was that the bomb would be used sometime between August 3 and 10.

Harry Truman was aboard the USS *Augusta* heading back to the United States when he learned that Hiroshima had been bombed. A telegram was handed to him while he was dining with enlisted men.

"This is the greatest news in history," he exclaimed to the messenger. Seconds later he broke the news to the crew. "Please keep your seats and listen for a moment," said the president as he tapped on a glass with a fork to get their attention. "I have an announcement to make. We have just dropped a new bomb on Japan which has more power than twenty thousand tons of TNT. It has been an overwhelming success." Moments later the White House issued a statement describing the blast. "Sixteen hours ago an American airplane dropped a bomb on Hiroshima . . . an atomic bomb. It is harnessing the basic power of the universe. The force from which the sun draws its power has been loosed against those who brought war to the Far East." The White House promised total annihilation should Japan fail to surrender. "Let there be no mistake; we shall completely destroy Japan's power to make war. . . . If they do not now accept our terms they may expect a rain of ruin from the air, the like of which has never been seen on earth."[33]

The impact of the blast was even greater than the scientists had estimated. Early reports indicated that approximately 80,000 people were killed from the initial explosion, much higher than Oppenheimer's prediction of 20,000. By year's end, somewhere in the neighborhood of 150,000 would perish, with many more suffering permanent burns, disfigurement, and radiation poisoning. The devastation was so total, so complete, so unimaginable that it took Japanese leaders two days just to establish communications with local officials and other eyewitnesses to the blast. During that time, Japan's Supreme Council for the Direction of the War—the group that controlled the nation's destiny—debated whether to accept the Potsdam Declaration's unconditional surrender terms. They remained deadlocked when news of a second blast in Nagasaki reached the prime minister's bunker in Tokyo. Even then, the hardliners continued to advocate for one last glorious battle to defend the mainland, in keeping with the concept of national honor. It took the extraordinary intervention of Emperor Hirohito—"I cannot bear to see my innocent people suffer any longer"—to convince them to finally accept surrender. "The time has come when we must bear the unbearable. . . . I swallow my own tears and give my sanction to the proposal to accept the Allied proclamation."[34] And with that, World War II came to an end.

"I was there. I did it. I would do it again."

From the moment he learned of the successful test in New Mexico until the day of his death, Harry Truman steadfastly insisted that the decision to drop the bomb was his and his alone. "Let there be no mistake about it," he wrote in his memoirs, "I regarded the bomb as a military weapon and never had any doubt that it should be used."[35] In interviews, speeches, diary entries, and private correspondences, the rationale was always the same: it would save American lives by shortening the war. On the day the second bomb was dropped on Nagasaki, Truman responded to a plea from highly regarded Senator Richard Russell to continue using atomic bombs until the Japanese had surrendered by assuring him that, while he regretted the "necessity of wiping out whole populations because of the 'pigheadedness' of the leaders of a nation," the purpose of the bomb was to "save as many American lives as possible," which he intended to do.[36] That same day Truman fired off a letter to the head of the Federal Council of Churches, who in an earlier telegram had begged him not to drop another atomic bomb. "Nobody is more disturbed over the use of atomic bombs than I am, but I was greatly disturbed over the unwarranted attack by the Japanese on Pearl Harbor and their murder of our prisoners of war. The only language they seem to understand is the one we have been using to bombard them. When you have to deal with a beast," it concluded, "you have to treat him as a beast. It is most regrettable but nevertheless true."[37]

In October of that year, Truman addressed a joint session of Congress as part of his effort to establish the Atomic Energy Commission. "Almost two months have passed since the atomic bomb was used against Japan," he began the speech. "That bomb did not win the war, but it certainly shortened the war. We know that it saved the lives of untold thousands of American and Allied soldiers who would otherwise have been killed in battle." Two months later at the annual Gridiron Dinner in Washington, Truman put it as plainly and bluntly as possible. "It occurred to me," he said of his thought process, "that a quarter of a million of the flower of our young manhood were worth a couple of Japanese cities. And I still think they were and are."[38]

If the president ever expressed regret or remorse over his decision, he never let on. He dismissed J. Robert Oppenheimer, the man most responsible for creating the bomb, as a "crybaby scientist" after the physicist complained of the "blood on his hands" to the president in a White House meeting. "Blood on his hands," the president was heard to have said, "Dammit, he hasn't half as much blood on his hands as I have. You just don't go around bellyaching about it."[39] Years later he would famously remark, "I never lost any sleep over my decision." The statement came, of course, with the disclaimer that the bomb had saved "half a million boys on our side."[40]

In the years following his time in the White House, Truman grew increasingly defensive about the subject when it would come up. Not one for introspection, he disliked reflecting on the matter, and was offended by the need to justify it. It was "not any decision you need to worry about," he testily scolded an assembly of students at Columbia University in 1959. The atomic bomb, he told them, was nothing more than "a bigger gun than the other fellow had to win a war and that's what it was used for." He challenged the students not to listen to the so-called experts—the "Monday morning quarterbacks"—because they didn't have a clue about his motives. "I was there. I did it. I would do it again."[41]

To historian Herbert Feis, who in 1962 began probing Truman's remembrances for a scholarly article on his decision to drop the bomb, the aging former president unleashed a torrent of invective in a letter that he ultimately decided against sending. The reason the weapon was used, he wrote, was to "end the Jap War. That was the objective." If the historian could think of any other "egghead contemplations," Truman taunts Feis, then he should "bring them out." But it wouldn't yield a different response. "You get the same answer—to end the Jap War and save a quarter of a million of our youngsters and that many Japs from death and twice that many on each side from being maimed for life." It was a good thing that Feis, and other "eggheads," didn't have to make the decision, Truman lectured, or "our boys would all be dead." The following year he had a similar explanation for *Chicago Sun-Times* columnist Irv Kupcinet, who had recently written a favorable column on Truman and the bomb. The former president repeated that the bomb saved 250,000 lives on both sides, and double that number from being crippled for life. Curiously, he added a new wrinkle to his defense, noting that the unprovoked attack on Pearl Harbor was tantamount to "plain murder," which evidently factored into his thinking. As usual, he had no regrets. "Under the same circumstances, I would do it again."[42] In the summer of 1964, he made his last "public" comment on the matter in a letter to a college professor who had written Truman inquiring about his motive for dropping the bomb. "The only reason the atomic bomb was used was because it was a weapon of war," he responded. He gave his usual justifications about saving lives and admonished her to read his memoirs. "I have never worried about dropping the bomb," Truman closed the note. "It was just a means to end the war and that is what was accomplished."[43]

To the very end, he never wavered on the rightness and logic of his decision. Even in his dying days, while infirmed at the Research Hospital in Kansas, the eighty-eight-year-old Truman was still making the case; what was supposed to be a five-minute visit with his former attorney general, Tom Clark, turned into a forty-five-minute discussion over his use of the bomb. It was one of the last conversations of his life. He would die three days later.[44]

* * *

The supposed "biggest decision in the history of the presidency," as it turned out, wasn't much of a decision at all. As David McCullough and other historians have noted, it would have been unthinkable for Truman—a little-known, barely regarded, and wildly uninformed vice president—to break ranks with FDR's intended desire to deploy the bomb as quickly as possible, and in the process flush $2 billion down the drain. The public would have considered it treasonous had it learned that the military possessed a weapon that could end the war in an instant but Truman chose not to use it. "If Truman had failed to use the bomb and invaded Japan instead," notes historian William O'Neill, "the resulting casualties would have destroyed him politically. Truman would never have been forgiven for sending hundreds of thousands of boys to their death when he had the means to spare them."[45] There almost certainly would have been calls for his impeachment, and conviction would not have been out of the question.

As for the moral component of the equation, the truth is that it never factored into the discussion in a meaningful way. To some extent, the world had been numbed to the notion of civilian deaths. Just a few months earlier, seventy thousand Japanese—most of them civilians—had perished during the hellacious fire bombings of Tokyo, where fifteen square miles of the city were charred beyond recognition. The inferno was straight out of Dante. American pilots reported smelling burning flesh from ten thousand feet above the city. Similar fire bombings had taken place at Dresden and Hamburg in Germany as well. By the summer of 1945 it was an accepted, though lamented, part of war.

Over the years, some have postulated that Truman didn't have to drop the bomb to win the war, that the Japanese were already defeated and looking for a way to surrender. He used it, the theory goes, to impress the Russians and keep them in check. There's no doubt that the military leaders in Japan knew the war was a lost cause. In fact, they had come to that realization in the summer of 1944 after their defeat at Saipan. Even so, defense of the home islands was considered something entirely different than merely waging war. They would be fighting for honor, tradition, and to preserve the spirit of the country. It was the same instinct that produced legions of kamikazes and made surrender on the battlefield unthinkable (and extremely rare). For many Japanese civilians—and virtually everyone in the military—dying on their soil was preferable to the shame and humiliation of surrender. They were gearing up for just that when Emperor Hirohito stepped in and accepted the Potsdam terms. Had he not, an invasion would have been necessary, the likes of which would have dwarfed that of Normandy.

That's not to say that Russia didn't enter into the equation at all. Truman came to regret asking Stalin (while the two were at Potsdam) to declare war on Japan as soon as possible (to which Stalin happily agreed). He quickly realized it was a mistake, for it meant that Russia would make territorial demands on postwar Japan. As it turned out, the second bomb was dropped just hours after Russia launched its attack on Japanese-occupied Manchuria. Whether a coincidence or not, it's impossible to know; Truman never made the connection in either his public statements or private correspondences.

Whether the decision was his, or it was made for him, this simple fact doesn't change: it's the single most identifiable act in presidential history.

Chapter 9

TRUMAN FIRES MACARTHUR

Printed with permission of the US Navy.

General, you don't have a staff. You have a court.
—George Marshall to Douglas MacArthur, 1943

He's not going to be allowed to quit on me. He's going to be fired!
—Harry Truman

President Truman must be impeached and convicted. His hasty and vindictive removal of General MacArthur is the culmination of a series of acts which have shown that he is unfit, morally and mentally, for his high office.
—Front-page *Chicago Tribune* editorial following MacArthur's dismissal

On April 11, 1951, President Harry Truman famously relieved General Douglas A. MacArthur from his position as commander of military operations in

Korea. The decision had been months in the making. Truman and MacArthur simply didn't see eye to eye on the prosecution of the Korean War, a point that MacArthur wasn't shy about making known. The firing unleashed an out-pouring of support for MacArthur and a tidal wave of abuse against Truman, and while the immediate aftermath looked unfavorably on Truman, hindsight and perspective have been much kinder to the former president.

* * *

Harry Truman said of his firing of General Douglas MacArthur that it was among the most difficult decisions of his presidency, an amazing sentiment given that Truman is perhaps best remembered for being the only president to deploy atomic weapons during wartime. At first blush his statement seems like a spat of hyperbole, but while the decision to fire MacArthur may not have posed the same moral dilemma as dropping the bomb, it was done in an effort to prevent a third world war and the widespread use of atomic weapons.

Harry Truman was not one for "wrestling with decisions." He trusted his gut and instinct as much as any president before or since, and prided himself on the ability to act quickly and decisively. He took seriously the admonition that sat on his desk—"The buck stops here"—and famously said of the pressure of the presidency: "If you can't take the heat, get out of the kitchen."[1]

But the decision to fire General MacArthur from his command position during the height of the Korean War was one that weighed on him for months. Years later, he would lament that he had waited too long to relieve MacArthur, that in hindsight he should have fired him months earlier. He never wavered on the correctness of the action, just the timing.

The Background

On the morning of June 25, 1950, the world learned that ninety thousand North Korean soldiers had stormed across the 38th parallel, an arbitrary line that was hastily created by Pentagon officials in the immediate aftermath of World War II. Their goal: to overrun South Korea and "unify" the peninsula.

Harry Truman got word of the invasion from Secretary of State Dean Acheson while Truman was in Missouri visiting with his wife. His call to the president wasn't Acheson's first—he had actually phoned the secretary general of the United Nations first to ask for an emergency Security Council meeting, knowing that Truman would ask for the same.

From the moment he learned the news, Truman knew that it would require US intervention. The "domino theory" of the day held that if a country fell to communism, that the entire region was likely to succumb. There was little choice, so the thinking went, but to meet it head-on. And while Korea was never officially declared a war—it was referred to as a "police action" so as to avoid a vote in Congress—it was understood that American soldiers were going to die.

There was never any doubt as to who would command the forces in Korea. General MacArthur, the hero of the Pacific theater, highest ranking active officer in the US military, and de facto ruler of Japan, was the logical candidate for the position. Truman needed someone with MacArthur's experience, stature, and brashness to stave off what looked like an imminent collapse of South Korea. The general's seventy-one years of age notwithstanding, nobody doubted his fitness for the job.

MacArthur didn't disappoint. Within days of taking command, he had mobilized the troops and secured a foothold in South Korea, and only weeks later had the United Nation forces—comprised largely of US troops—on the offensive. Just three months after the start of hostilities, MacArthur pulled off what many consider the finest amphibious landing of its type at the port of Inchon as the Marines split the enemy force in two and forced their hasty retreat above the 38th parallel. In a single thrust he had changed the momentum of the war, and was bragging to reporters that he would get "the boys home by Christmas."[2]

Still basking in the glory of Inchon, MacArthur reiterated to Truman, at a quickly convened summit on Wake Island that would mark the only face-to-face encounter of their lives, that things were solidly in control. He gave an emphatic assurance that China would not enter the fray. It was an important guarantee for Truman, one that he took seriously. While both men agreed on unifying the peninsula for South Korea, Truman was adamant about not provoking the Chinese and the Russians. He took at face value MacArthur's promise that the war would not widen.

As it turned out, the dramatic landing at Inchon and the rendezvous with Truman that followed would represent the high point for their relationship, as well as the war effort in general. The day after Thanksgiving, just two months after the Inchon landing, the Chinese launched an intense counterattack, pouring 260,000 troops into Korea and forcing MacArthur into one of the greatest military retreats in history. It caught everyone by surprise—especially MacArthur—and eliminated any chance for a quick victory. Truman's fear had been realized—the war had expanded beyond just the Koreans—and with it stood the real threat of another world war. The seeds had been sown for a showdown.

The Showdown

Though they had only met that one time on Wake Island, Truman and MacArthur had little regard for each other. Truman thought the general was a "supreme egoist," a "prima donna, brass hat" and a "play actor" who thought of himself as "something of a God," while MacArthur dismissed Truman as just another fickle politician who failed to grasp the complexities of war.[3]

Many historians contend that MacArthur actually goaded Truman into firing him—that he wantonly disobeyed the president because he wanted to exit the war as a "martyr"—but there's no hard proof of this. There's plenty of evidence, however, that suggests that MacArthur purposely violated direct orders, so much so that those around Truman thought it was a clear-cut case of insubordination. In their opinion, the general went out of his way to contradict the president in an effort to widen the war.

One such incident occurred during the height of the preparations for the Inchon landing, when the Associated Press published a speech that MacArthur had given to the Veterans of Foreign Wars in which he defended Chang Kai-shek's control of Formosa—something Truman disagreed with—and seemingly called the president an appeaser. "Nothing could be more fallacious than the threadbare argument by those who advocate appeasement and defeatism in the Pacific that if we defend Formosa we alienate continental Asia," MacArthur told the veterans.[4] The speech sent Truman into a rage—many around him were recommending he sack MacArthur on the spot. But he knew it wasn't the right time. He didn't want to derail the daring counteroffensive that was just days away, and looked the other way as MacArthur made final preparations.

It wouldn't be the last time that MacArthur contradicted the president—the commander in chief—in the press. As the Chinese counteroffensive gained steam and American losses mounted, MacArthur began lobbying the president in the press to expand the war in China, something Truman desperately wanted to avoid. The general told *US News & World* that the administration's prohibition from entering Chinese territory amounted to "an enormous handicap, without precedent in military history"—an outrageous charge on its face—which he repeated to the United Press International and other media outlets.[5] Truman's response: He issued a presidential gag order that forbade military commanders from talking to the press without clearing it with the Pentagon first—an order that MacArthur gleefully ignored on dozens of occasions.

In the spring of 1951, MacArthur pushed his luck a bit more when, in the words of Secretary of State Dean Acheson, he committed "insubordination of the grossest sort" and a major act of sabotage with the issuance of a direct communiqué to the Chinese demanding their surrender or face "imminent military collapse" at his hands.[6] The timing of MacArthur's missive couldn't have been worse; it came as Truman was preparing to issue his own communiqué to the Chinese seeking peace—a plan that Truman was forced to scrap in light of MacArthur's bombshell.

MacArthur's ultimatum to the Chinese left Truman in a state of disbelief. He would later write in his memoirs that it was "an act totally disregarding all directives to abstain from any declaration on foreign policy. . . . This was a challenge to the President under the Constitution. . . . By this act MacArthur left me no choice—I could no longer tolerate his insubordination."[7]

And yet he did for another month. With his Gallup poll ratings at an all-time low in the high 20s, Truman did not have the political capital to quickly sack MacArthur; he needed to make the case both inside the Pentagon—some in the military actually favored MacArthur's approach to widen the war—and to the public that MacArthur had to go.

The final straw came on April 5, 1951, when Joe Martin, Republican minority leader in the House of Representatives, read a letter from MacArthur on the House floor in which the general strongly endorsed the notion of enlisting Chiang Kai-shek's forces in Formosa into the fight so as to meet the enemy with "maximum counterforce." "If we lose the war to communism in Asia the fall of Europe is inevitable," he concluded the letter. "Win it and Europe would most probably avoid war and yet preserve freedom. As you pointed out, we must win. There is no substitute for victory."[8] The Martin letter sent into motion the final chain of events that would lead to MacArthur's dismissal.

The Fallout

For Truman, the reaction following MacArthur's dismissal was swift and severe. The invective came from all directions. Several prominent Republicans, including Senate minority leader Robert Taft, Senator Joe McCarthy, and Senator William Jenner of Indiana, called for immediate impeachment proceedings, as did a handful of national media outlets such as the *Chicago Tribune* and *Time* magazine. "President Truman must be impeached and convicted," wrote the *Chicago Tribune* in a rare front-page editorial. "His hasty and vindictive removal of General MacArthur is the culmination of a series of acts which has shown that he is unfit, morally and mentally, for his high office."[9]

And it wasn't just the Republicans howling in protest. Many Democrats, particularly the Southern conservatives, thought that Truman had erred in his judgment, and publicly said so. Four state legislatures from Florida, Michigan, Illinois, and California took the extraordinary step of passing resolutions condemning MacArthur's firing, while protesters in several cities burned the president in effigy as enraged citizens flew the flag at half-mast. According to one estimate, over 44,000 telegrams were sent to members of Congress in the forty-eight hours following his dismissal; all but 344 condemned Truman's action. A few prominent liberals, most notably Eleanor Roosevelt and Supreme Court Justice William O. Douglas, came to Truman's defense, but the support was mostly drowned out by the chorus of abuse hurled his way.

MacArthur, on the other hand, fared much better. Ten thousand raucous supporters greeted his arrival at the San Francisco airport, the first time he had touched base on US soil in fourteen years. It took him over two hours to make his way from the airport to his hotel. In New York, he was met with the largest ticker-tape parade in the city's history as 7 million admirers cheered him on—double the number that greeted Eisenhower following his return from World War II. His Gallup approval rating stood at 69 percent. Congress made the extraordinary gesture of inviting him to address a joint session—an honor typically reserved for heads of state and other foreign dignitaries.

His appearance before Congress was unlike anything in that chamber's history. Over 30 million Americans watched and listened as a defiant MacArthur once again accused the administration of appeasement, wondering aloud why he was prevented from taking the fight to China. He reminded his fellow citizens that there could be "no substitute for victory"—a line he used in the Martin letter—and wrongly asserted that the Joint Chiefs shared his point of view. He was interrupted by applause thirty times during a thirty-four minute address, the loudest coming at the closing with the stirring rhetorical flourish "old soldiers never die—they just fade away"—the line which has come to immortalize the speech.[10]

"The Biggest Fight of Your Administration"

In some respects, Truman's decision to fire MacArthur was an easy one: no general could survive multiple acts of insubordination, and this was no exception. Truman believed it was important for military leaders to respect civilian authority. Allowing MacArthur to get away with blatant insubordination sent the wrong signal.

But he struggled with it nonetheless. Firing MacArthur, Dean Acheson warned, would lead to the "biggest fight of your administration" at a time when Truman was in no position for a fight; his approval ratings were as low as MacArthur's were high, and there was even talk of impeachment should MacArthur be dismissed.[11] Truman, and most of those around him, understood that they weren't taking on just a general, but rather a living legend—a man who had come to symbolize "total victory" in a world made complicated by atomic annihilation. For a guy known to act impulsively on occasion, Truman uncharacteristically approached the MacArthur situation from every conceivable angle before making a decision. It may have been the only time in his career.

Interestingly, as he began to ponder relieving MacArthur of his command, Truman did something out of character: research. He was curious to know if there were parallels in history, perhaps something he could learn from. During the winter of 1950–51 he assigned White House staffer Ken Helcher to search the Library of Congress for historical precedents. Helcher would spend weeks on the task.

A history buff of sorts, Truman knew that Abraham Lincoln had a tense and acrimonious relationship with General George B. McClellan, the commander of the Union army during the early years of the Civil War. What he didn't know, however—and learned from Helcher's research—was just how similar his predicament was to Lincoln's.

Like MacArthur, General McClellan possessed an oversized ego and contempt for the president to match. He despised Lincoln, and wasn't above openly mocking him to acquaintances and strangers. But the real problem was that McClellan refused to follow military orders (though ironically he was overly cautious instead of aggressive), and was all too happy to share his political views with the press. He was a constant irritant to Lincoln, and after months of McClellan's ignoring orders and belittling the presidency, Lincoln had no choice but to relieve him.

"Lincoln was patient," Truman would later write, "for that was his nature, but at long last he was compelled to relieve the Union Army's principal commander. And though I gave this difficulty with MacArthur much wearisome thought, I realized that I would have no other choice myself than to relieve the nation's top field commander."[12]

Did the McClellan firing convince Truman that MacArthur had to go? No—Truman had mostly made up his mind by the early months of 1951. But Helcher's research—he presented Truman with a detailed written report on Lincoln-McClellan—certainly eased his mind that axing the highest-ranking commander during wartime was not without precedent. And he took comfort in knowing that a century after the Civil War, Lincoln was universally considered among the greatest presidents while McClellan was regarded as an unmitigated bust.

In the end, the McClellan situation was simply another piece to the puzzle—an important one—and buoyed his confidence at a time when little was going his way. Ulysses S. Grant succeeded McClellan and led the Union to victory; Truman was hoping for a similar outcome.

Building Consensus

Rarely was Harry Truman mistaken for a consensus seeker in his decision making. He let his instincts guide him on most calls, unafraid of being wrong on occasion. He was quick and decisive in finding solutions, rarely reaching beyond a handful of advisors. It was one of the qualities that the American people most admired about him. But Truman understood his limitations; he knew that a snap decision on MacArthur could be disastrous. There was too much at stake, and he lacked the political capital to act unilaterally without bringing others along.

When it came to the subject of Douglas MacArthur, Truman sought counsel from a small group of advisors that he respected and trusted—Secretary of Defense George Marshall, Secretary of State Dean Acheson, Chairman of the Joint Chiefs of Staff Omar Bradley, and former commerce secretary and special envoy Averell Harriman. He listened closely to their advice, but rarely showed his hand, even to them. Truman didn't want his thoughts on the matter too widely shared; he knew it was an explosive situation that could ignite at any moment.

In his wisdom, Truman was aware that he couldn't get too far in front of any decision regarding MacArthur. The general was simply too popular—much more popular than Truman in fact—for the president to lead the charge for his dismissal, and both men knew it. Truman needed the military brass, in particular the Joint Chiefs, to reach that conclusion on their own. If it was forced on them, they would likely reject it.

Truman believed that given enough rope, MacArthur would eventually hang himself. His instincts proved right. With each act of seeming insubordination, MacArthur further alienated the military establishment. By the time the Martin letter was made public, he had little remaining support within the administration or the military.

As historian David McCullough noted in his Pulitzer-winning biography of Truman, even after he had decided to fire MacArthur, Truman held one final "speak-now-or-forever-hold-your-tongue" meeting with the Joint Chiefs to give them a last say and get their decision on record. The room was in full agreement with Truman, and when a young aide suggested to the president that the press release should make mention of the unanimity, Truman cut him off. "Not tonight son. . . . I'm taking this decision on my own responsibility as President of the United States and I want no one to think I'm trying to share it with anyone else. . . . [It is] my decision alone." Historian David Halberstam described it as one of the finest moments of his presidency.[13]

Playing for History

Harry Truman was known for having a quick temper and a short fuse. Diplomacy wasn't always a strong suit, patience sometimes a fleeting virtue. His political opponents understood this. On more than one occasion he was goaded into ill-conceived responses against his better judgment.

Sometimes it was reporters who got the better of him. When *Washington Post* music critic Paul Hume wrote a scathing review of Truman's daughter Margaret's singing concert before 3,500 people at Constitution Hall, he responded with a nasty letter that ended with a threat to punch him in the nose. Truman's staff was horrified to read it in the next day's paper.

MacArthur's allies in the Senate—Joe McCarthy, Bob Taft, Richard Nixon among them—relished baiting the president with a chorus of personal attacks against George Marshall and Dean Acheson, two of his closest advisors, for their refusal to grant MacArthur free rein in widening the war. McCarthy went so far as to call Acheson a traitor and Marshall—one of the most revered military leaders in the country—a "living lie." He referred to Truman as a "son of a bitch" and would later suggest that the president was drunk when he axed MacArthur. Calls for the president's impeachment were practically a daily occurrence, and while he generally ignored the partisan sniping and histrionics, it took all his restraint from returning volley on some of the more outlandish ripostes.[14]

There's no doubt that Truman would have enjoyed responding to the near-constant goading, but in the end it would have accomplished little. The president had nothing to gain and everything to lose by letting loose on his tormentors. A war of words with the far right could have easily alienated the military brass and even some in his own party. The stakes were too high—in Truman's mind, World War III hung in the balance—and he thought better against risking it all with a few ill-chosen words for peripheral players.

Truman was a shrewd politician with sharp instincts. It wasn't lost on him that he would pay dearly in the short term for sacking MacArthur. He fully expected to take a hit from the daily newspapers, elected officials, and even a few in his own party. But in some ways they weren't his primary audience. History was. In his mind, future generations would remember MacArthur as an out-of-touch megalomaniac who refused to recognize civilian authority over the military and therefore had to be removed from command.

Several advisors had floated scenarios that would allow MacArthur to save face, such as recalling him home to be a "special advisor" to the president or letting him keep his post in Japan while giving up Korea, but Truman would have none of it. He wanted MacArthur to suffer the indignity of being fired, and he wanted history to record it that way. He might suffer in the short term, Truman reasoned, but it was MacArthur who would pay the price in the long run. Truman was certain that the historians would vindicate his decision, irrespective of what the columnists and editorial writers of the day had to say.

In some regards, Truman made it easy for historians to make his case by leaving such a copious paper trail. On more than one occasion he foreshadowed MacArthur's dismissal in his diary, including the day after the Martin letter was revealed, writing that "this looks like the last straw—rank insubordination. I've come to the conclusion that our Big General in the Far East must be recalled."[15]

But he didn't leave it at that. On April 13, Truman took to the airwaves with a televised address that outlined, in no uncertain terms, why he had removed MacArthur from command. "I believe that we must try to limit the war in Korea for these vital reasons: to make sure that the precious lives of our fighting men are not wasted; to see that the security of our country and the free world is not jeopardized; and to prevent a third world war. A number of events have made it evident that General MacArthur did not agree with that policy. I have therefore considered it essential to relieve General MacArthur so that there would be no doubt or confusion as to the real purpose and aim of our policy. It was with the deepest personal regret that I found myself compelled to take this action. General MacArthur is one of our greatest military commanders. But the cause of world peace is more important than any individual."[16] The speech did little to quiet the storm of protest directed at Truman, but in hindsight it reads like a sober and even-handed assessment of MacArthur's reckless behavior.

In the weeks following the firing, the Senate Foreign Relations and Armed Services Committees held joint hearings to investigate the matter. Truman found the proceedings bothersome and petty, but he also understood that it was an important chance to continue building his case for posterity. Truman couldn't testify himself—that would be unseemly—but George Marshall, Omar Bradley, and the Joint Chiefs did, coming strongly to the president's defense for nineteen days. The Joint Chiefs again rejected MacArthur's claim that they were in agreement on his strategy. Marshall characterized MacArthur's firing as a "very distressing necessity" but one that was needed to keep the war a limited one. Omar Bradley produced the most memorable line from the hearings when he said that MacArthur's plan to bomb China and widen the war would "involve us in the wrong war, at the wrong place, at the wrong time, and with the wrong enemy." The message from the generals was unmistakable: Truman was right; MacArthur was wrong. And they weren't subtle about it.[17]

The hearings marked a turning point of sorts for Truman. Day after day for three weeks, some of the nation's most respected military figures spoke with one voice about the necessity of Truman's action. Not surprisingly, it took its toll on the general's reputation and popularity. By the time the hearings were over, the country had begun to move on from the entire incident, and a level of calm had returned to the country. MacArthur seemed less heroic and more ordinary, and talk of Truman's impeachment had quickly become a distant memory.

Old Soldiers Never Die

He may not have faded away from public life, but Douglas MacArthur certainly receded to the background shortly after coming home. There was talk of a presidential candidacy, but it never materialized; he wound up endorsing conservative Republican Senator Bob Taft over Dwight Eisenhower at the 1952 Republican convention. Ironically enough, his keynote speech for Taft was a massive flop. Some contend that it contributed to Eisenhower's easily winning the Republican nomination, and in the process bruised some feelings. As a result, MacArthur declined to endorse Eisenhower in the general election. The two generals were on the outs for several years. They would eventually patch things up toward the end of Ike's presidency.

While Truman had no intention of seeking reelection (despite the passage of the Twenty-Second Amendment, Truman could have been "godfathered" in), the MacArthur firing made it a virtual impossibility as it drove his approval ratings to the lowest levels in modern memory. Truman's preferred candidate was General Eisenhower. On several occasions—including as late as the winter of 1951—he tried to convince Ike to seek the Democratic nomination, but the general declined. It would create a bitter rift between the two for the remainder of their lives.

Truman didn't campaign much for the Democratic nominee, Illinois governor Adlai Stevenson. He understood that the stalemate in Korea and the specter of communists in the government were the defining issues of the campaign, and that his presence would likely hurt Stevenson. Eisenhower benefited from the anti-Truman sentiment and trounced Stevenson. He would trounce him again in their rematch four years later. It would be years later before historians began to rethink Truman's presidency.

Chapter 10

EISENHOWER, KENNEDY, AND THE RACE TO THE MOON

Courtesy of the John Fitzgerald Kennedy Library.

I would rather have a good Redstone [rocket] than hit the Moon, for we don't have any enemies on the Moon!
—President Dwight Eisenhower, 1957

Everything we do really ought to be tied in to getting on the Moon ahead of the Russians; otherwise we shouldn't be spending that kind of money, because I'm not interested in space. The only justification is because we hope to demonstrate that instead of being behind by a couple of years, by God, we passed them.
—President Kennedy to his NASA director, James Webb, in 1963

What we attained when Neil Armstrong stepped down on the moon was a completely new step in the evolution of man. . . . For the first time, life left

187

its planetary cradle and the ultimate destiny of man is no longer confined to these familiar contents that we have known so long.
　　　　　　　　　　　　—Werner von Braun, father of the modern rocket

On the morning of October 4, 1957, Americans awoke to the faint pings of the first-ever artificial satellite orbiting the Earth. Called Sputnik, *the Russian-made orb was twenty-three inches in diameter and circled the planet once every two hours. The launch came as a shock to the American public. It had been assumed that the United States was years ahead of its communist rivals in rocketry, satellite technology, and overall scientific know-how. In an instant, that illusion had been shattered, and less than a month later it would be completely demolished with the orbit of* Sputnik 2, *a one-ton satellite that contained the first space passenger, a thirteen-pound Samoyed terrier named Laika. A succession of breakthroughs would follow, and by decade's end the Soviets enjoyed a comfortable lead in the "race to dominate space." For its part, the Eisenhower administration dismissed the Russians' accomplishments as little more than fancy parlor tricks. Ike had no interest in blowing a hole in the federal budget just to keep pace with the Russians in a pointless space race. Across the globe, however, allies and foes saw the competition differently. To some, the Soviets' newfound advantage in science, technology, and innovation stood as proof that communism was at least the equal to capitalism—perhaps superior. If it was a contest to win the hearts and minds of peoples around the globe in the titanic struggle between freedom and totalitarianism, then the finish line would have to be redefined for the United States to win.*

* * *

One would be hard pressed to find consecutive presidents, considered by most to be moderates, as dramatically different in style, temperament, and approach as Dwight Eisenhower and John Kennedy. Eisenhower was among the oldest to serve in the office; Kennedy, the second youngest. Ever the military man, Ike instilled rigid discipline and clear lines of authority with his staff; Kennedy, much like his idol Franklin Roosevelt, held an advanced degree in "informational interloping." Eisenhower shunned the bully pulpit and was perfectly content to allow others to shape administration policy. Kennedy loved the stage and the arena and being at the center of attention. Eisenhower avoided risk; Kennedy courted it. Perhaps the only similarity was their shared dislike of their respective vice presidents.

They differed on policy, too. Ike favored balanced budgets and fiscal austerity; Kennedy preferred tax cuts and robust growth. Eisenhower, interestingly enough, was wary of the rapid expansion in the "military-industrial" complex—a phrase he coined—as the Cold War settled in. He believed the concentration of power among those interested in making war was unhealthy and dangerous. Kennedy, on the other hand, spoke of the growing missile gap and the need to meet force with even greater force. The Cold War, in his view, was an epic contest to be won at all costs. Eisenhower reluctantly enforced what few civil rights existed; Kennedy sought to expand them.

But their greatest departure came in the area of space policy. Or more specifically, the notion that the United States and the Soviet Union were locked in a "space race." Eisenhower thought the whole thing was pure folly. Trying to one-up the other guy, in his estimation, amounted to nothing more than an expensive publicity stunt for which he refused to take part. He couldn't see the value of besting the Soviets in a meaningless endeavor devoid of tangible benefit, or so he thought. On some level, Kennedy agreed. In and of itself, space exploration held little significance for him. It was the competition that mattered. And with the world picking sides between the two systems, providing a reason to choose America would be paramount.

Early Cold War

As many in the Truman White House had predicted—and feared—the end of World War II was greeted by the beginnings of a cold war with the Soviet Union. The former ally wasted little time in extending a sphere of influence over Eastern Europe, its dominance soon threatening Western Europe. In Asia, things were no better as Mao Zedong's rebel forces overtook Nationalist China, bringing with it the specter of communism throughout the entire continent. President Truman responded with the Marshall Plan, the $25 billion aid package meant to prop up the European economy, and the policy of containment, which held that the

United States would provide aid to any country struggling to resist the forces of communism. In August of 1949, the Cold War turned colder on the news that the Soviets had detonated their first atomic bomb. The test caught the White House and Pentagon off guard; it was assumed that the Soviets were years away from acquiring nuclear weapons. Americans had taken comfort in the knowledge that the Russians lacked the bomb. Now that was no longer the case.

The early 1950s was a difficult time for the United States. At home, Senator Joseph McCarthy had whipped the country into a frenzy over his search for communists in government. In the process, civil liberties were trampled, morale suffered, and thousands were chased from government service though few Reds were ever found. The McCarthy witch hunt remains one of the ugliest episodes in American history. Overseas, the United States military—the same one that had saved the world from Nazi and Japanese fascism—was stuck in a bloody stalemate in faraway Korea against an enemy it didn't understand. The American people were baffled—and frustrated—by the unsatisfying outcome. A few years later Americans could only watch helplessly as the Soviet army brutally crushed a democratic uprising in Hungary. By the middle of the decade, the American public had come to accept the terms of this new reality: the world was divided between two ideologies for which friendly coexistence seemed impossible.

Dwight Eisenhower was swept into office in 1952 and reelected in 1956 on the strength of his military credentials. Who better to keep the Russians in check than the Supreme Allied Commander, the man who liberated Western Europe from Nazi rule. Ike was so popular, in fact, that Gallup polls in the spring of 1952 showed him leading both the Republican and the Democratic primaries, even though his party affiliation was unknown.[1] His trouncing of Adlai Stevenson in 1952, and again in 1956, was a testament, in many ways, to his legacy as one of the greatest military leaders in American history.

It was expected that Eisenhower would meet the Red menace head-on. In the minds of some Americans, the problem stemmed from the previous Democratic administrations. Franklin Roosevelt, according to their logic, had "given away" Eastern Europe at the Yalta Conference, too ill and naïve to recognize Stalin's treachery and ambition. Truman only made matters worse. He had "sold out" Chiang Kai-shek to Mao's

Red army and in the process "lost" a billion people to communism. And when Douglas MacArthur had the temerity to suggest using nuclear weapons to break the Korean stalemate, he was promptly fired by the unpopular president. Ike would change all that; he would get tough on the Reds.

He did and he didn't. Eisenhower certainly appreciated the gravity of the Soviet threat; he suffered no illusion that the typical tenets of diplomacy were applicable in this new Cold War. "From behind the Iron Curtain," he said during his first State of the Union address, "there are signs that tyranny is in trouble and reminders that its structure is as brittle as its surface is hard."[2] But for Americans expecting him to behave like Douglas MacArthur—a chest-thumping cowboy all too eager to "take the fight" to the "Commies"—they were sorely disappointed. Eisenhower believed that the best deterrent to Soviet aggression was a sound economy; a well-developed transportation infrastructure that included interstate highways, tunnels, and bridges; and advanced weaponry that could take the place of large troop commitments around the world. "There is no amount of military force that can possibly give you real security," he said at one of his first press conferences, "because you wouldn't have that amount unless you felt that there was almost a similar amount that could threaten you somewhere in the world."[3]

In his view, a strong economy meant a balanced budget, low interest rates, and sustainable growth. Eisenhower has been fairly described as being obsessed with keeping spending in line with revenues. He considered deficits a moral failing and something of a disgrace. To that end, he achieved a balanced budget in three of his eight years—the last Republican president to do so—and on two occasions cut federal spending in real dollars, the most recent president to accomplish that feat. This singular focus on keeping spending under control, inflation in check, and government expansion at bay colored his thinking on virtually everything. Decisions big and little were filtered through the same prism: what would it mean for the federal budget? Eisenhower was loathe to invest in anything—including tax cuts favored by his own party—that wasn't supported by revenues. It went doubly so for programs that he believed provided little value. In this light, the notion of a space race must have seemed alien to the penurious president.

Little Red Moon

"Here in the capital responsible men think and talk of little but the metal spheroid that now looms larger in the eye of the mind than the planet it circles around," is how CBS news reporter Eric Sevareid described the mood in Washington on October 6, 1957, two days after the launch of *Sputnik*. "The wisest of men does not know tonight whether man in his radiance or man in his darkness will possess the spinning ball."[4]

It was a legitimate question. Most Americans—including politicians and the press—were puzzled at how the Soviets, long thought to be dramatically inferior in science and technology, could send an object into outer space. And more importantly, they wondered, could that same technology be used to launch intercontinental ballistic missiles against the United States? The prospect of a Soviet first-strike capability—once considered remote—no longer seemed so far-fetched. "For the first time," writes one student of the era, "geography had ceased to be a barrier, and the U.S. mainland lay exposed to enemy fire. In that respect, Russia's rockets were infinitely more frightening than the Japanese bombers that had attacked Pearl Harbor sixteen years before."[5]

Publicly, the administration tried to downplay the significance of the Soviet accomplishment. "The importance should not be exaggerated," said the official White House response the following day. "What has happened involves no basic discovery." The only reason the Soviets were able to pull it off, it went on, was because they had inherited the program from the Nazis. "The Germans had made a major advance in this field and the results of their effort were largely taken over by the Russians when they took over the German assets, human and material, at Peenemunde, the principal German base for research and experiment in the use of outer space." The statement conceded that "despotic societies" could achieve spectacular accomplishments by "commanding the activities and resources of all their people," but it didn't prove that "freedom is not the best way."[6]

Privately, however, the White House was in a panic. Eisenhower was seething after learning from his secretary of defense that the United States could have put a satellite in orbit two years earlier—had it only been a priority. "We might have to go to a Manhattan Project type approach in order to get forward in this matter," he told the cabinet.

"Get the Redstone [rocket] people into the business of putting a satellite into orbit as soon as possible."[7]

The press, from the administration's perspective, wasn't helping matters. "Listen now for the sound that will forever more separate the old from the new," reported NBC as it broadcast the pinging tones from *Sputnik*'s orbit live on its airwaves. The *New York Times* reserved six column inches on its front page—a size typically allotted for presidential deaths or declarations of war—to blare that "Soviet Fires Earth Satellite into Space; Sphere Tracked in Four Crossings over U.S." The wildly Republican *New York Herald Tribune* conceded that it represented "a grave defeat." *Newsweek* pondered the obvious question: "What effect would the Soviet achievement have on the nation's security?" *Time* magazine, writing of *Sputnik*'s "chilling beeps," pulled no punches as it lamented that "in vital sectors of the technology race, the U.S. may have well lost its precious lead." For Edward Teller, the man behind the hydrogen bomb, the little orb was nothing less than "a technological Pearl Harbor."[8] *Pravda*, the official paper of the Soviet Politburo, had fun rubbing America's nose in it. *Sputnik*, in their view, was simply further proof to "our contemporaries" that the "freed and conscientious labor of the people of the new socialist society makes the most daring dreams of mankind a reality."[9]

The Democrats in Congress, sensing their best opportunity in years to score political points against the popular Eisenhower, wasted no time in stoking the flames of fear. It was "a devastating blow," said Washington Senator Scoop Jackson, to the "prestige of the United States as the leader in the scientific and technical world." To Senator Stuart Symington, it was evidence of the "growing Communist superiority in the all-important missile field." Not to be outdone, Senator Richard Russell, the powerful and well-respected elder statesman from Georgia, posited—somewhat misleadingly—that "the Russians have the ultimate weapons—a long-range missile capable of delivering atomic and hydrogen explosives across continents and oceans." Should America fail to close the technological gap, he warned, it would compromise the "position of the free world." Senate Majority Leader Lyndon Johnson, who would later chair President Kennedy's Space Council, quickly convened a congressional investigation that eventually produced a three-thousand-page report detailing America's technological shortcomings.

"Our country," it opined, "is disturbed over the tremendous military and scientific achievements of Russia. Our people believed that in the field of scientific weapons and in technology and science that we were well ahead of Russia. With the launching of *Sputnik* . . . our supremacy and even our equality have been challenged."[10] Eisenhower's response: "Johnson can keep his head in the stars; I'm going to keep my feet on the ground."[11]

The furor from the press and Democrats was too much to leave unanswered. On October 9, less than a week after *Sputnik* had become a household word, Eisenhower held a press conference, ostensibly to defuse the situation and reassure the nation that there was little to be concerned about. What he thought would be a routine affair was anything but, as a hostile press took him to task for the better part of an hour. Ike had barely finished greeting reporters when Merriman Smith of United Press International cut in with the first question. "Mr. President," he demanded to know, "Russia has launched an earth satellite. They also claim to have had a successful firing of an intercontinental ballistics missile, none of which this country has done. I ask you, sir, what are we going to do about it?" The president fumbled through an answer and it went downhill from there. Did he agree with Khrushchev that "planes, bombers, and fighters will be confined to museums because they are outmoded by the missiles which Russia claims she has now perfected?" Not exactly. "I believe it would be dangerous to predict what science is going to do in the next twenty years." Was it a mistake not to recognize that we were in a race with the Soviets? Not at all, responded Eisenhower, since "the value of that satellite going around the earth is still problematical." As for the American satellite program, was he confident that it would be "up to par" with Russia? "Well now," he said solemnly, "let's get this straight: I am not a scientist."[12]

And so it went. It was a sloppy performance, bordering on reckless, and did little to provide assurance to an increasingly edgy public. Things went from ugly to worse following the launch of *Sputnik II* on November 2, which carried a 1,100-pound payload that included Laika the dog, the first world's first astronaut. Under intense pressure to respond in kind with an American satellite, the navy (which at this time was in charge of rocketry) rushed a premature attempt in early December. The resulting explosion was dubbed "flopnik" and "kaputnik" by the press and left the administration embarrassed and angry. "I am saddened and humiliated by the cheap and gaudy manner in which the Administration has gone about the business of trying a last-ditch rush to launch a satellite," said Hubert Humphrey, the presumptive Democratic frontrunner for the 1960 election.[13]

Though the United States would eventually reach orbit, it lagged well behind the Soviet Union in milestones and achievements for the remainder of the decade, a point that Nikita Khrushchev joyfully reiterated at every possible occasion. The *Sputnik* program, he told world leaders toward the end of 1957, "demonstrates that the USSR has outstripped the leading capitalist country—the United States—in the field of scientific and technological progress." It was, he emphasized, evidence of a "change in favor of the socialist states in the balance of forces with capitalist states."[14] He would repeat the line often.

As much as Eisenhower wanted to avoid the notion of a space competition between the two countries, he couldn't resist the pressure to create a new agency that would spearhead America's exploration of the cosmos. In July of 1958, the National Aeronautics and Space Administration (NASA) was created, and within a few months—nearly a year to the day after *Sputnik*'s faithful journey—it had begun developing a program to send humans to the stars.

Even so, Ike never warmed to the idea of manned space flight. He couldn't shake the belief that it was costly, dangerous, and ultimately pointless since it didn't deepen scientific understanding or produce technologies that couldn't be attained elsewhere more cheaply. It would simply bust the budget, ratchet up the Cold War, and divert attention from other important matters, such as fighting inflation and improving the nation's infrastructure. With that being the case, there was no way the president was going to allow the country to get "involved in a pathetic race." As for exploring the moon, that was out of the question. "I'd rather have a good rocket than be able to hit the moon," he told advisors. "We don't have any enemies on the moon!"[15] To underscore the point, Eisenhower nixed NASA's proposed plan to put a man in lunar orbit by 1969 with just months left in his presidency. It was too impractical and expensive, he reasoned—nothing more than a grandiose "publicity stunt." And with that, he believed, the notion of space race was done and buried for good.[16]

"The torch has been passed to a new generation of Americans"

John Fitzgerald Kennedy entered the national consciousness in the summer of 1956 at the Democratic National Convention in Chicago. It was there that the handsome, skinny, thirty-nine-year-old senator from Massachusetts with the sharp accent came within a whisker of joining Adlai Stevenson as his running mate on the Democratic ticket. In losing the public floor vote to Tennessee senator Estes Kefauver, Kennedy delivered a gracious and rousing concession speech, one that made a lasting impression on the delegates in attendance and television viewers at home. To anyone who saw Kennedy that night, there was little doubt that he would be heard from again.

For those already familiar with Kennedy, it was common knowledge that he was far from a traditional northeast liberal. He came from a wealthy family led by its isolationist and increasingly conservative patriarch; sported a moderate voting record in the Senate; and frequently drew criticism from his own party for having been neutral on the "McCarthy issue" and siding with Republicans on matters of national defense and the Cold War.[17] For Kennedy, Eisenhower's failure to keep pace with the Russians on missile and rocket technology was simply further proof that the country was in desperate need of new leadership and direction. America, he believed, wasn't about to best the Soviets by nickel and diming on technology investments and defense spending. It called for a more aggressive and creative approach, with a dash of inspiration thrown in for good measure. It required, he believed, a leader such as himself.

Kennedy would hit on this theme time and again during the 1960 election against Richard Nixon, who as Eisenhower's vice president carried the baggage of *Sputnik* and the missile gap at a time when the president's standing was at an all-time low. At campaign stops, Kennedy reminded voters that "we are in a strategic race with the Russians and we have been losing."[18] He particularly liked to mock Nixon over his famous "Kitchen Debate" with Soviet premier Nikita Khrushchev, where the vice president boasted to the Russian dictator, "You may be ahead of us in rocket thrust, but we are ahead of you in color television." Kennedy's typical retort: "I will take my television in black and white. I want to be ahead in rocket thrust!"[19] If that didn't get under Nixon's skin, his debate line about "the first living creatures to orbit the earth in space were dogs named Strelka and Belka, not Rover or Fido—or even Checkers [Nixon's departed mutt]" certainly did.[20]

Kennedy took his most serious jab at Eisenhower—and by proxy Nixon—at a rally in Portland two months before Election Day. "It seems to me, and this is most dangerous for all of us," he said sternly, "that we are in danger of losing the respect of the people of the world. . . . The people of the world respect achievement. For most of the twentieth century they admired American science and American education, which was second to none. But now they are not at all certain about which way the future lies. The first vehicle in outer space was called *Sputnik*, not *Vanguard*."[21]

It was a valid point. In the battle to win the hearts and minds of "undecideds" around the world in the struggle against the Red Menace, milestones and accomplishments mattered. So did propaganda and perception. How else could people in faraway regions of the globe be convinced that democracy and capitalism were superior to totalitarianism and communism except by comparing their respective achievements? Kennedy understood this. Ironically, so did Nixon. But like others in the administration, he was unable to convince Eisenhower that beating the Soviets in space was a noble and strategic cause worthy of a well-funded and spirited effort. There's no doubt that the perceived "technology gap" contributed to Nixon's razor-thin defeat.

In some ways, Kennedy's victory began a new chapter in the Cold War. What had been a somewhat abstract, mostly ideological, and at times rhetorical struggle evolved into an all-out competition. The playing field would be everywhere: politics, culture, sports, espionage, technology, weaponry—even chess. Most of those landscapes were pretty settled. Kennedy wanted a new canvas—something bold, dramatic, that America could win. Something that would unequivocally put to rest the debate over which system was superior. A race to the moon.

"I'm tired of America being second in space!"

When John F. Kennedy was sworn in on January 20, 1961, as the thirty-fifth president of the United States, sending a man to the moon was hardly on his mind. The economy, Fidel Castro, military readiness, and civil rights were. Other than taking potshots at Nixon and exploiting the "*Sputnik* gap" for political gain, Kennedy hadn't given the cosmos much thought at all. He had a vague understanding that NASA was working toward manned space flight, but beyond that it was a bit of mystery. He certainly had no long-term vision or plan for space exploration.

That all changed on April 12, 1961, when Yuri Gagarin became the first human to leave Earth. Like *Sputnik* four years earlier, the news of the cosmonaut's four-day orbit came as a shock to the American people, setting off a similar wave of fear, panic, and finger-pointing. At a press conference that same day, a beleaguered and surprised Kennedy, responding to a reporter's question regarding a recent remark from a congressman that he was tired of seeing the Soviets make history, let his frustration show. "However tired anybody may be, and no one is more tired than I am, it is a fact that it is going to take some time. . . . We are, I hope, going to go in other areas where we can be first, and which will bring perhaps more long-range benefits to mankind. But," he conceded, "we are behind."[22]

Behind the Iron Curtain, Khrushchev was up to his old tricks. He hailed Gagarin as "the new Christopher Columbus" and dared the young president to "catch up with our country." *Pravda* went even further. In their humble opinion, the Cold War was all but over, the Soviet Union having delivered the knockout blow: "In this achievement are embodied the genius of the Soviet people and the powerful forces of communism. The Gagarin flight was . . . evidence of the global superiority of the Soviet Union in all aspects of science and technology."[23]

Two days after Gagarin's flight, Kennedy convened an emergency meeting of his top space advisors, including James Webb, the head of NASA, and his deputy, to assess the situation. Was there anything on the horizon, Kennedy wondered, that could give them a meaningful "first" in the space race? The feedback was discouraging. In all likelihood, the Soviets would be the first to build a space station, put crews of two and three in space, and orbit the moon. "Is there any place we can catch them?" the president heatedly asked. "What can we do? Can we leapfrog?" There was really only one option: the moon. If NASA embarked on a Manhattan Project–style crash program, the group told Kennedy, it might be possible to put an American on the lunar surface before the end of the decade. It would be an enormous gamble, fraught with risk and danger, and require upwards of $20 billion—a staggering sum. Kennedy was alarmed at the price tag but conceded that "there's nothing more important."[24]

What began as a bad week for the president—with Gagarin triumphantly circling Earth—ended even worse, with the CIA's botched attempted overthrow of the Cuban dictator Fidel Castro at the Bay of Pigs. Though the plan to ouster the island's strongman dated back to the Eisenhower administration, the young and inexperienced Kennedy was saddled with its failure. The bungled operation was an embarrassing setback for the fledgling administration and another blow to America's prestige around the world. And according to historian Michael Beschloss, it left Kennedy in desperate "need of something that would divert the attention of the public and identify him with a cause that would unify them behind his administration."[25]

In the wake of Gagarin's ride and the Bay of Pigs fiasco, Kennedy summoned Vice President Lyndon Johnson—whom he had recently appointed chairman of the previously dormant Space Council—to the White House for an urgent strategy session on April 20. He handed the startled Johnson a memo with a list of questions. "Do we have a chance of beating the Soviets by putting a laboratory in space, or by a trip round the moon, or by a rocket to land on the moon, or by a rocket to go to the moon and back with a man? Is there any other space program which promises dramatic results in which we could win? . . . How much additional money would it cost? . . . Are we working 24 hours a day on existing programs? . . . Are we making maximum effort? Are we achieving necessary results?" He told Johnson to investigate the answers as quickly as possible.[26]

After canvassing NASA officials, the secretaries of defense and state, leaders on Capitol Hill, and even the famed rocket scientist Werner von Braun, Johnson returned to the White House a week later with the answers Kennedy wanted. His feedback was blunt, unapologetic, and left no doubt as to the best course of action. "Largely due to their concerted efforts . . . the Soviets are ahead of the United States in world prestige attained through impressive technological accomplishments in space," wrote Johnson. This occurred, in part, because the United States had "failed to make the necessary hard decisions and to marshal those resources to achieve such leadership." If this continued to be the case, Johnson warned, "other nations, regardless of their appreciation of our idealistic values, will tend to align themselves with the country which they believe will be the world leader—the winner in the long run. Dramatic accomplishments in space are being increasingly identified as a major indicator of world leadership." The Soviets, the memo concluded, held an advantage in most facets of space exploration, with the notable exception of a lunar circumnavigation and landing. "With a strong effort, the United States could conceivably be first in those two accomplishments by 1966 or 1967." It wouldn't come cheap, or easy, but it was achievable.[27]

The only remaining hurdle was getting NASA's top administrator, James Webb, on board. He liked the challenge of going to the moon, but understood—perhaps better than anyone—the enormous resources, commitment, and national fervor it would require. As a longtime Washington hand, he knew that government funding could be fickle: here today, gone tomorrow. He also knew that failure would be laid at his feet. To win Webb over, Kennedy wisely dispatched Johnson—who as Senate majority leader had perfected the art of "arm-twisting"—to make his case. In reading Johnson's notes from the meeting, one can assume how the conversation unfolded. "We are here to discuss not WHETHER, but HOW—not WHEN, but NOW," wrote the vice president.[28]

Webb got the message. Less than a week later, he delivered a letter to the administration charting a new direction for NASA, one that would land Americans on the moon before 1970. "This nation," he wrote, "needs to make a positive decision to pursue space projects aimed at enhancing national prestige. . . . Lunar and planetary exploration are, in this sense, part of the battle along the fluid front of the Cold War. . . . We recommend that our National Space plan include the objective of manned lunar exploration before the end of this decade." Circumnavigation wasn't enough. In Webb's estimation, the orbiting of "machines" was "not the same as the orbiting or landing of man. It is man, not merely machines, in space, that captures the imagination of the world."

A failure to accept this challenge, he concluded, would be interpreted as "a lack of national vigor and capacity to respond."[29]

Kennedy discussed the matter with his full cabinet on May 10. He was heartened by Alan Shepard's brief (fifteen minutes), suborbital flight of a week earlier. It might not have been as dramatic as Gagarin's joyride, but it was a start. Still, the cabinet had reservations. The budget director was concerned about the enormous price tag for a mere matter of "national prestige." The secretary of labor challenged the notion that the spending would stimulate the economy. As was later noted by one of the participants, Secretary of Defense Robert McNamara—a supporter of the program—shut down remaining dissent by positing that the aerospace industry, which was suffering from his military cutbacks, needed the Apollo program to stave off massive layoffs. "This," the observer recalled, "took away all arguments against the space program."[30]

"We choose to go to the Moon in this decade and do the other things, not because they are easy but because they are hard"

On May 25, 1961, President Kennedy went before Congress to deliver his State of the Union address. It was slightly unusual in that he had given his first State of the Union just months earlier. "While this has traditionally been interpreted as an annual affair," he noted at the top of his remarks, "this tradition has been broken in extraordinary times. These are extraordinary times."

They were certainly trying times. America's standing in the world was at its lowest point in decades; the Soviet Union seemed to be on an unstoppable roll; and there was a feeling of unease as to what the future held. Kennedy covered a lot of ground in the speech, but reserved the most time for the moon challenge. It was here that America could strike a blow against the Soviet Union and galvanize the world to its side again. "If we are to win the battle that is now going on around the world between freedom and tyranny," he said bluntly, "the dramatic achievements in space which occurred in recent weeks should have made clear to us all, as did the *Sputnik* in 1957, the impact of this adventure on the minds of men everywhere, who are attempting to make a determination of which road they should take." It was time for "a new American enterprise"—a great challenge—that would restore America as the undisputed leader in scientific achievement. The blame, Kennedy wasn't shy to point out, rested with the previous administration, since "we have never made the national decisions or marshaled the national resources required for such leadership." Acknowledging the "many months of lead-time" currently enjoyed by the Soviets, Kennedy refused to accept it as an excuse. "We cannot guarantee that we shall one day be first, we can guarantee that any failure to make this effort will make us last." With that being the case, Kennedy put forth a clear challenge: "I believe that this nation should commit itself to achieving the goal, before this decade is out, of landing a man on the moon and returning him safely to the earth. No single space project will be more impressive to mankind . . . or so difficult or expensive to accomplish."[31]

Curiously, the president left a sliver of wiggle room to back away from the challenge should it fail to catch on with Congress and the public. "I believe we should go to the moon," he said in closing, "but I think every citizen of this country as well as the Members of the Congress should consider the matter carefully in making their judgment . . . because it is a heavy burden, and there is no sense in agreeing or desiring that the United States take an affirmative position in outer space, unless we are prepared to do the work and bear the burdens to make it successful. If we are not, we should decide today and this year." It was an odd, defensive note to close out the section, but a smart political hedge. If we were going to do this, it was Kennedy's way of saying, then everyone had to be on board.[32]

Vice President Johnson got Congress to fall in line. He saw to it that the Apollo program received all the funding it needed. Even so, the president remained nervous about the enormous cost. The $20 to $30 billion it would take, he was reminded by advisors, could be used in myriad other ways that would be more beneficial to Democrats in Congress. It weighed so much on his mind that Kennedy raised the idea of a cooperative moon expedition with Khrushchev at their first summit meeting in Vienna just a month after his speech. The Soviet premier brushed aside the proposal, but it wouldn't be the last time that Kennedy visited the topic. In the fall of 1963, just weeks before his death, he again invited the

Soviets to jointly shoot for the moon in a speech before the United Nations. "Why, therefore, should man's first flight to the moon be a matter of national competition?" he asked. "Surely we should explore whether the scientists and astronauts of our two countries—indeed of the world—cannot work together in the conquest of space. Let us do big things together." Khrushchev was closely reviewing the offer when Kennedy was tragically assassinated.[33]

Even with congressional backing, Kennedy had plenty of critics for what some in the press had dubbed "moondoggle." Perhaps the most persistent and outspoken was former president Eisenhower, who told a friend shortly after Kennedy's speech that his plan to spend billions of dollars to beat the Soviets to the moon was "immature" and "hysterical." In August of 1962, Ike went public with his displeasure in a wide-ranging piece that he penned for the *Saturday Evening Post*. Reaching for the stars was well and good, opined Ike, so long as it didn't bankrupt the nation in the process. "By all means," he agreed, "we must carry on our explorations in space, but frankly I do not see the need for continuing this effort as such a fantastically expensive crash program." The United States, in his estimation, didn't have to prove anything. "Why the great hurry to get to the moon and planets? We have already demonstrated that in everything except the power of our booster rockets we are leading the world in scientific space exploration." Ike's suggestion: "From here on, I think we should proceed in an orderly, scientific way, building one accomplishment on another, rather than engaging in a mad effort to win a stunt race."[34]

Eisenhower's criticism of Kennedy's space priorities didn't sit well with the astronauts themselves. One of them, Frank Borman, who as commander of the Apollo 8 mission would become the first man to orbit the moon along with Jim Lovell and Bill Anders, penned a testy note to the former president taking exception to his calling the Apollo program a stunt. "What I have criticized about the current space program is the concept under which it was drastically revised and expanded just after the Bay of Pigs fiasco in 1961," replied Eisenhower in a long and thoughtful letter. "The President of the United States announced that this nation challenged the Russians to a race to the moon, implying that the prestige of the U.S.A. would be riding on this issue. This, I thought, unwise." Ike didn't back away from his contention that it was little more than a public relations ploy. The Apollo missions "took one single project or experiment out of a thoughtfully planned and continuing program involving communications, meteorology, reconnaissance, and the future military and scientific benefits and gave the highest priority—unfortunate in my opinion—to a race, in other words, a stunt."[35]

The funding issue—nor the critics—never completely went away. Kennedy understood the importance of maintaining public support and enthusiasm. At press conferences and other events, he was forever reiterating the need for regaining the admiration of the world through great accomplishments like the moon landing. In the fall of 1962, he gave his most expansive speech on the topic while visiting Rice University. Addressing what he found to be a bothersome and nagging question— why a moon landing?—Kennedy delivered one of the most memorable lines of his presidency. "We choose to go to the moon. We choose to go to the moon in this decade and do the other things, not because they are easy, but because they are hard, because that goal will serve to organize and measure the best of our energies and skills, because that challenge is one that we are willing to accept, one we are unwilling to postpone, and one which we intend to win, and the others, too." He spoke of other benefits to the pursuit—job creation, scientific discovery, new defense technologies—but left no doubt that the biggest motive was simple inspiration. "Many years ago the great British explorer George Mallory, who was to die on Mount Everest, was asked why did he want to climb it. He said, 'Because it is there.' Well, space is there, and we're going to climb it, and the moon and the planets are there, and new hopes for knowledge and peace are there. And, therefore, as we set sail we ask God's blessing on the most hazardous and dangerous and greatest adventure on which man has ever embarked."[36]

* * *

Kennedy's grand gamble paid off. On July 20, 1969, with an estimated 450 million people around the world watching, Neil Armstrong became the first human to set foot on another celestial body, his words immortalized for all eternity: "That's one small step for [a] man, one giant leap for mankind."

Though he wouldn't live to see it, the moon landing is arguably the greatest accomplishment of Kennedy's presidency. For sheer size, scope, ambition, and breadth of scientific achievement, it ranks alongside the Manhattan Project and the building of the Panama Canal as the most impressive feats of the twentieth century.

Did it accomplish Kennedy's goal of restoring America's prestige around the globe as the undisputed leader in science and technology? Without question. People who lived through it still recall with wonder how the United States put a man on the moon in less than a decade. For later generations, it all seems a bit fantastical. The images of Armstrong, Aldrin, and those who came after, plodding across the lunar horizon with impish delight, remain among the most iconic in all of history, forever emblazoning American ingenuity at the summit of man's greatest conquest. In that sense, it was worth every penny of the estimated $40 billion it took to put them there.

To say that it was done solely with the best of intentions—to further scientific discovery, satisfy a genuine curiosity about our closest heavenly neighbor, invite cooperation and understanding with the dreaded Soviets—would be misleading. First and foremost, it was a competition. Kennedy, and later Johnson, believed that besting the Soviets was critical to strengthening America's standing in the world. "Everything we do really ought to be tied in to getting on the Moon ahead of the Russians," Kennedy directed NASA director Webb. "Otherwise, we shouldn't be spending that kind of money, because I'm not interested in space."[37]

But it was more than just that. In his speech at Rice University—his most eloquent one on the topic—President Kennedy reminded the nation that the journey to the moon would yield untold scientific insight and breakthroughs, as well as preserve this new frontier for peaceful exploration. "We set sail on this new sea because there is new knowledge to be gained, and new rights to be won, and they must be won and used for the progress of all people. For space science . . . has no conscience of its own. Whether it will become a force for good or ill depends on man, and only if the United States occupies a position of preeminence can we help decide whether this new ocean will be a sea of peace or a new terrifying theater of war."[38]

Ironically, the Soviets never got out of the starting blocks. The Gagarin orbit, as it turned out, marked the high-water mark of their space program. Plagued by ruinous droughts, a collapsing economy, and unstable leadership, the country that had achieved so many firsts could only watch as America zoomed ahead in the mid-1960s. For years, they denied ever having a lunar program, but recent documents show, indeed, that the Soviets were racing for the moon, too. They gave up shortly after Armstrong's landing, years away from ever leaving Earth's orbit.[39]

In the end, John Kennedy, with his challenge to reach for the moon, changed the way the world viewed the United States. The Apollo program demonstrated, once and for all, that America was the unrivaled leader in scientific achievement. Never again could the Soviets proclaim technological superiority. It may be Kennedy's greatest legacy.

Chapter 11

LYNDON JOHNSON AND CIVIL RIGHTS

LBJ Library photo by Cecil Stoughton.

I do not know where you could have gotten the idea that I am supporting the "so-called bill for civil rights legislation now before Congress." . . . The bill that has been introduced is one to which I am very much opposed, as I do not believe it would advance any legitimate cause.
   —Lyndon Johnson responding to an irate constituent who fumed that he was "selling out the South" by supporting the 1957 Civil Rights Act

Well, what the hell is the presidency for?
   —Lyndon Johnson to aides who were counseling him against pushing too aggressively for a civil rights measure

I think we just delivered the South to the Republican Party for a long time to come.
   —Lyndon Johnson to aide Bill Moyers, hours after he signed the Civil Rights Act of 1964

On November 27, 1963, a grief-stricken and still unsteady Lyndon Johnson went before a joint session of Congress to reassure the nation—and himself— that the "forward thrust of America" that John F. Kennedy had begun would continue beyond his death. He reaffirmed the slain president's "dream of conquering the vastness of space" and of a "Peace Corps in less developed nations." He reminded Americans about the need for educating "all of our children" and providing "care for the elderly." He spoke of creating "jobs for all who seek them and need them" and urged the "early passage of the tax bill for which he fought all this long year." But he saved his most extended remarks for the cause of civil rights. "Above all," he said with growing confidence and resoluteness, "the dream of equal rights for all Americans, whatever their race or color—these and other American dreams have been vitalized by his drive and by his dedication." With that being the case, he went on, "no memorial oration or eulogy could more eloquently honor President Kennedy's memory than the earliest possible passage of the civil rights bill for which he fought so long. We have talked long enough in this country about equal rights. We have talked for one hundred years or more. It is time now to write the next chapter, and to write it in the books of law. . . . There could be no greater source of strength to this Nation both at home and abroad." It was a watershed moment for a nation that was beginning to come apart at its racial seams. And the driving force behind it was the first Southern president in over a century, a son of the segregated South. How did this come to pass?

* * *

Lyndon Johnson ranks alongside Richard Nixon and perhaps Bill Clinton as among the most complicated, fascinating, contradictory characters ever to occupy the office. Like his two successors, he had a brilliant, intuitive political mind that relished the minutiae of legislation and policy. He was prone, like Nixon and Clinton, to wild mood swings and bouts of self-pity and grandiosity, and wasn't above being consumed by hatred of his enemies, both perceived and real. And he was seemingly encased in layer upon layer of insecurity and self-loathing, a vestige, some have speculated, from his humble upbringing. That's not to put a value judgment on his presidency, or deem it a failure. He had a long list of accomplishments—civil rights, Medicare, scores of antipoverty programs that came to define the Great Society, the space program, to name a few—and one thunderous failure, Vietnam. Rather, it's meant to point out the enormous complexity of the man.

Nowhere was it more apparent than the area of civil rights. As a political conundrum, it called upon his mastery of the legislative process, mined the depths of his political acumen, and benefited from his considerable gift of deception and feigned sincerity. As a moral blight, it touched a deep reservoir of compassion and a genuine belief that all people—irrespective of race or standing—deserved an equal opportunity in life.

But more than anything, civil rights challenged Lyndon Johnson—the person, the legislator, the president—in a way that no other issue could. For all Southern politicians from that era, racial inequality—and the simmering tension that came with it—served as a backdrop to their public and private lives, never far removed from their consciousness or votes. Reminders were everywhere of how separate, unequal, and tragically unfair the promise of America remained for African Americans living south of the Mason-Dixon line. For Southern officials with upwardly mobile ambition, championing anything that resembled racial equality was a surefire path to an early retirement. For much of the twentieth century, the old Confederacy states operated as one-party territories. Go against the party on civil rights? Unheard of.

So how did an ambitious, calculating longhorn from the prairies of Texas, mentored by the leading segregationist in the Senate and cursed with an insatiable need to be loved by everyone, do more than any president in history save Lincoln to bring racial justice and equality to the United States? That's the story of Lyndon Johnson.

Race, Ambition, and the South

It has been said that Lyndon Johnson's political career was shaped by two competing forces: his Southern roots and his appetite for ever-expanding political power. They were competing, in the sense that, for politicians reared in the Deep South, the parochial attitudes of the region had historically acted to collar those with national ambition. Sure, the old Confederacy states had produced the occasional Speaker of the House and

Senate majority leader (including Johnson himself), but the White House was a different matter. For the better part of a century prior to Johnson's election in 1964, it remained tantalizingly out of reach for aspirants groomed in the South. The primary culprit: virulent racism. For most Northerners and Westerners, the practice of forced segregation, vigilante justice, and racial separation at the hand of Jim Crow laws and barbaric lynchings was an alien concept, as appalling as it was offensive. It made little sense, an unenlightened anachronism from a bygone era. And in some ways, it had become an automatic disqualifier—or at least a weighty albatross—for Southerners in search of national prominence. The country simply wasn't going to countenance a president who tacitly endorsed the legal subjugation of the races. For Dixie politicians who aspired to the highest office in the land, it would be an insurmountable obstacle for decades on end.

That's not to say that Lyndon Johnson was an unabashed racist or militant segregationist like so many of his cohorts, or that he aspired to become president from the moment he set foot in Congress in 1937. To the contrary, his views on race, status, and even poverty were decidedly more progressive than those around him. On a personal level, he was remarkably compassionate and magnanimous in his treatment of blacks and Hispanics at a time when it was considered perfectly acceptable—some would even say fashionable—to behave otherwise. Stories abound about his genuine concern for minorities and those less fortunate. As a young schoolteacher in a heavily Hispanic district, he stood apart from the other instructors for his commitment to seeing that the Mexican-American students received an education equal to that of the white children. "I was determined," Johnson would reminisce to biographer Doris Kearns Goodwin after leaving the White House, "to spark something inside them, to fill their souls with ambition and interest and belief in the future."[1]

Johnson may have been a product of the segregated South, but he was never an enthusiastic participant; he understood that the horrible treatment of blacks was wrong, immoral, and ultimately unsustainable. "During the 1940's and 1950's," noted LBJ biographer Robert Dallek, "[Johnson] had said more than once: 'The Negro fought in the war, and . . . he's not gonna keep taking the shit we're dishing out. We're in a race with time. If we don't act, we're gonna have blood on the streets.'"[2]

LBJ's total consumption with politics—and the ambition that went along with it—was evident from his earliest days as a congressional aide and later as a member of Congress. Over the years, former colleagues and friends would marvel at Johnson's singular focus and drive toward furthering his political career. "He had the narrowest vision of anyone you can imagine," remembered one former roommate. "Sports, entertainment, movies—he couldn't have cared less." Recalled another friend, who frequently invited Johnson to Washington Senators baseball games to help broaden his interests, "Lyndon would go along because he didn't want to be left behind. But he didn't give a hoot about the game. He would keep on arguing politics through every inning."[3] Said Johnson of himself at the time: "I never think of politics more than 18 hours a day."[4]

With the guidance of powerful mentors, notably Speaker of the House Sam Rayburn and President Franklin Roosevelt, and after getting a taste of how the levers of government could be manipulated to benefit his constituents, LBJ's fascination with the raw gamesmanship of politics slowly metamorphosed into a lust for pure power. As the youngest representative in the House his freshman year of 1937, he quickly earned the reputation as the consummate insider—someone who understood how to get things done. "He knew how to operate in Washington better than some who had been here twenty years before him," it was said of Johnson during his early years on Capitol Hill.[5] During his six terms in the House of Representatives, LBJ was an avowed champion of the rural poor and assiduously cultivated an image as a progressive New Dealer. He wisely avoided taking high-profile positions on issues of race, segregation, and civil rights, knowing full well that a point of view—one way or the other—could become a liability should he seek national office someday. Even then, Johnson knew that his ambition and the issue of racial inequality were on a collision course.

After a decade in the House of Representatives, Lyndon Johnson graduated to the United States Senate with a razor-thin victory in one of the nastiest elections in Texas history. Charges of voter fraud flew back and forth, both sides accusing the other of stealing votes. Was Johnson the beneficiary of foul play? "It's impossible to penetrate through the layers of truths, half-truths, and lies to determine what really happened," writes one student of the era. "To this day, the facts remain murky. It does seem clear, however, that both sides committed fraud."[6] The two-hundred-vote margin of victory earned Johnson the ironic nickname "Landslide Lyndon."

It was in the Senate where LBJ first came to national prominence. Within four years, he was voted minority leader by his Democratic colleagues—the most junior person in that chamber's history to achieve leader status—and two years later he became majority leader when the Democrats regained control of the Senate. He was now one of the most powerful men in the country. Legislation didn't happen without his consent. Deals weren't cut unless he approved. Even President Eisenhower had to court the Texan if he hoped to achieve anything on the domestic front. But it wasn't enough for Johnson. There was still one office he had an eye on. And there was only one way to get there.

The 1957 Civil Rights Act

Lyndon Johnson came to the United States Senate with little fanfare or promise. As part of a class that included notable standouts like Minneapolis's reform mayor Hubert Humphrey; Southern progressive Estes Kefauver; Russell Long, son of legendary Louisiana governor Huey "Kingfish" Long; and Clinton Anderson, Harry Truman's former secretary of agriculture, it was understandable. Few had expectations of great things from the relatively unknown former representative from the 10th Congressional District of Texas.

But Johnson's rapid ascent to leadership wasn't by accident or luck. He quickly surmised that power in the Senate was predicated upon one simple thing: relationships. He focused all his energies on understanding the interests, wants, and needs of his colleagues, mastering the minutiae of their states and tailoring his approach to match their sensibilities. Within short order, he had become something of a professional chameleon, mimicking the tenor and disposition of those in his presence. When speaking to senators from the North, his Southern drawl was replaced by a clipped, crisp accent. With Westerners, he adopted a folksy, breezier style. Among his colleagues from the South, he was just another good ol' boy, same as them. He didn't think twice about using the word "nigger" or "nigra" in their company, oftentimes to belittle the black attendants serving them—something he rarely did in polite company. There was no harm in letting the segregationists think he stood in union on the issue they cared about most, or so he thought.[7]

No relationship was more critical to Johnson's development as a national figure than with Senator Richard Russell of Georgia, the "dean" of the Southern bloc. An unapologetic racist and champion segregationist, Russell was revered by his colleagues from the old Confederacy. His opinion was so valued, his leadership so trusted, that he effectively spoke for the two dozen senators from the region on matters of segregation and civil rights. For any Southern Democrat who went against Russell on the issue, his tenure in the body was destined to be short lived and forgettable.

Johnson made a point of befriending Russell from the second he set foot in the upper chamber. A lifelong bachelor and workaholic, the Georgian had few close relationships and even fewer trusted confidants. His weekends were spent toiling in solitude in his Senate office, rummaging through legislative arcana and familiarizing himself with the following week's docket. Johnson won Russell's trust by laboring alongside him those long Saturdays and Sundays. Over time, their relationship blossomed into a genuine friendship. Before long, Russell was a regular visitor at the Johnson house for weekend brunches and barbeques, talking politics for hours on end with his young protégé. How much time did the two spend together? Johnson's children took to calling Russell "Uncle Dick."

It was Russell who elevated Johnson to Democratic leader, and it was Russell who convinced him that higher office was in his future. His motive was straightforward: Russell knew that Johnson, with his moderate stance (in his estimation) on segregation and civil rights, was the only Southerner with the potential to be elected president or vice president someday. That being the case, he gave LBJ a "free pass" when it came to endorsing his harsh rhetoric on the subject. With the drumbeat of civil rights coming louder and harder, Russell encouraged Johnson to keep his distance from the Southern bloc on the explosive issue so as to avoid being branded a segregationist.

This lesson was drilled home to Johnson and Russell at the 1956 Democratic Convention in Chicago, where LBJ's upstart candidacy for president was quickly aborted after Northern delegates saddled him with the label of "Southern candidate"—a tag Johnson wanted desperately to avoid. In some ways, the experience was a turning point in Johnson's career. As LBJ biographer Robert Caro points out in his seminal work on Johnson's Senate years, the debacle in Chicago convinced the dispirited candidate that the road to the White House invariably went through the North. Should he decide to make another go of it in 1960, he knew it would require a more progressive stance on civil rights. "The lesson he had pounded into him in Chicago," observes Caro, is that "you couldn't win the nomination as the 'Southern candidate' . . . you had to have substantial Northern support, and that Northern antipathy to him ran very deep. [This] had devastating implications for his chance to win the nomination in 1960." Johnson, writes Caro, "understood now that there was only one way to change his image in liberals' eyes: to support the cause that mattered to them above all . . . civil rights."[8]

Was it a cynical reading of Johnson's motives for shepherding the 1957 Civil Rights Act through the Senate? Perhaps. But by his own admission, Johnson wanted to do just enough to secure passage of *a* civil rights bill—the first in nearly a century—yet have it watered down to the point of rendering it effectively meaningless. He brilliantly persuaded Richard Russell and the other leading segregationists to forgo a filibuster—which they had successfully employed on six previous occasions over the past decade to thwart similar legislation—by convincing them that a toothless law made more sense than a bill-killing filibuster that would undoubtedly bring the scorn of the country upon them and eventually lead to even more sweeping reforms. It was the perfect solution, at least for Johnson's political aspirations. Northerners would see him in an entirely new light—civil rights champion—while his friends in Dixie would be indebted to his political acumen for staving off real reform. "Now we've got to do something about this," he reminisced to Doris Kearns Goodwin years later in describing his approach to Richard Russell. "We've got to give them [African Americans] a little something, just enough to quiet them down, not enough to make a difference. For if we don't move at all, then their allies will line up against us and there'll be no way of stopping them, we'll lose the filibuster and there'll be no way of putting a brake on all sorts of wild legislation. It'll be Reconstruction all over again."[9]

In September of 1957, President Eisenhower signed the first civil rights law since 1875. In theory, it was supposed to extend voting rights to the 80 percent of the African American population that remained disenfranchised. In reality, it was powerless to do much of anything, a fact illustrated in the South when fewer African Americans voted in the 1960 election than in 1956. Nonetheless, passage was considered a victory for Johnson, and a milestone of sorts. Political observers noted that it was a case study in threading the political needle; against all odds, he had somehow managed to gain the esteem of Northern colleagues without alienating Richard Russell and his Southern base. No other politician in the land had the political dexterity, or motivation, to pull off such a remarkable feat. But some on both sides of the divide were beginning to wonder: where did his true sympathy lie?[10]

"Until justice is blind to color, until education is unaware of race, until opportunity is unconcerned with the color of men's skins, emancipation will be a proclamation but not a fact"

John F. Kennedy's election as the thirty-fifth president of the United States has long been the stuff of political lore. It's been said that were it not for some voting irregularities in Illinois and Texas, where Kennedy won by the slimmest of margins, Richard Nixon would have been president.[11] It's impossible to prove or disprove the claims, but one thing is for certain: Lyndon Johnson played a decisive role in Kennedy's triumph. Johnson campaigned tirelessly on behalf of the ticket, his efforts helping secure crucial Southern states—notably Texas, Louisiana, North Carolina, South Carolina, and Georgia—that would have otherwise gone to Nixon. Had Kennedy given the veep nod to one of the other leading candidates—Adlai Stevenson, Stuart Symington, Hubert Humphrey—it very likely would have cost him the election.

Johnson had mixed feelings about being vice president. On the one hand, he knew it was the best steppingstone to someday becoming president. After eight years of serving at Kennedy's side, he figured to be the presumptive heir in 1968. But it was also a major downgrade in power and influence for the former majority leader. Whereas once he had lorded over the Senate with unquestioned dominion, he now found himself a fringe player in an administration that didn't value his judgment or experience. For someone who craved action, thrived on attention, prided himself on getting things done, and knew more about the "workings of Washington" than any man in town, it was a humiliating experience. "I detested every minute of it," he would confess to Doris Kearns Goodwin about his tenure as vice president.[12] Johnson became so despondent, in fact, that at one point he toyed with the notion of not seeking reelection, though it's uncertain how seriously he entertained the idea.

Aside from the space program, the one area where Johnson believed he could make a difference was civil rights. It stood to reason: having been the driving force behind the 1957 and 1960 Civil Rights Acts, he had an instinctive grasp of the legislative complexities, potential pitfalls, and leadership required to bring about real change. But it went even deeper than just offering his congressional wizardry on the matter. In some ways, LBJ had become more progressive than Kennedy—in fact more progressive than many Democrats—on racial equality. Having been liberated, in a sense, from the need to pay fealty to Richard Russell and the Southern segregationists, Johnson began to see the issue from a different perspective. He knew that the 1957 and 1960 laws were a sham, mostly because of his handiwork. He also knew that his beloved South would never be fully integrated into the union—politically, economically, culturally, morally—until it did away with the practice of racial subjugation. And he was moved by the sacrifice, courage, and dedication of those on the front lines of the fight for racial justice that the nation was witnessing every day. It stirred in him memories from his youth of the fierce racial divisions and how debilitating it was for blacks and Hispanics. "Civil Rights was really something that, by this time, was burning pretty strongly in Johnson," recalled Harris Wofford, a leading civil rights advocate in the Kennedy administration. James Farmer, the founder of the Congress of Racial Equality (CORE) and leader of the freedom rides across the Deep South, was struck upon meeting the vice president at his fervor for the cause. "He was sincere, he was very interested, almost a passionate concern came through," remembered Farmer. "He came through as one who was not merely working on this because it was politically expedient, but because he had a strong belief in it. And I was convinced of that."[13]

Johnson was bitterly disappointed that President Kennedy didn't ask him to serve as point person for the administration on civil rights. As consolation, Kennedy appointed him head of the Committee on Equal Employment Opportunity (CEEO), a largely symbolic body that was powerless to effect change. It wasn't a total lost cause, however; Johnson used the perch to better understand the depth of the problem beyond just integration in the South, and quietly began piecing together a network of allies, supporters, and activists inside and outside of government—a move that would pay dividends in the future.

In the opinion of many Democrats outside the South, Kennedy's record on civil rights for the first two years of his administration was unimpressive, bordering on abysmal. It simply wasn't a priority. But by early 1963, notes historian Robert Dallek, the "pressure to do something about black rights in the South had reached fever pitch." Much of the nation was sickened by the images of mob violence, fire hoses, attack dogs, and baton beatings that flashed across their television screens every night. The brutish tactics of Southern leaders like Bull Connor, George Wallace, and other rabid segregationists brought international shame to America, leaving President Kennedy little choice but to enter the fray, though he still feared the political repercussions of moving too aggressively.

Unaware—purposely kept out of the loop—that the president was only days away from going on national television to introduce a new civil rights bill, Lyndon Johnson made an impassioned plea for racial justice in an elegant and moving speech at Gettysburg on Memorial Day weekend. In what many regard as the finest address of his career, Johnson spoke plainly and bluntly about America's failure to honor Lincoln's immortal words a century earlier. "One hundred years ago, the slave was freed," he solemnly intoned. "One hundred years later, the Negro remains in bondage to the color of his skin. The Negro today asks justice. We do not answer him—we do not answer those who lie beneath this soil—when we reply to the Negro by asking, 'Patience.' . . . To ask for patience from the Negro is to ask him to give more of what he has already given enough." He closed with a simple observation: "Until justice is blind to color, until education is unaware of race, until opportunity is unconcerned with the color of men's skins, emancipation will be a proclamation but not a fact. To the extent that the proclamation of emancipation is not fulfilled in fact, to that extent we shall have fallen short of assuring freedom to the free."[14]

A week later Kennedy delivered an address of his own to the American people that in many ways echoed Johnson's sentiment. "One hundred years of delay have passed since President Lincoln freed the slaves, yet their heirs, their grandsons, are not fully free," said the president. "They are not yet freed from the bonds of injustice. They are not yet freed from social and economic oppression. And this Nation, for all its hopes and all its boasts, will not be fully free until all its citizens are free."[15]

Kennedy failed to follow his stirring words with a bold piece of legislation. The bill sent to Congress, the contents of which Johnson only learned from reading the *New York Times,* was muddled, cautious, and destined for failure. Prevented from conferring directly with Kennedy on the matter, Johnson, in a phone call with close Kennedy aide Theodore Sorenson, relayed a message to the president: turn civil rights into a moral crusade. In Johnson's opinion, the only way the bill would survive is if Kennedy "goes down there [to the South] and looks them in the eye and states the moral issue and the Christian issue, and if he does it face to face, these Southerners at least respect his courage."[16]

As he did throughout much of his presidency, Kennedy ignored Johnson's counsel. Though he understood that failure to secure a civil rights bill could imperil his entire legislative agenda, perhaps even his reelection, the president refused to "take the fight" to the ever-dwindling and increasingly isolated segregationists in Congress and statehouses across the Deep South. It was a shame, too, because a good many Southerners, Johnson believed, were ready to abandon segregation if confronted by an unyielding and morally insistent federal government. But it wasn't to be the case. Kennedy's "attempt to find a middle ground," opines one historian of the era, "made him less effective in a fight that required unqualified expressions of faith in the righteousness of the case. . . . He certainly could have made it the one great domestic moral cause of his presidency."[17] Of course, he would never get the chance to see it through.

"And should we defeat every enemy, and should we double our wealth and conquer the stars, and still be unequal to this issue [of civil rights], then we will have failed as a people and as a nation"

Lyndon Johnson spent his first evening as president of the United States dictating plans, sharing observations, and prioritizing his agenda to three aides while lying in bed in his silk pajamas. He rambled on for half the night, filling several of their notebooks. Exhausted, his voice shot, Johnson finally nodded off shortly past three in the morning.

The new president wasn't being insensitive or disrespectful to the memory of John F. Kennedy. He was simply making up for lost time. Having spent the past three years largely on the periphery, LBJ suddenly found himself the most powerful man in the free world. He had clear vision of how he wanted to approach the weeks and months ahead and was eager to get started.

There was never any doubt in Johnson's mind that civil rights legislation would be at the top of the agenda. By this point in his career, he had become a full-fledged convert to the cause. The years of straddling the middle, playing both sides off each other, watering down legislation, and kissing up to Richard Russell were behind him. He had disagreed with Kennedy's bill—in fact his entire approach—and that, too, was behind him. He was now in charge. He knew that the segregationists were ripe to fall. He wasn't about to let the moment pass. When a somewhat skeptical Roger Wilkins, head of the NAACP, asked Johnson why the sudden fervor over civil rights after years of indifference, the president paused, arched a brow, and grinned while mouthing Dr. King's transcendent refrain: "Free at last, free at last. Thank God Almighty, I'm free at last." The message was unmistakable: I'm free to follow my heart.[18]

In some ways, forging ahead on civil rights was an easy call for Johnson. Like Truman and the bomb, all the momentum was pointing in one direction. The country was deeply in mourning. The American people were eager to find ways to immortalize their slain president. The political winds would be at his back for months. It was the perfect opportunity to break the segregationists' grip on the Senate once and for all.

And politically, it was something Johnson knew he had to do. Liberals were still suspicious of the new president. Nobody in the Democratic Party, for that matter, was quite sure what to make of him, mostly because he had been so far under the radar the previous three years. Ever the political animal, Johnson feared that he might not receive the nomination in 1964 without winning the trust of Northern progressives. "I knew," he told biographer Doris Kearns Goodwin years later, "that if I didn't get out in front on this issue, they [the liberals] would get me. They'd throw up my background against me, they'd use it to prove that I was incapable of bringing unity to the land. . . . I couldn't let that happen." And it couldn't be toothless bills like the ones in 1957 and 1960—that wasn't going to cut it. "I had to produce a civil rights bill that was even stronger than the one they'd have gotten if Kennedy had lived," he suggested to Goodwin. "Without this, I'd be dead before I could even begin."[19]

Historical posterity played a role, too. Johnson had a keen understanding that future generations would look favorably upon the president who put an end to racial subjugation and fulfilled the promise of the Declaration of Independence and the Emancipation Proclamation. "I'm going to be the president who finishes what Lincoln began," he boldly predicted to aides and supporters.[20]

Johnson smartly used his address before Congress just five days after the assassination to put the country—and more importantly the Senate—on notice that civil rights was happening. "We have talked long enough in this country about equal rights. . . . It is time now to write the next chapter, and to write it in the books of law."[21] The message couldn't have been more direct or menacing to his old segregationist cohorts like Russell and Eastland: I'm no longer on your side. If Russell didn't fully grasp the passion behind the president's words, he did the following week in a private White House meeting with his old protégé. "Dick, you've got to get out of my way," warned Johnson. "If you don't, I'm going to roll over you. I don't intend to cavil or compromise." Russell was quick with a retort. "You may do that, but it's going to cost you the South, and cost you the election." Responded Johnson: "If that's the price I have to pay, I'll pay it gladly."[22]

Johnson meant it. He knew that a holy war over civil rights would probably cost him the South, but so be it. The legislation he sent to Capitol Hill was exactly as had been advertised to civil rights leaders and liberals—dramatically more far-reaching and impactful than Kennedy's bill. Among other things, it would put an end to municipal and state government discrimination, segregation in public facilities, and the unequal application of voter registration requirements. And more importantly, it would greatly expand the federal government's enforcement powers, something that had been missing from previous efforts.

Drawing on his favorite poker analogy, Lyndon Johnson told friends and foes alike that he was "shoving his stack in the middle" on this one; there would be no negotiations or compromises. Either he was going to get his bill, or Russell would defeat it with a filibuster. Johnson knew what he was doing. Public sentiment ran strongly in favor of decisive action, and the civil rights community, liberals in Congress, and even moderate Republicans were firmly behind him. Just as he had counseled Kennedy to make the moral case on Southern soil, he heeded his own advice. Before the Georgia state legislature, the president admonished lawmakers "not to heed those who would come waving the tattered and discredited banners of the past, who seek to stir old hostilities and kindle old hatreds." It was time to join the rest of the nation, he lectured them, and "insure that every man enjoys all the rights secured him by the American Constitution." In Miami, he promised to "press forward with legislation . . . until we have eliminated the last barrier of intolerance."[23]

In a delicious piece of historical symmetry, the final battle in the struggle for civil rights was fought in the very chamber where the leading segregationist of the era once mentored the man who stood to obliterate their prized system, once and for all. On some level, Russell knew that he was outmatched by Johnson. "We would have beaten Kennedy," he confided to a reporter in the days leading up to the showdown. "Now it will be three times harder." Russell, it turns out, had taught his student well. "He knows more about the use of power than any man."[24]

Russell and his brethren didn't go down without a fight. They waged a seventy-three-day filibuster—to this day the longest in history—that brought the nation's business to a grinding halt. Their goal was to demoralize, frustrate, and hopefully outlast the president. But it was Johnson who played the final, triumphant card. He convinced his old friend, Republican minority leader Everett Dirksen, to join forces with moderate Democrats to cut off debate, making it only the second successful cloture (up to that point) in Senate history. With the filibuster defeated, the reconciled bill easily passed both houses of Congress, and on July 2, Lyndon Johnson signed the 1964 Civil Rights Act into law.[25] With that, a century of legal segregation had finally come to an end.

* * *

Back on his ranch in Texas after leaving the White House, Lyndon Johnson famously boasted to Doris Kearns Goodwin that "some men want power to strut around the world and hear the tune of 'Hail to the Chief.' Others want it to build prestige. . . . Well, I wanted power to give things to people—all sorts of things to all sorts of people, especially the poor and the blacks."[26] Was it a case of historical posturing or a heartfelt sentiment revealed in a moment of candor? Probably a little of both.

Even his most devout critics would be hard pressed to deny that Lyndon Johnson had always carried deep-seated misgivings about the appalling injustice African Americans were forced to endure in the Jim Crow South, that over time he developed a fervent belief in the cause of equality. To be sure, he was motivated in part by a blinding ambition to be president someday, but it doesn't explain why he went "all in" on the most turbulent issue of the era when compromise would have sufficed. One explanation: Machiavellian stratagem had given way to genuine concern, a crusader's zeal, and an intuitive sense to seize the moment and chart a new course for the nation.

Lyndon Johnson was puzzled at why his former colleagues in the Senate would limit their political careers for the sake of trying to preserve a dying system premised on hate. He once remarked to aide Bill Moyers that Senator Bill Tillman of South Carolina could have been president were he not such a bigot. "I'd like to sit down with him and ask how it was to throw it away for the sake of hating."[27] He felt the same way about his old mentor Richard Russell. "Jim Crow put a collar on more smart men as sure as if they were sentenced to a chain gang in Georgia. If Dick Russell hadn't had to wear Jim Crow's collar, Dick Russell would be sitting here now instead of me."

The Civil Rights Act of 1964, and the subsequent Voting Rights Act of 1965, are undoubtedly the defining acts of Lyndon Johnson's presidency, and arguably the most impactful legislative achievements of the twentieth century. Johnson knew that the Democratic Party would suffer at the ballot box in the Deep South for decades to come, and he was correct. In the span of a few years, the old Confederacy states had transformed from Democratic bastions to Republican strongholds, a reality that persists to this day. It was a predictable consequence, one he was willing to endure.

Chapter 12

RICHARD NIXON VISITS CHINA

Courtesy of the Nixon Presidential Library and Museum.

If there is anything I want to do before I die, it is to go to China. If I don't, I want my children to go.
   —Richard Nixon in an interview with *Time* magazine in the fall of 1970, a full year before it was revealed that he would visit China

This is the most important communication that has come to an American president since the end of World War II.
   —Henry Kissinger to Richard Nixon following their receipt of a formal invitation from the Chinese government for a presidential visit

We have been here a week. This was the week that changed the world.
   —Nixon toasts his Chinese hosts on the final day of his historic trip

On the evening of July 15, 1971, Richard Nixon appeared on live television from a studio in Burbank, California, to inform the nation that he would be

225

embarking on a historic trip to China early the following year. "There can be no stable and enduring peace," he prophesied to stunned viewers, "without the participation of the People's Republic of China and its 750 million people." The visit, said Nixon, was the culmination of several years of back-channel negotiations with the Chinese government, the most recent round having only concluded just days earlier with the secret excursion of National Security Advisor Henry Kissinger to the faraway land. The news was met with shock and bewilderment. Up to that point, the United States had virtually no diplomatic, economic, or cultural ties to the communist colossus. Many, in fact, still viewed Taiwan, with its government-in-exile led by Chiang Kai-shek, as the "legitimate" authority for the people of China—a position that the United Nations obstinately clung to by recognizing the island nation instead of the People's Republic. But with the three-and-a-half-minute speech, Richard Nixon—the same man who two decades earlier had shot to prominence as a rabid anticommunist—concluded one chapter and began another with the world's most populous nation. It was a brilliant, daring, diplomatic stroke—perhaps the boldest of the twentieth century—and undoubtedly would have been the defining act of his presidency were it not for Watergate.

* * *

As with everything about Richard Nixon, the study and analysis of his motives for forging diplomatic relations with communist China can be difficult, complicated, and at times, frustrating. Though his presidency was well chronicled by himself, contemporaries, journalists, historians, and even his own taping system, there is precious little consensus as to what it all means. Sadly, but understandably, most observers bring their own filter to understanding Nixon—the man, his accomplishments, his indiscretions, his legacy. Few figures in American history, let alone the presidency, arouse the passion, vitriol, revulsion, head-scratching, and plain curiosity as the thirty-seventh president. It's hard to imagine that ever changing.

Ever the cynic, Nixon himself was not naïve about how future generations would regard his time in office. "I will be known historically for two things," he accurately predicted less than a year before his death, "Watergate and the opening to China. One bad, one good." It was a somewhat cruel and unfair fate, he complained, because it overlooked other notable achievements, but he was resigned to it nonetheless. "Those two things are going to stand out, and that's the way it is."[1]

Though he's primarily remembered for Watergate and China, it's not with equal weighting. By far, the Watergate scandal and subsequent resignation is the singular event that has come to define Richard Nixon's four decades in public service. To the extent that normalizing relations with China is mentioned in the same breath, it remains a distant second. And with the continued public release of the White House audio tapes, it's unlikely that gap will close anytime soon. The portrait of a paranoid, duplicitous, vengeful, and emotionally unstable Nixon has only grown more graphic with the sound of Nixon's voice as the memory of the brilliant strategist and geopolitical savant recedes to the background.

Be that the case, it doesn't minimize the historical significance of Nixon's trip to China in the winter of 1972. Just because it lurks in the shadow of the worst scandal in presidential history shouldn't nullify the accomplishment. Henry Kissinger immodestly described the telegram from Mao's representative to Nixon extending an invitation to visit China as the "most important" communiqué since 1945. Still, he may well have been right. As a diplomatic feat, it certainly has no rival in the twentieth century—perhaps none in American history. It required endless patience, broad vision, a mastery of the subject matter, a natural gift for negotiation, and a willingness to ruffle feathers that few presidents possess. As far as shaping America's foreign policy, normalized relations with China deserve consideration alongside the building of the Panama Canal, the creation of Lend-Lease, the dropping of the atomic bomb, and the acceleration of the arms race with the Soviet Union under Reagan as seminal moments of the twentieth century. Put another way, it is difficult to overstate its significance.

Our purpose here is not to re-litigate Nixon's presidency or debate his place in history. That's for others to determine. It's simply an examination of his decision to extend an olive branch to the People's Republic of China.

Nixon the Cold Warrior

In *Star Trek VI: The Undiscovered Country*, the final installment of the *Star Trek* movies with the original cast, the aging but still logical Mr. Spock, in trying to convince the volatile Captain Kirk to accompany the Klingon chancellor to Earth for peace negotiations, quotes an ancient Vulcan proverb: "Only Nixon could go to China." How the phrase made it into the Vulcan lexicon is unclear, but the meaning was unmistakable: Kirk, who had been fighting the hated Klingons his entire career, was the sole Starfleet officer with the credibility and stature to seek a peaceful resolution with the dreaded enemy. Not surprisingly, it worked, disaster once again averted.

The Vulcans, or rather the screenwriters of the *Star Trek* series, had it right. In many ways, Richard Nixon was the best-positioned statesman—some would argue the only—of his generation to attempt normalization with the People's Republic of China, which had been estranged from the world community since the end of World War II. Even to casual political observers, it was conventional wisdom that any overtures to Red China would require someone with an unassailable pedigree as a committed anticommunist, someone who could quell the moderates and conservatives in Congress who were bound to view diplomatic overtures to Mao as treasonous to their longtime friend and ally in Taiwan, Chiang Kai-shek.

As fate would have it, Nixon earned his political stripes as an accomplished "Red baiter" during the height of the Cold War in the late 1940s and early 1950s. He won his seat in Congress, in fact, by falsely and maliciously claiming that his opponent, respected five-term incumbent Jerry Voorhis, was a communist sympathizer, a charge that Nixon would later admit was patently false.[2] He did the same thing four years later in his successful campaign for the Senate against former Hollywood starlet and three-term Congresswoman Helen Gahagan Douglas, whom he dubbed the "Pink Lady" and chortled was "pink right down to her underwear."[3] He won both elections in landslides.

It was the Alger Hiss spy case that catapulted Nixon to national prominence in the late 1940s, making him something of a household name and solidifying his credentials as the leading anticommunist of the day along with Senator Joe McCarthy of Wisconsin. As a member of the

House Un-American Activities Committee (HUAC), Nixon stood alone in urging his colleagues to press forward with a treason investigation against the seemingly reputable Hiss when few believed the evidence warranted it. Nixon's gambit paid off with the blockbuster testimony of Whitaker Chambers, which proved unequivocally that Hiss had indeed been a Soviet agent. While Hiss was found guilty of perjury and shipped off to a federal penitentiary, Nixon was rewarded with the vice presidential slot on Dwight Eisenhower's ticket, where he expertly played the role of unrelenting hatchet man for the general, who quietly despised him.

As far as Nixon was concerned, there were only two issues in the campaign: The Truman administration's appeasement of the Soviets and the fall of China to the communists. Adlai Stevenson, the Democratic nominee, was not to be trusted safeguarding America's liberties since, according to Nixon, he held a "Ph.D. from the Acheson College of Cowardly Communist Containment." As for the "fall of China" and the loss of its "600 million inhabitants to communism"—that was the legacy of "Trumanism" and the "spineless school of diplomacy" that he practiced.[4] Throughout the campaign, and even beyond, Nixon would return to that theme time and again: the Democrats were responsible for Mao's victory and Chiang Kai-shek's humiliating retreat back to Taiwan. In Nixon's mind, it had nothing to do with Chiang's incompetence as a leader, the rampant corruption in his government, or Mao's tactical brilliance, and everything to do with Truman and Acheson's failure to adequately fund his forces and stiffen their resolve. It was the same reason, he believed, why the United States could only muster an embarrassing stalemate against little North Korea: Truman didn't have the will or guts to allow MacArthur to take the fight to China. The fact that Eisenhower, in his first two years in office, failed to live up to campaign promises such as "liberating" Eastern Europe, "unleashing" Chiang on mainland China, and unifying the Korean peninsula meant little to Nixon, for in the larger scheme of things it was still the Democrats' fault. "The Acheson policy," opined Nixon in the fall of 1954, "was directly responsible for the loss of China." And by that reasoning, "if China had not been lost, there would have been no war in Korea, and there would be no war in Indochina today."[5]

Did Nixon truly believe that Truman, Acheson, and the "striped-pants" diplomats in the State Department were responsible for the birth of Red China, or was it simply a matter of serving "red-meat" rhetoric to the Republican faithful on the campaign trail? It may have been a little of both. Among Republicans, Nixon certainly wasn't alone in postulating that America's setbacks in Asia—Korea, the fall of China, the war in Indochina—had resulted from naïve policies and years of neglect by the Democrats in power. That had been their standard line for years. When it made political sense, Nixon aggressively pushed that theory, and later when it became a liability, he quietly retreated from it. It's clear that he softened his position on China during his second term as vice president, most likely at the urging of Eisenhower, who believed that the Republican mythology around the communists' victory in China was nonsensical fantasy. That's not to say that Nixon began dreaming of rapprochement with China at this time; it would be another decade before the thought would seriously enter his mind. But unlike the other Red-baiters of the era, Nixon had the intellectual capacity to expand his horizons, consider the issue from another perspective, and evolve his views over time. It may have initially been spurred by political expediency, but it was genuine nonetheless, and would mark the beginning of the journey that would ultimately lead him to Peking.

The Long View of History

With his painfully narrow loss to John F. Kennedy in 1960, and humiliating defeat two years later in a scrambled bid to become governor of California, Richard Nixon had plenty of time to ponder and reassess his views on America's place in the world, and his role in it. He spent a good deal of time during his "wilderness years" traveling abroad, reconnecting with world leaders he had visited while vice president, cultivating old relationships and forging new ones, and committing his thoughts to paper in the form of books and scholarly articles. Though he had bitterly vowed to the press corps, following the gubernatorial debacle, that it wouldn't have "Nixon to kick around anymore," the truth is that the presidency was never far from his mind. Few around him believed that the world had heard the last from Richard Nixon.[6]

As he did with everything in his life, Nixon methodically went about constructing a blueprint that would someday return him to power. On a tactical level, it meant piecing together a nucleus of staffers that would serve him loyally; replenishing his political coffers by hitting the road to stump and raise money for Republican candidates in the 1964 and 1966 elections; spending time in critical swing states that had cost him in 1960 and would likely prove pivotal again; and gently transforming his image from a partisan, at times immature, hatchet man to a seasoned, well-traveled, statesman.

On this last point, it was where Nixon had the most ground to make up. Undoing two decades of being caricatured as little more than a one-dimensional reactionary would require something other than just skillful image crafting. He had gone that route several times in the past, only to have it crumble upon closer inspection by the press and interrogatory Democrats. To be considered a balanced, measured, thoughtful statesman with the stature and gravitas requisite for holding the highest office in the land, he needed to *become* a balanced, measured, thoughtful statesman, and that meant reexamining party dogma and revisiting some long-held beliefs.

Nixon had always been more interested in foreign policy than domestic affairs, probably because he had a natural, instinctive feel for geopolitics, diplomacy, the need to balance long-term strategic interests with short-term considerations that he simply lacked when it came to issues closer to home. He focused most of his intellectual energies during these years on the pressing global matters of the day (a trend that would continue into the presidency), particularly the war in Vietnam, America's tense relationship with the Soviet Union, and China's continued isolation from the world community.

Nixon would write years later that his position on communism began to evolve around this time. It wasn't an epiphany as much as a subtle, but noticeable, awakening. "Unlike some anticommunists who think we should refuse to recognize or deal with the Communists lest in doing so we imply or extend an ideological respectability to their philosophy and their system," he had come to realize, "we can and must communicate and, when possible, negotiate with the Communist nations." They were, he reasoned, simply "too powerful to ignore." The sensible and safer approach meant communicating with the Soviets and Chinese instead of "living in icy cold-war isolation or confrontation," a tack that a young Richard Nixon would have found hard to swallow.[7]

In some ways, the seeds of détente with the Soviets and normalization with China were sown during the wilderness years. Away from the pressures of elected office, he had the chance to deliberate on long-range concerns such as rising tension in Soviet-Sino relations, America's strategy in Asia after Vietnam, and Russia's growing influence in the Middle East in a way that would later serve him well as president. It was his commentary about China, however, that most aggressively challenged conventional wisdom on the Republican fringe, and in doing so helped Nixon shed the image of a narrow partisan incapable of reaching beyond his base. In a highly acclaimed piece for *Foreign Affairs*, a well-respected scholarly journal, Nixon committed the ultimate act of right-wing apostasy with his declaration that continued isolation of the world's most populous nation no longer made sense. Neither, for that matter, did the fanciful notion of "liberating" mainland China from Mao's grip with a preemptive war in partnership with Chiang's army. He even dismissed the idea of a Soviet-US alliance against China on the grounds that it would give the appearance of "white v. non-white," which Nixon perceptively observed would have "catastrophic repercussions throughout the rest of the non-white world in general and Asia in particular." So where did that leave US policy toward China? Nixon didn't offer any concrete solutions, but did hint toward the direction of engagement. "Taking the long view, we simply cannot afford to leave China forever outside the family of nations, there to nurture its fantasies, cherish its hates and threaten its neighbors. There is no place on this small planet for a billion of its potentially most able people to live in angry isolation. . . . It means pulling China back into the world community."[8]

For Nixon, the rationale for opening lines of communication with China wasn't merely a case of hollow words in an elitist publication. While on a tour of Asian allies in the summer of 1967, he made a stop in Taiwan to see his old friend Chiang Kai-shek, who urged him to champion the idea of a joint American-Taiwanese invasion of the mainland. The time was right, he tried to convince America's most high-profile private citizen, for the Nationalists to retake the country. Nixon wasn't buying it, and told him so. "Chiang was a friend and unquestionably one of the giants of the twentieth century," he wrote years later, "but my pragmatic analysis told me he was wrong. . . . It was totally unrealistic in view of the massive power the Communists had developed." He gave similar counsel to President Johnson during a White House briefing at the president's request. "When I leave this office, Bobby [Kennedy], Hubert [Humphrey], or you will have the problem of China on your hands," Nixon recalled Johnson telling him. "Mr. President," he responded, "now is the time to confront them on the diplomatic front." He sensed that Johnson agreed with his counsel but simply wasn't in the position to act on it. Nixon wondered if he would someday have the chance to pull it off himself.[9]

The Week That Changed the World

Unlike Truman and the bomb, or Johnson and civil rights, it was no certainty that Richard Nixon would visit China during his first term as president. He clearly was intrigued by the notion, and believed, for many reasons, that it was the smart, strategic course of action. But he was also a realist. There would be many obstacles to meeting Mao on Chinese soil, not the least of which was ascertaining if the Chinese leadership reciprocated the sentiment. For the better part of two decades, the United States had virtually no diplomatic contact with the People's Republic of China. Just figuring out how to communicate with them would prove to be a challenge.

For reasons hard to understand, Nixon also considered his own State Department, and to a lesser extent the Defense Department, potential road blocks as well. Why this is the case is unclear. But with his appointment of Harvard professor Henry Kissinger as national security advisor, he put both agencies on notice that foreign policy would be conducted directly from the White House—the first president since Woodrow Wilson to do so.[10] Having the brilliant Kissinger report directly to him allowed Nixon to bypass the "foreign policy establishment," giving him total control over direction and policy making. The odd structure turned out to be invaluable not only for opening relations with China, but for his other foreign policy triumphs as well.

What made it invaluable, of course, was Kissinger. Though the two were opposites in many regards—Nixon never understood Kissinger's obsession with the Washington social scene or his proclivity for dating starlets—they were on the same page where it mattered most: understanding the global chessboard and the movement of its pieces. It helped that neither man was saddled by fidelity to an ideology or a static view of America's role in the world. Prior to ever meeting, each had reached the conclusion that the Cold War strategies of containment and regional confrontation made little sense given that half the world was under communist rule. For that matter, the objective of the Cold War itself—the defeat of global communism—was something of an open question, seeing how victory seemed nowhere on the horizon. To their thinking, global peace and stability—and by virtue prosperity for America—represented a more achievable outcome. The best way to go about it: by moving away from a bipolar system premised on confrontation to a strategy that sought a balance of power among nations according to geography, interests, and resources. Under that model, unyielding ideology, hardened principles, and fixed rules gave way to practical considerations, case-by-case analysis, and goal-oriented solutions. The approach would come to define their time together.

Over the years, there has been much speculation as to Kissinger's role in the decision to reach out to China. Was he merely executing the president's plan or drawing the blueprint? For his part, Kissinger has been known to refer to the historic breakthrough as "our China initiative," the implication being that it was a collaboration from the inception. Much of the evidence, however, suggests otherwise. It's apparent from Nixon's writings that he began pondering the notion in the mid-1960s. His article in *Foreign Affairs* couldn't have been clearer on that point. When Nixon first interviewed Kissinger for the national security advisor position in the winter of 1968, he suggested to the Harvard professor the need to "re-evaluate our policy towards communist China" and recommended he study his *Foreign Affairs* article on the topic.[11] For all his credit grabbing after the fact, Kissinger was initially skeptical of Nixon's desire to go to China. "Our leader has taken leave of reality," is how he characterized the president's intention to his aide, Alexander Haig. "He just ordered me to make this flight of fancy come true." His misgivings were mostly philosophical in nature, as he doubted "whether we want China to be a world power like the Soviet Union, competing with us, rather than their present role which is aiding certain insurgencies." Even as late as the winter of 1969, months after initial back-channel communications had been made, Kissinger remained skeptical about the prospects of pulling it off. "Fat chance," he responded to chief of staff Bob Haldeman when told that the president was insistent on meeting Mao.[12]

In reality, the notion of reconciliation with China was much less far-fetched than either Kissinger or even Nixon could have known. As it turns out, the Chinese leadership was equally as interested in opening lines of communication with the newly elected president. Contemporary accounts indicate that Prime Minister Zhou Enlai, Mao's longtime right-hand man, was keeping close tabs on Nixon's writings and public statements regarding his country. The *Foreign Affairs* article in particular had caught his attention. This was somebody they could do business with, he counseled Mao. With tensions on their Russian border escalating, the time was right to consider a new relationship with the United States. Perhaps it would give China leverage in their talks with the Soviets over territorial disputes, or at least make them nervous. Like Nixon, Zhou was convinced that it was worth exploring.[13]

Having been isolated from one another for over two decades, neither side was entirely sure how to begin the process of normalizing relations. It wasn't as straightforward as simply extending an invitation since there were no formal channels of communication. Beyond that, the prospect of rejection was a real concern, particularly for Nixon, who was terrified that the Chinese would rebuff his overtures—and worse yet, leak it to the world. This could potentially cripple his administration, to be avoided at all cost. Secrecy and caution were required, and above all, patience.

Initial contact between the two countries was made through their respective ambassadors in Warsaw, Poland. Following instructions from Kissinger, the US envoy let it be known to his Chinese counterpart that the United States was interested in establishing long-term relations with their government, including a possible high-level summit.[14] Similar overtures proposing a meeting were made from the US consulate in Romania, too, though in the form of a letter from respected US journalist Theodore White, who had written extensively about China during World War II, to Zhou Enlai.[15] The initial feedback was encouraging.

Things progressed slowly, however. Nixon's increased bombings in Vietnam and ill-advised excursion into Cambodia put a temporary damper on the nascent talks. It was at this time that Nixon seized the initiative, telling *Time* magazine that he wanted to visit China. "If there's anything I want to do before I die, it is to go to China." Mao promptly reciprocated the feeling in the fall of 1970 through *LIFE* magazine with an offer to host Nixon as "either a tourist or as president."[16] The most dramatic step toward a breakthrough, however, came not through formal channels but rather sport—specifically, ping-pong. Zhou Enlai—wrongly thinking that a serendipitous gift exchange between flamboyant American ping-pong player Glenn Cowan and Chinese superstar Zhuang Zedong at the World Championships in Japan had been coordinated by the State Department—extended an invitation to the US team to play an exhibition in Peking. The offer caught everyone by surprise, not the least of which was Nixon. "The world was suddenly transfixed by the spectacle of ping-pong diplomacy," noted Kissinger biographer Walter Isaacson. Zhou capitalized on the moment to send a veiled message to Nixon. "You have opened a new chapter in the relations of the American Chinese people," he praised the players in a banquet at the Great Hall.[17] Weeks later, China further signaled its intentions with the release of Bishop James Walsh, an American clergyman who had been wrongly imprisoned as a spy for over a decade. It was the clearest indication yet that China was ready for normalization.

For his part, Nixon continued to give subtle, reassuring hints, to Mao and Zhou about his desire to visit China. In his annual foreign-policy report to Congress, he noted that bringing China's "750 million talented and energetic people" into a "constructive relationship with the world community" would be a positive development. In the spring of 1970, he told a group of newspaper editors that he was prepared to liberalize trade and travel restrictions. "If they want to have Chinese come to the United States, we are ready. We are also ready for Americans to go there." And on several occasions, he made public declarations that the bombings in Laos and Cambodia were not intended to threaten China. He was concerned that escalation of the war would derail the slow but steady progress.[18]

The final breakthrough came through a series of back-channel notes between the two governments with the president of Pakistan acting as the courier. Though the missives had the awkwardness of a high-school courtship, the back-and-forth negotiations proved effective. From Zhou: "In order to discuss the subject of the evacuation of Chinese territories called Taiwan, a special envoy of President Nixon's will be most welcome in Peking." Kissinger's response: the United States would gladly send a special envoy to China to discuss a "broad range of issues." As for America's role in Taiwan, Kissinger didn't commit to anything, other than to point out that "the policy of the United States government is to reduce its military presence in the region of East Asia and the Pacific as tensions in the region diminish." It was a subtle, potentially ruinous, dig at China for its support of North Vietnam, but Kissinger assured Nixon that it wouldn't derail the process. He was right. Undeterred, Zhou stood by the offer: "The Chinese government reaffirms its willingness to receive publicly in Peking a special envoy of the President of the United States (for instance, Mr. Kissinger) or the U.S. Secretary of State or even the President of the U.S. himself for a direct meeting."[19] Nixon replied with an offer to send Henry Kissinger to Peking for a secret, preliminary meeting with Zhou that would lay the groundwork for a presidential visit the following year.

This was the moment that Nixon had been waiting for. Should the Chinese accept, it was all but certain that he would be visiting their country sometime in 1972. On June 2, the Pakistani ambassador delivered a response to Nixon's latest letter. A breathless Kissinger, flush from having chased down the president as he was heading back to the residence following a state dinner, handed the note to Nixon, calling it the "most important" communication received by a president since World War II. "Chairman Mao Tse-tung has indicated that he welcomes President Nixon's visit and looks forward to the occasion," it read in part. "Premier Zhou En-lai welcomes Dr. Kissinger to China as the U.S. representative who will come in advance for preliminary secret meeting."[20] An overjoyed Nixon retrieved an old bottle of Courvoisier and the two men toasted their monumental achievement. Here's to the "generations to come who may have a better chance to live in peace because of what we have done," boasted Nixon as he raised his glass. It marked the beginning of a new era between the United States and China.[21]

* * *

One could argue that Nixon's trip to China was little more than political theater on the world's biggest stage. Aside from a joint communiqué that declared, among other things, that "earnest and frank discussions were held between President Nixon and Premier Chou En-lai on the normalization of relations between the United States of America and the People's Republic of China, as well as on other matters of interest to both sides," nothing of major significance was accomplished during the week-long visit. There were no dramatic policy shifts on either side. The Taiwan issue, in particular, remained unresolved, as did the war in Vietnam. China continued to flaunt human-rights violations at every turn, political pressure notwithstanding. Even trade between the two countries was still years away.

But that would miss the point. Nixon and Zhou knew that one summit could not undo decades of estrangement. That was neither's intention. Both could see the bigger picture, that the two countries were on a collision course of sorts in which fear, ignorance, and mistrust would only make matters worse. Better understanding of the other's point of view might mitigate future conflicts and perhaps lead to areas of cooperation. In the least, it would bring about normalized relations, which it did. Simply establishing open lines of communication was a necessary first step.

Nixon had his reasons for reaching out to China. Part of it was that he genuinely believed that the country was a sleeping giant, a force to be reckoned with for decades to come. With its massive population, copious natural resources, and homogenous culture, there was little doubt in his mind that it would someday be a superpower. He was clairvoyant in his belief that China, not Russia, posed the greatest long-term threat to America's prosperity and standing in the world. To the extent that it made the Soviets uneasy, even better. Nixon sensed that relations with China would give him leverage in his talks with the Kremlin. He was right.

Part of it was that he knew a dramatic trip to the exotic land would prove invaluable come reelection time. On that score, too, he was correct. Democrats, moderate Republicans, the media elite, and virtually everyone else save conservatives considered it a diplomatic coup. It yielded the most positive press coverage by far of his checkered career. It was Nixon at his finest, and he wisely milked it for everything it was worth. It made moderates and even some liberals temporarily comfortable with him, no doubt contributing to his landslide victory over

McGovern later that year. For a short while it made people forget about the old Tricky Dick.

And of course history played a role. Nixon understood that a breakthrough of this magnitude would position him well for posterity. He had spent his career idolizing the giants of the twentieth century—men like Eisenhower, Churchill, de Gaulle—even chronicling them in several of his books. In his mind, China was his shot at immortality, a chance to be included among the pantheon of greats. It nearly did.

Chapter 13

FORD PARDONS NIXON

Courtesy of the Gerald R. Ford Library.

In giving the former President Nixon an inappropriate and premature grant of clemency, President Ford has affronted the Constitution and the American System of Justice. It is a profoundly unwise, divisive and unjust act.
—The opening paragraph of the *New York Times* editorial on September 9, 1974, the day after the pardon was issued

Damn it, I don't need the polls to tell me whether I'm right or wrong.
—Gerald Ford to an aide shortly before announcing his pardon of Richard Nixon

Anybody who can't keep his enemies in his head has too many enemies.
—Gerald Ford commenting on Nixon's "Enemies List"

On September 8, 1974, President Gerald R. Ford, almost one month to the day after being sworn in as president under the Twenty-fifth Amendment, issued former president Nixon a "full, free, and absolute pardon" for all offenses that may have been committed against the United States during his five years in the

White House. It was an extraordinary event, though not totally unforeseeable. Most Americans wanted to see the judicial system play out before clemency was to be considered. It was the timing of Ford's pardon—not even a month after Nixon had left office—that surprised and outraged many in the country. In an instant, Ford's approval ratings plummeted, and the trajectory of his presidency had been inexorably altered.

* * *

Gerald R. Ford never aspired to be president of the United States. Having served in the House of Representatives for a quarter century—the final decade as minority leader—his sole remaining ambition was to someday become Speaker of the House. Like many Republicans, he thought that 1972 would be their best chance in decades to take back the House of Representatives. When Nixon's landslide victory over George McGovern failed to put a dent in the Democrats' huge majorities in Congress, however, he became resigned to the fact that it would likely never happen.[1] Following the election, he made a pledge to his wife, Betty, that his 1974 reelection would be the last.

Little could he know that fate had chartered a different course. When Vice President Spiro Agnew was forced to resign after pleading no contest to charges of bribery and tax evasion in December 1973, a politically weakened Richard Nixon chose Gerald Ford to fill the position. Nixon selected Ford mostly because the amiable congressman was bound to face little opposition during the confirmation process. Nixon knew that he didn't have the political capital to take on the House Democrats.[2]

Ford spent most of his eight months as vice president on the road trying to rally the Republican faithful to Richard Nixon's cause. He publicly defended the president with zeal, but as Nixon's situation worsened, Ford began to focus his attention on the possibility that he could soon become president. On the evening of August 8, 1974, Richard Nixon addressed the nation for a thirty-seventh and final time to announce that he was resigning the presidency the following day. It was hard to imagine that a man who had all but given up on public service only a year earlier was about to ascend to the highest office in the land. But the question still lingered: what would become of Richard Nixon?

A Thirty-One-Day Presidency

Although he served for 895 days as president of the United States, in many ways Gerald Ford's presidency can be measured by thirty-one days, for on the thirty-second day everything changed. Never in American history has a presidential term been as clearly demarcated by a single event as Ford's pardon of Nixon.

Ford certainly never intended for that to be the case. He came to the office with a sense of purpose—to restore confidence and integrity to the White House—and with a simple mandate to focus on the nation's business after two years of neglect. On that front, there was more to be done: In addition to being traumatized by Watergate, the country was going through one of the worst economic patches in memory, with rampant inflation, record-high interest rates, spiraling energy costs, and a ballooning trade deficit contributing to a jittery stock market and nagging recession. Preoccupied with his unraveling situation, Nixon was both indifferent to, and incapable of, course-correcting the economy, which only contributed to the atmosphere of cynicism and distrust. His focus was on his own survival—not that of the country.

Ford viewed his quick ascent as a chance for a clean break from Nixon and his policies. He was aided by the fact that in temperament, style, and personality, the two could not have been more different. There were a few similarities: they came from humble beginnings, began their careers in the House of Representatives, had a tireless work ethic, and were adherents to party loyalty more than ideologically fastidious. But that's mostly where the comparisons ended.

Scores of books have been dedicated to Nixon's shortcomings—which we've noted ourselves. There is little point in rehashing here. But for as devious, imbalanced, and emotionally insecure as Nixon was, he was also undeniably brilliant, particularly in the area of foreign policy, as we have seen. He approached global geopolitics like a chess master would, looking three steps ahead in an effort to outmaneuver his adversaries. He thought in bold, sweeping terms and wasn't afraid to part with conventional wisdom when it served a larger purpose. Many observers, including some detractors, consider Nixon among the ablest foreign policy strategists to hold the office.[3]

Few would categorize Gerald Ford as a brilliant thinker or master visionary. The word most often used to describe Ford was *decent*. He was a decent man, a humble public servant, well regarded by everyone. He had a strong sense of purpose and was devoted to serving his constituents— and later the country—in an honest and forthright manner. Unlike Nixon, he was remarkably comfortable in his own skin; there was nothing conniving or manipulative about him, and people sensed that. Even the most partisan Democrats in Congress liked and respected Gerald Ford. He was, as it would be said throughout his career, a *good* man.

Ford understood his strengths and limitations as well as any politician. He had been around long enough to know that he shouldn't expect a typical "honeymoon" period accorded a newly elected president. But he also realized that there was a reservoir of good will toward him, something he intended to capitalize on. With that being the case, he sought to clearly delineate between his approach and Nixon's in ways big and small, and wasted little time in setting a different tone. One of his first orders of business as the new president, in fact, was to invite to the White House members from the Congressional Black Caucus—an organization that had been shunned by Nixon for years—followed by a group of Equal Rights Amendment (ERA) supporters shortly thereafter, much to their shock. He even brought in the head of the AFL-CIO—another organization that Nixon cared little about—for a discussion about labor. At a state dinner for King Hussein and Queen Alia of Jordan, Ford did the unthinkable when he invited some of Nixon's noisiest detractors, including former secretary of defense Robert McNamara, Congressman Pete McCloskey of California, and several reporters on Nixon's famed enemies list. So accommodating to former personae non gratae was Ford that humorist Art Buchwald noted that the Ford White House was "working from an old Nixon enemies folder, which they mistakenly believe was the President's social list."[4]

And it wasn't just symbolic gestures. Within weeks of taking office, Ford reversed Nixon's policy of prosecuting Vietnam War draft dodgers and deserters by offering limited amnesty, a bombshell he dropped during a speech before the Veterans of Foreign Wars convention in Chicago.[5]

Time magazine hailed it as "courageous," while Ford biographer and fierce critic Richard Reeves noted that "it was the most striking example to date that Richard Nixon was gone, showing a president compassionately aware of the division among Americans."[6]

Not long after, he took on the conservative wing of his own party with the nomination of Nelson Rockefeller, the liberal governor of New York, to be his vice president, something he knew would cause a tizzy among conservatives. Ford wanted a strong vice president, someone with the gravitas to step into the office at a moment's notice, and Rockefeller fit the bill perfectly. He knew that Rockefeller's selection could leave him vulnerable to a potential primary battle with a conservative stalwart like Ronald Reagan, but it didn't weigh on his mind; country came before party in his book.

Perhaps the most noticeable difference was their relations with the media. Nixon despised virtually everyone in the press—in his mind, reporters were out to get him, plain and simple—and he obsessed over ways to make their lives difficult. As a consequence, the press corps had virtually no access to Nixon as he assiduously avoided public settings where he could be questioned. Ford would have none of that. As a congressman, he had always enjoyed good relations with the media; he understood that reporters craved access more than anything else, and he employed that approach at the White House, too. He invited reporters to visit him in the Oval Office and provided for informal gatherings while on the road. Ford was a big believer in press conferences—he held a staggering fifty-seven while vice president—and was more than happy to let reporters ask follow-up questions, a practice that Nixon abhorred. He even appeared on CBS's *Face the Nation* program while president, another gesture that Nixon would have found unthinkable.[7]

Four weeks into his presidency, Gerald Ford was riding high in the polls with a 71 percent job approval and only 3 percent disapproval.[8] The media had a big role in his popularity, as reporters seemingly competed to produce the most gushing coverage of the new president. Ford's "everyman sensibility" was of particular fascination as they wrote breathlessly about his penchant for making his own breakfast (a toasted English muffin), wearing short-sleeve shirts, picking up his newspaper from the porch while in his bathrobe, and his utter lack of pretense and pomp. Wrote *Time* magazine: "Last week Washington and the nation seemed satisfied to rejoice in such simplicities as having a Chief Executive who worked in his shirtsleeves, who said what he meant and meant what he said, who by his honesty and accessibility was swiftly exorcising the pinched ghosts of the Nixon era from the White House."[9] None of it was lost on Ford. "In the first month of my presidency," he wrote in *A Time to Heal*, "I had received the kind of press coverage that every politician loves but almost never gets." But Ford knew it couldn't last, lamenting that he had "been in politics long enough to realize that popularity of this magnitude wouldn't continue forever."[10]

"The hate had to be drained and the healing begun"

Gerald Ford knew that he wouldn't enjoy a 71 percent approval rating or the unending adulation of the press core for his entire presidency—no president ever does. But he was unprepared for the magnitude and ferocity of the dissent over his pardon of Richard Nixon. It came at him like a storm, and since he never anticipated it, he also never factored it into his thinking.

So how did Ford reach the conclusion to pardon Richard Nixon? What drove his decision making? For a situation as complicated, uncharted, and unprecedented as pardoning a disgraced former president staring at a criminal indictment, Ford took a more intuitive approach, whereby deep analysis, consensus building, and political expedience gave way to instinct, confidentiality, and loyalty.

It wasn't in his nature to be overly reflective with big decisions like a Franklin Roosevelt or Bill Clinton; he was more like Truman, a gut-and-hunch sort of guy. He greatly admired Truman for his decisiveness and principles, and his willingness to sacrifice political expedience for what he knew was right.[11] During his first week in office, Ford gave little thought to Nixon's situation. He was preoccupied with settling the country, facilitating a smooth transition of power, and getting a handle on the economy. To the extent that he thought about Nixon, it was mostly about his health—he had heard reports that Nixon's physical condition had deteriorated rapidly[12]—and what to do with his voluminous papers and notorious recordings.[13]

But by his second week on the job, Ford found himself increasingly spending time huddled with lawyers sorting out the complicated legal issues surrounding the custody of Nixon's papers. It was a thankless and unrewarding task, not the least bit of interest to him, though he understood the legal importance of preserving the documents and tapes and avoiding the appearance of abetting their premature return to Nixon. But it was quickly becoming a time drain, something Ford had little to spare. "It intruded into time that I urgently needed to deal with a faltering economy and mounting foreign policy problems all over the world," reasoned Ford. "With these critical issues pressing upon me— and the nation—I simply couldn't listen to lawyers' endless arguments about Nixon's tapes and documents or answer constant questions about his legal status."[14]

At 2:30 in the afternoon on August 28, President Ford held his first press conference. At the suggestion of his press secretary, Jerry terHorst, he decided to change things up. Instead of going with Nixon's imperial blue curtain as the backdrop, the conference was moved to the East Room of the White House across from the Grand Entrance Hall. The feeling was that it would create a friendlier and more open atmosphere, which it did (so much so that the practice is still used today). Ford was hoping that the focus would be on the economy and the other pressing issues, but with United Press International reporter Helen Thomas's first question, it became clear that Nixon remained the dominant story among the press corps. "Mr. President," she asked from her customary seat in the front row, "aside from the Special Prosecutor's role, do you agree with the bar association that the law applies equally to all men, or do you agree with Governor Rockefeller that former president Nixon should have immunity from prosecution? And specifically, would you use your pardon authority, if necessary?"[15]

And so it went. Nearly a third of the press conference was spent on Nixon-related matters, much to Ford's surprise and chagrin. Never a great speaker, Ford was simply unprepared and overmatched by the onslaught of Nixon questions as he fumbled, dodged, and contradicted his way through the lengthy conference. He had performed poorly, and he knew it. Following it, he canvassed aides if this would be the pattern for future press conferences; most agreed that the former president's situation would dominate the news for as long as he remained in criminal jeopardy.[16] It was just too big a story for the press not to be consumed by it.

It was at this moment, Ford writes in his memoirs, that he began to seriously contemplate pardoning Nixon. In something resembling an epiphany, it dawned on him that it would be impossible to govern the country—tame inflation, breathe life into the economy, manage the Middle East and Vietnam—with the spectacle of a cornered and defiant Richard Nixon, battling to stay out of jail, playing out on the nightly news for years to come. It was an untenable situation with no endgame in sight. A quick pardon, as he saw it, was the only way out. "This story would overshadow everything else," he surmised. "No other issue could compete with the drama of a former president trying to stay out of jail. It would be impossible for me to direct public attention to anything else." But it wasn't just about putting the sordid episode in the past so that he could tackle more pressing matters. That was part of it—a large part of it—but it ran deeper than just governing; it was about bringing closure to Watergate—and everything it stood for—so that the nation could begin to close the divisions and look to the future. "The hate had to be drained and the healing begun."[17]

One question has vexed commentators and historians over the years: what role did friendship play in Ford's decision? A larger one than previously thought, as it turns out. In his memoirs and other contemporary writings, Ford's relationship with Nixon is described as a professional one. They had served in Congress together in the late 1940s and crossed paths many times after that, but nothing out of the ordinary. By all accounts, Richard Nixon had very few friends, either personal or political. Ford was thought to be just another political acquaintance who had served in the arena with him. Toward the end of his life, however, Ford began to paint a different portrait of their relationship, one that can't be overlooked when analyzing the pardon. "I believe I was a better friend to Dick Nixon than anyone [else] over a longer period of time," he told Bob Woodward for his 1999 book, *Shadows*.[18] After Ford's death, Woodward published private conversations with the former president that depicted a much more intimate friendship between the two former presidents (conversations that Ford insisted not be made public until after his death). "I looked upon him as my personal friend," Woodward quoted Ford for a *Washington Post* story titled "Ford, Nixon, Sustained Friendship for Decades," which ran just days after the president's passing in 2006. "And I always treasured our relationship. And I had no hesitancy about granting the pardon, because I felt that we had this relationship and that I didn't want to see my real friend have the stigma."[19]

Did their friendship shape his thinking? Unquestionably. Ford clearly liked Nixon the person (a book unto itself), and didn't want to see his friend suffer. But was it the primary determinant? Not by a long shot. Ford firmly believed that it was in the best interest of the country to move on; he couldn't begin to heal the country with Nixon's legal battles still blanketing the airwaves. Their friendship probably made the decision easier, and may have prevented regret or "pardon remorse" from setting in, but it wasn't at the heart of the matter.

Deal or No Deal

Over the years, an alternative explanation—one with more sinister motives at the center of it—has been cultivated to make sense of Ford's pardon of Nixon. In this contrarian point of view, the proffered reason for the pardon was that a secret deal existed between the two men whereby Nixon agreed to relinquish the presidency in return for clemency. Why else, some have surmised, would Ford have issued a blanket pardon of Nixon so soon after taking office, and with the special prosecutor's work a long way from over, were it not for some kind of clandestine deal? For many, it seemed—and still seems—like the most plausible explanation.

Gerald Ford steadfastly and adamantly maintained throughout his life that there had been no such deal, testifying as much before a House subcommittee and stating so in numerous public forums. But Ford readily conceded in his testimony before the House of Representatives that he had an uncomfortable meeting with Nixon's chief of staff, Al Haig, just days prior to Nixon's resignation in which the topic was broached. And it was this meeting which has fueled the conspiracy theorists' insistence that a secret deal indeed existed.

What really took place during the encounter? Well, according to Gerald Ford's recounting in his memoir, on August 1, eight days before Nixon would eventually resign, Al Haig called Ford and asked for a private meeting. Haig insisted on no aides being present so that they could discuss the president's options. Ford writes that Haig outlined a bunch of scenarios[20] that could play out, one of them being that Richard Nixon would resign and receive a pardon from Ford. He contends that Haig merely presented Nixon's dwindling options, and that there was no linkage or quid pro quo of any kind between resignation and a pardon. "He asked if I had any suggestions as to the courses of action for the President," Ford writes. "I didn't think it would be proper for me to make any recommendations at all, and I told him so."[21] Ford was curious to know, however, if the president even had the power to issue a pardon to an individual prior to a formal criminal indictment, and posed the question to Haig. Haig's understanding, so writes Ford, was that he did have the power, and the matter rested there.

Not surprisingly, Al Haig tells a different story. In his version of events, he merely informed Vice President Ford that resignation could be imminent and that he needed to prepare for that eventuality. Haig's only public comment on the topic came during his confirmation hearing to become Ronald Reagan's secretary of state. "At no time did I ever suggest in any way an agreement or 'deal' that Mr. Nixon would resign in exchange for a pardon from Mr. Ford," he told the Senate Foreign Relations Committee. "When I met alone with Vice President Ford on August 1st, 1974, I went to that meeting to tell him of President Nixon's inclination to resign, and to emphasize to him that he had to be prepared to assume the presidency within a very short time—perhaps within a day."[22]

Following the meeting, Ford consulted with several confidants over what to make of Haig's pardon suggestion, which would seem to lend more credence to his version of events. Ford's aides were horrified by the "monstrous impropriety"[23] of Haig's mere mentioning of the pardon, and wisely brought in well-respected Washington super-lawyer Bryce Harlow for a second opinion. Bryce counseled Ford to phone Haig back in the presence of several witnesses and firmly reiterate that he would not make any recommendations to President Nixon on potential courses of action. Ford went so far as to write out his statement in longhand and then proceeded to deliberately read it to Haig so as to avoid any ambiguity and preserve it for the historical record. "I want you to understand," he slowly intoned to Haig, "that I have no intention of recommending what the President should do about resigning or not resigning and that nothing we talked about yesterday afternoon should be given any consideration in whatever decision the President may wish to make."[24]

Some observers contend that Ford's silence in the meeting with Haig (he never objected to Haig's mentioning of the pardon scenario; he merely listened and agreed that they should keep in close contact) could have been interpreted by Haig that Ford was amenable to a pardon deal, and reported as such back to Nixon.[25] Given Nixon's distressed state of mind during those final weeks in office, it is certainly *conceivable* that Nixon—after listening to Haig's recounting of the meeting—could have believed that some kind of deal had been struck. Robert Hartmann poses the question in his 1980 memoir. "Is it possible that Nixon believed that he had a deal before he resigned," he writes. "Who knows what Haig reported back to Nixon (and others) after his private talks with Vice President Ford."[26]

At the end of the day, there is simply no concrete evidence suggesting there had been a pardon deal. And there is no indication that the specter of a potential pardon influenced Richard Nixon's decision making those final days. In fact, Nixon was so despondent, his behavior so erratic toward the end, that it's hard to understand any of his decision making. As Ford himself points out in his memoir, he didn't need to strike a pardon deal to convince Nixon to leave office because after the "smoking gun" tape of June 23[27] was made public there was no doubt that Nixon would have to leave office (either voluntarily or through impeachment). Simply put, Ford knew—as did those around him—that he was going to become president, irrespective of any pardon deal. It was only a matter of time.[28]

The Last Piece of the Puzzle

The decision to pardon Richard Nixon was a relatively quick one. The endless meetings with lawyers, the Nixon-dominated press conference, and the daily distraction of new revelations from the special prosecutor all convinced Gerald Ford that a pardon was the only answer. There was some suggestion, among aides, that he at least wait until after a trial and conviction before considering such a drastic move; why do it prematurely when he may be found not guilty, they reasoned. But Ford wouldn't hear of it. It would take years for the legal case to wind its way through the courts, during which time it would be nearly impossible to govern effectively.

Throughout the process, Ford sought the counsel of just a few close confidants, mostly to serve as a gut check. He knew what he wanted to do (given an unconditional pardon), and when to do it (very quickly), but one nagging question remained: did he actually have the power to issue a pardon prior to a criminal indictment or conviction? In his infamous meeting with Al Haig while he was vice president, Haig seemed to suggest that the president did have the power, but Ford wanted to be dead certain. The last thing he needed was to exacerbate the confusion by issuing a legally dubious pardon.

Ford turned to Benton Becker, a brilliant staff lawyer, for the answer. "Does a pardon erase a criminal act or does it only erase criminal punishment?"[29] he asked the young aide. In Ford's mind, there was a big difference. If it was said to wipe out a criminal act, the public would be furious; were it only to erase the punishment, and include an admission of guilt, it would be more palatable (or so he hoped). Becker found the answer Ford was looking for in a 1915 Supreme Court case, *United States v. Burdick*, which held that the president does, in fact, have the power to issue a pardon prior to a criminal indictment, and moreover it carries an admission of guilt.[30] With that information, Ford was convinced that a pardon was the right thing to do: the burden would be on Nixon to affirmatively accept the pardon, and with it the imputation of guilt that it carries.

Of course, there was no guarantee that Nixon would actually accept the pardon. In the weeks following his resignation, the disgraced former president had been experiencing a roller coaster ride of emotions, from defiance to depression and everything in between. Depending on the day, his mood, or something else, he was prone to give conflicting answers on the subject of the pardon. But in the end, he had no choice. The prospect of a long legal fight with possible jail time was enough to convince Nixon to accept the pardon and all that it meant.

On Sunday, September 8, shortly after returning from church, Gerald Ford addressed the nation from the Oval Office and formally signed the pardon of Richard Nixon. He spent several minutes explaining his reasons, closing with the most powerful: "My conscience tells me that only I, as President, have the constitutional power to firmly shut and seal this book. My conscience tells me it is my duty not merely to proclaim domestic tranquility but to use every means that I have to ensure it."

Ten minutes later, Richard Nixon released his response. "Looking back on what is still, in my mind, a complex and confusing maze of events, decisions, pressures and personalities," it read in part, "one thing I can see clearly now is that I was wrong in not acting more decisively and more forthrightly in dealing with Watergate, particularly when it reached the stage of judicial proceedings."

And with that, the saga of Watergate had come to a close.

* * *

The immediate aftermath of the Nixon pardon was not pretty for Gerald Ford. His longtime friend and press secretary, Jerry terHorst, quit on the spot after learning the news shortly before Ford was about to address the nation to announce the pardon. Other staff were equally outraged, and White House morale took a nose dive. The press's reaction was near-universal condemnation; just about every newspaper editorialized against it with a mixture of shock, befuddlement, disappointment, and outright anger. In an instant, Ford's Gallup poll rating plummeted from 71 to 49, and with it all the goodwill that had been created with the Democrats and the media in the first month of his presidency had vanished.

Protestors began appearing at his public appearances, usually chanting "Jail Ford" or "terHorst in '76." Congress took the extraordinary step of asking him to appear before a House committee to give a full accounting of the pardon, which he voluntarily complied with, making him the only sitting president in history to testify before Congress.[31] Some on the far left went so far as to call for his impeachment, but the sentiment didn't gain much traction. Ford writes in his memoirs that Nixon called him a week after the pardon to express his gratitude. "Jerry, I know this is causing you great political difficulty and embarrassment, but I also want you to know I'm appreciative and grateful," he told Ford. "I did it for the reasons I stated publicly," Ford responded. "I expected an adverse reaction. It's been worse than I thought, but I've done it, and I'm convinced it was the right decision, and I think history will prove my point."

Ford was right on all counts. The initial reaction was worse—much worse—than he had anticipated, and yet many today believe that history, indeed, has proven him right. "As the years have passed, I have become more and more convinced that Ford made the correct decision in pardoning Nixon. . . . A pardon was the only way of ending the public's and media's obsession with his predecessor's future," wrote Bob Woodward in his book *Shadows*—a far cry from his initial reaction in 1974.[32] Longtime *New York Times* columnist Anthony Lewis expressed a similar sentiment, confessing that among his "greatest regrets as a newspaper columnist is how I underrated Gerald Ford when he was in the White House. It is time, past time, to acknowledge what a model of decency and respect for the law he has been."[33] Perhaps nobody did a greater about-face than historian and columnist Richard Reeves, who publicly apologized for his scathing 1975 book, *A Ford, Not a Lincoln*, with an essay for *American Heritage* magazine entitled "I'm Sorry, Mr. President." He concludes his long mea culpa with "you have my respect and thanks, Mr. President."[34]

In 2001, Gerald Ford was the recipient of the Profiles in Courage Award from the John F. Kennedy Library Foundation, an award so named after the late president's Pulitzer Prize–winning book. The honor is perhaps the strongest evidence yet that history has come to view the decision in a different light.[35] In his remarks at the awards ceremony, Senator Ted Kennedy reminded the audience that he was "one of those people who spoke out against the action then. But time has a way of clarifying past events, and now we see that President Ford was right. His courage and dedication to our country made it possible for us to begin the process of healing and put the tragedy of Watergate behind us."

Of course, it's almost universally accepted that the pardon cost Ford the 1976 election and a chance for a full term as president. Carter wisely made the contest a referendum on the crimes of the "Nixon-Ford" administration and Ford's ill-conceived pardon, and it paid off handsomely. It was smart politics, and with the margin of difference a mere 2 percentage points, there's little doubt that the pardon more than accounted for the difference. How different history might have been had Ford not pardoned Nixon. Chances are, there would have been no President Carter, and perhaps no President Reagan, too. One can only speculate.

As for Richard Nixon, the road to redemption was a winding, twisting, torturous path that ultimately led to nowhere. He spent the remainder of his postpresidency trying to rehabilitate his image—with some success—by authoring several critically acclaimed books, entertaining political leaders in small gatherings, providing counsel to presidents and foreign heads of state, and opining on the great issues of the day. Through hard work and sheer will, Nixon managed to achieve something resembling "elder statesman" status on the world stage before his death.[36] Most of the good work, however, has since come undone with the release of the remaining White House tapes, which clearly show an even greater level of paranoia, insecurity, and emotional instability than was even suspected. After listening to the tapes, there can be no doubt that Nixon was a troubled soul who put his own whimsical urges before the Constitution and well-being of the country.

Chapter 14

REAGAN AND THE EVIL EMPIRE

Courtesy of the Ronald Reagan Library.

Reagan Denounces Ideology of Soviets as "Focus of Evil"
> —*New York Times* headline, March 9, 1983

If anyone in the State Department read it, they just read the first few paragraphs and set it aside. They didn't know it was going to be a foreign policy speech. On the face of it, it wasn't a foreign policy speech.
> —Aram Bakshian Jr., director of speechwriting for the
> Reagan White House

I hate to admit it, but it's true: history has shown . . . I was wrong. That phrase, the Evil Empire, allowed Reagan to speak truth to totalitarianism.
> —David Gergen, who as a Reagan aide opposed the
> "evil empire" reference

I have seen the rise and fall of Nazi tyranny, the subsequent cold war and the nuclear nightmare that for fifty years haunted the dreams of children everywhere. During that time my generation defeated totalitarianism. As a result, your world is poised for better tomorrows. What will you do on your journey?

—Ronald Reagan in a speech before the Oxford Union Society in December 1992

On March 8, 1983, Ronald Reagan went before the National Association of Evangelicals to discuss the relationship between morality, religion, and the coarsening popular culture. It was expected to be a routine address, typical fare for an evangelical gathering. But Reagan had something different in mind that night. Disturbed by the growing momentum of the "nuclear freeze" movement within religious communities, as well as Congress, he sensed it was time to "expose" the Soviet Union for what it was—an "evil empire." He was particularly incensed that some church leaders refused to make a moral distinction between the two countries and their ideologies. "In your discussions of the nuclear freeze proposals," he told the unsuspecting audience, "I urge you to beware the temptation of pride—the temptation of blithely declaring yourselves above it all and label both sides equally at fault, to ignore the facts of history and the aggressive impulses of an evil empire, to simply call the arms race a giant misunderstanding and thereby remove yourself from the struggle between right and wrong and good and evil." The speech made front-page news around the world. Reagan was roundly criticized by newspaper editorials, Democrats, and other opinion leaders for the recklessly antagonistic jab. Even some Republicans, including a few on his own staff, thought the president went too far with the remark. But Reagan refused to back away from the sentiment. He believed that Soviet totalitarianism was a dying system, that victory in the Cold War was in sight. He considered harsh rhetoric simply another tool at his disposal to keep the pressure on, and wasn't shy about using it. It would prove to be a prescient instinct.

* * *

"The aggressive impulses of an evil empire"—it's one of the most memorable lines in presidential history, though the speech itself was fairly unmemorable. Few presidents author one notable phrase, let alone two—"Mr. Gorbachev, tear down this wall" being Reagan's other iconic utterance. Even rarer still is that both declarations dealt with the same subject: Soviet totalitarianism.

These memorable lines put Reagan in elite company alongside Lincoln—"government of the people, by the people, for the people"; "Four score and seven years ago our fathers brought forth on this continent, a new nation, conceived in Liberty, and dedicated to the proposition that all men are created equal"; "With malice toward none, with charity for all"—and perhaps Franklin Roosevelt—"The only thing we have to fear is fear itself"; "A date which shall live in infamy."

With the Cold War two decades in the past, it's easy to forget how jarring and impolitic the evil empire reference truly was. And unconventional. The United States had spent the better part of the previous decade in "détente" (or a relaxing of tensions) with the Soviets, the brainchild of Richard Nixon. The hope was that thawing relations would lead to arms control, increased trade and cooperation, a lessening of hostilities, and perhaps some kind of understanding about territorial ambitions. For a short while it did, but détente came to a sudden halt with the Soviet invasion of Afghanistan in the winter of 1979 and the later crackdown of the Polish solidarity movement. Still, most Americans feared an escalation of tension with the Russians back to the Cuban Missile Crisis levels of the early 1960s. The prospect of World War III over a misunderstanding or inconsequential "test of wills" between the two countries was real and worrisome in the minds of many. This concern helped fuel, in fact, the rapid growth in the "nuclear freeze" movement (the central principle of which was to convince the United States and Soviet Union to halt production of all new nuclear weapons), which was cresting in the early 1980s. Ratcheting up bombastic rhetoric for no apparent reason hardly seemed reassuring.

Yet none of that deterred Ronald Reagan in the least. It wasn't that he was impervious to the sentiment around him. He simply came to the office with cemented beliefs about the Soviet Union, which he wasn't about to change as president. And he was itching to tell the world what he really thought of the Cold War adversary.

* * *

Early in his presidency, Ronald Reagan was dubbed the Great Communicator by the press and Washington pundits for his ability to connect with the American people. Even his harshest critics—and there were many—conceded that the actor-turned-politician was an unusually gifted speechmaker, adept at delivering a phrase or sound bite. His folksy mannerisms, dulcet voice, breezy confidence, and years of acting served him well in that capacity. But it was more than just theatrical performance that set him apart. What his detractors could never understand—or accept—was that his success as an orator hinged on two things: his mastery of the written word, and a coherent worldview rooted in a few simple but transformative principles.[1]

For all his considerable talent as a speechmaker, what is generally overlooked is that Ronald Reagan was an equally brilliant *speechwriter*. As biographer Lou Cannon points out, his love for the written and spoken word can be traced to his time at Eureka College. "People who had gone to college with Reagan told me that he had memorized Franklin D. Roosevelt's famous 1933 inaugural address that carried the phrase, 'the only thing we have to fear is fear itself,'" Cannon wrote in *USA Today* just days after the former president's passing. "He could do the speech with a broomstick microphone. He also liked to use Roosevelt's phrases, such as 'rendezvous with destiny.'"[2] Reagan discovered his skill as a writer during the 1950s while criss-crossing the country on behalf of General Electric giving talks to plant workers as part of his 'goodwill ambassadorship' for the company. His traveling companions were impressed at how he meticulously wrote each speech on dozens of index cards, then committed them to memory—a practice he would continue through the White House years. The years of speechmaking culminated during the fall of 1964 in what has become known in Reagan lore as "the speech"—his thirty-minute, nationally televised endorsement of Barry Goldwater just days before the election. Though his candidate was trounced, "the speech" gave birth to the "draft Reagan" movement in California that would take him to the statehouse two years later. He continued the practice of writing his own speeches as governor of California, and further honed his skills while delivering over one thousand national radio addresses between 1975 and 1980. By the time he took office in January of 1981, Ronald Reagan had written and given thousands of speeches, remarks, and radio and television addresses, and with it had developed a masterful grasp of cadence, imagery, and storytelling. After decades of trial and error, he had come to understand the enormous impact that a few well-chosen words could have. As it stands, few presidents in the twentieth century spent more time with the written word than Ronald Reagan, a fact often underappreciated. There's no doubt it contributed mightily to his success in communicating his vision to the country.[3]

It would also be fair to say that few presidents in the twentieth century—perhaps in all of American history—had a deeper understanding or greater fidelity to their convictions than Ronald Reagan. He was certainly the most ideological office holder, maybe with the exception of his childhood hero, Franklin Roosevelt. Ironically enough, he spent the first four decades of his life as a Roosevelt Democrat, but liked to joke that he didn't leave the Democratic Party as much as it had left him. By the early 1960s, he had become a "movement conservative" whose political philosophy could be distilled to four precepts: the need to reduce the size and scope of government through tax cuts and deficit reduction; the importance in reestablishing American pride and patriotism; the belief that Soviet expansion and the spread of communism should be aggressively confronted; and a stout commitment to rebuild the military. He campaigned on those issues in 1976 and nearly defeated the sitting president for the Republican nomination. He followed the same playbook four years later and trounced Jimmy Carter. Upon taking office, he was determined not to lose sight of the few things he wanted to accomplish. Sure, other issues would breach the national consciousness now and again, but in the end it was these four that mattered most.

Some observers at the time confused this narrow (the word today would probably be *disciplined*) approach for simplicity. Anyone who could summarize a worldview on a 3 × 5 index card must be a simpleton, held conventional wisdom—a man possessing an uncurious and lazy intellect. Perhaps there's a kernel of truth in the sentiment. Reagan certainly wasn't a policy wonk like Clinton or obsessed with the legislative process like Johnson. Aside from tax cut legislation and defense authorizations, he had little interest in the minutiae of lawmaking. And he wasn't exactly searching for new ideas, either. He was sixty-nine years old when he came to the office, set in his thinking about the world around him. It would have been out of character for him to suddenly question or challenge decades-old beliefs.

But in retrospect, it's hard to argue against the success of this approach. The presidency, in many ways, resembles a narrative—a story with a beginning, middle, and end. The ones who stand out—Jackson, Lincoln, both Roosevelts—have memorable arcs: a few big accomplishments that shaped or altered the direction of the nation. Whether one agrees with Reagan's politics or not, there's no denying that his narrative closely resembled the tenets on those index cards, a fact that then-candidate Barack Obama, much to his handlers' dismay, pointed out during the 2008 Democratic primary. "Ronald Reagan changed the trajectory of America in a way that Richard Nixon did not, and a way that Bill Clinton did not. We want clarity, we want optimism, we want a return to that sense of dynamism and entrepreneurship that had been missing."[4] Obama took heat from the Clintons and other Democrats for the remark, but it revealed an understanding of the presidency that explains—and to some extent, Reagan's legacy— his decision to tackle healthcare reform.

"Freedom is one of the deepest and noblest aspirations of the human spirit"

"We win, they lose. What do you think of that?" Reagan interrupted his future national security advisor Richard Allen, who was gently probing his strategy for dealing with Soviet communism. It was sometime in 1979, and even those closest to Reagan weren't entirely sure what he meant by "winning the cold war."[5] It wasn't so much that his thoughts on the Soviet totalitarianism were unclear; Reagan, as biographer Richard Reeves put it, had long rejected the notion of "détente," and its predecessor, "containment," because both approaches assumed the Soviet system would remain in place for an indeterminate future—a prospect he found unacceptable. "Reagan rejected coexistence and agreed with the orthodox conservative view that containment was a losing strategy in the face of determined revolutionists," writes a historian of the era.[6]

It was the concept of winning *itself* that threw advisors for a loop. Ever since Harry Truman conceived the policy of containment in the years following World War II, the general approach of the United States government had been to thwart Soviet expansion using whatever means available: aid to allies, covert operations, military action, negotiations, even cooperation on occasion. To be sure, presidents routinely emphasized one tactic over another, but the construct and objectives varied little; the goal was to prevent the spread of Soviet totalitarianism to democratic nations.

Ronald Reagan came at it differently. As Richard Reeves put it, he "wanted to destroy communism." He had no doubt that Soviet communism was inferior to democratic capitalism. In his mind, it wasn't an "economic or political system," but rather a "from of insanity—a temporary aberration which will one day disappear form the earth because it is contrary to human nature."[7] Reagan never bought into coexistence because he didn't believe totalitarianism was sustainable. "Freedom is one of the deepest and noblest aspirations of the human spirit," he said in his second inaugural address, a phrase he used many times over the years. Perhaps other presidents felt similarly, but none made it foundational to their foreign policy. For Ronald Reagan, it was *the* bedrock of his worldview, the lens through which he filtered the Cold War. And it gave him supreme confidence that the West would ultimately prevail.[8]

This was a confidence that few shared in 1980. After all, the Soviets were on the march in Afghanistan, soaring energy prices had brought the economy to its knees, the government was powerless to free the hostages in Iran, and Vietnam and Watergate had badly eroded morale at home and support around the world. Jimmy Carter had tried to rally the nation from its doldrums, but the best he could offer was carpooling and to lower thermostats. In its final issue to close out the 1970s, *Newsweek* noted that there was "a growing sense that the country's institutions and leaders were no longer up to managing problems that were simply too complex to grasp."[9] When candidate Reagan met with reporters from the *Washington Post* in June of 1980 and boldly declared that an arms race would "get the Soviets to the negotiating table" given that they "couldn't compete with us," few in the room believed him.[10]

Voters did, however, or at least they were ready for something new. Reagan's thumping of Carter—he won 489 electoral votes to 49—remains the most lopsided margin against an incumbent.[11] If there was any doubt that the new president would try a different tack with the Soviets, it was put to rest on January 29 during his first press conference. Dismissing a question from Sam Donaldson about the prospects of détente by noting that "so far [it's been] a one-way street that the Soviet Union has used to pursue its own aims," he volunteered his take on the Soviets' intentions. "I know of no leader of the Soviet Union since the

revolution, and including the present leadership, that has not more than
once repeated in the various Communist congresses they hold their
determination that their goal must be the promotion of world revolution
and a one-world Socialist or Communist state, whichever word you want
to use." As for doing business with them, Reagan wasn't ruling it out, but
made it clear that since "the only morality they recognize is what will further their cause, meaning they reserve unto themselves the right to
commit any crime, to lie, to cheat," it seemed unlikely they would find
common ground. "We operate on a different set of standards."[12]

What Reagan offered that day was more than just a doctrinal shift or
new policy direction. It was an attitudinal sea change. The language was
defiant, bordering on coarse, unapologetic, judgmental, and menacing—
dramatically more confrontational than anything previously uttered by a
president. And a bit frightening to many Americans. In case it was mistaken for an aberration, Reagan repeated the sentiment a month later in
an interview with Walter Cronkite. "They can resort to lying or stealing
or cheating or even murder if it furthers their cause," he explained. "If
we're going to deal with them, we have to keep that in mind."[13] The language was reminiscent of Senator Joe McCarthy during the height of the
Red-baiting era. Presidents simply didn't talk this way.

Except Reagan. As the American people would soon learn, he had
every intention of matching his words with deeds, and those deeds were
considerable. The new Reagan Doctrine, as it would become known,
included a massive increase in defense spending; controversial aid to
"resistance fighters" in Africa, Asia, and Latin America to roll back
Soviet puppet regimes; more sophisticated missile technologies; and
investment in the Strategic Defense Initiative (SDI—better known as
"Star Wars"), which underscored the administration's intention to recon-
sider the long-standing theory of Mutually Assured Destruction (MAD)
as official policy, which held that a strong (and ever-growing) nuclear
arsenal was needed to deter the Soviets from attempting a first strike.[14]
It was this point that most concerned the Soviets—and the American
public for that matter—for SDI signaled that the president had not ruled
out the possibility of acquiring first-strike capability (by employing SDI
technology to prevent Soviet missiles from hitting the United States).
This, in turn, made the notion of a "winnable" nuclear war seem more
plausible, which only further destabilized an already tense relationship

between the two superpowers. All of this, of course, stemmed from Reagan's singular belief that victory in the Cold War was achievable in his lifetime.

In Reagan's world, words mattered. The harsh rhetoric was a way to keep pressure on the Soviets while he raced to implement his program that hopefully would push their economy to the brink. "They are in very bad shape," he wrote in his diary just days before nearly losing his life to an assassin's bullet. Soon enough, "they'll have to yell 'uncle' or starve."[15] He offered a similar line to Senate Majority Leader Howard Baker, who would later become his chief of staff. "We must keep the heat on these people," he confided to the somewhat skeptical Republican. "What I want is to bring them to their knees so that they will disarm and let us disarm; but we have to do it by keeping the heat on. . . . We have them on the ropes economically."[16]

In a practical sense, "keeping the heat on these people" meant driving them to economic ruin with an unsustainable arms race, among other things. Reagan was content to instigate stratospheric deficits if it meant bankrupting the Russians in the process. But it also meant pushing the rhetoric to uncomfortable extremes, too. He couldn't shake the notion that language could make a difference. One particular word—*evil*—perfectly encompassed everything he believed about Soviet totalitarianism. It eloquently captured the moral judgment—*his moral judgment*—that democratic capitalism was intrinsically better than state-imposed communism. He first explored the theme some fifteen years earlier in "the speech" on behalf of Goldwater, noting that "we are faced with the most evil enemy mankind has known in his long climb from the swamp to the stars."[17] He was looking for the right opportunity to revisit the notion as president.

There was a deep divide in the White House regarding Reagan's penchant for overheated language. The moderates—men like Secretary of State Al Haig, Chief of Staff Jim Baker, communications director David Gergen, among others—were on constant vigil to scrub impolitic phrases from the president's speeches and remarks. While they didn't necessarily disagree with his objectives, they favored a more sober, even-handed approach to diplomacy and policy making. The "movement conservatives" housed in the speechwriting group, however, felt no similar constraints. They were ideologues, people who swore allegiance to a set of ideas and principles, not "bilateral communications." They were less interested in finding common ground with the Soviets and more interested in poking them in the eye. Ronald Reagan enjoyed his weekly meetings with the speechwriters.

The president initially tested the "evil theme" on May 27, 1981, at the commencement ceremony for the cadets at West Point. It was only his second public address since nearly being assassinated two months earlier, and he was anxious to get it "on the record." Reagan was reminded that "at Trophy Point [there were] links of a great chain that was forged and stretched across the Hudson to prevent the British fleet from penetrating further into the valley." Today, he told the graduate class, "you are that chain holding back an evil force that would extinguish the light we've been tending for 6,000 years."[18] The remark went largely unnoticed, though that wasn't the case a week earlier with his commencement speech at Notre Dame, where he predicted that the "years ahead will be great ones for our country, for the cause of freedom and the spread of civilization. The West will not contain Communism; it will transcend Communism. We will not bother to denounce it, we'll dismiss it as a sad, bizarre chapter in human history whose last pages are even now being written."[19]

In November of that year, Reagan gave his most comprehensive remarks about the Soviet Union at the National Press Club. Billed as a "major foreign policy address," he unveiled *his* version of arms reduction called "the zero option," which essentially held that if the Soviet Union dismantled all of its intermediate-range missiles, the United States would "forgo deployment of Pershing and cruise missiles" in Western Europe. The proposal was so one-sided, so outlandish, that even the State Department opposed it. Reagan went ahead anyway, probably because he knew it would offend the Soviets. And it did. It was a "formula for unilateral disarmament by our side," observed the Soviets' chief arms negotiator in Geneva, "and frankly, an insult to our intelligence."[20]

That suited the president just fine. He had no intention of negotiating arms reductions with the Soviets on the verge of collapse, as he saw it. In fact, just the opposite: Now was the time to ratchet up the rhetoric with the hope of incensing them into poor decisions.

Reagan found the perfect opportunity to do just that in June of 1982 with his address before the British Parliament, the first sitting president accorded such an honor. His staff had been fighting for weeks over the speech. The moderates, led by the National Security Council and State Department, wanted something forceful but temperate in tone— "bureaucratese," as one observer put it. The true believers in the speechwriting shop didn't quite see it that way. For months, they had been conspiring to slip a line borrowed from legendary anticommunist author Whitaker Chambers—"I see in communism the focus of concentrated evil in our time"—into a speech, but couldn't seem to navigate past the editing process. This time around, they went so far as to plead their case directly to the president—the hope being that he would overrule the moderates. To their disappointment, the language was purged from the final text without explanation. Whether Reagan approved the edit remains a mystery, but even without the phrase, the speech was still a blockbuster, producing one of his most memorable lines—"the march of freedom and democracy will leave Marxism-Leninism on the ash-heap of history."[21] It also produced a torrent of negative reaction from the press and even some British officials. "The speech was very strong, very striking, and extremely hard line," opined Peter Jay, the former British ambassador to Washington. "He seemed to almost be declaring non-military war on the Soviet Union. If he does mean it, it's very frightening."[22] The *New York Times* was only slightly less hysterical, going with the headline "Soviet Says Crusade by Reagan May Risk Global Catastrophe." *Time* put it more bluntly: "It was a bad week for relations between Moscow and Washington." When the president returned to the States, he was greeted by 700,000 protesters demonstrating "their support of nuclear freeze in New York's Central Park."[23]

And so it went. Reagan spent the months prior to the 1982 midterm elections jabbing the Soviets here and there, but as one biographer put it, he "deliberately held below the radar of press and public" his "hard inner determination."[24] With the economy in recession, deficits piling up, and his poll numbers plummeting, he had little choice but to stay on script. His "real feelings," observed another, "were not part of most of his own speeches."[25]

But that couldn't last forever. By the spring of 1983, it had been a little over two years and he still hadn't unleashed his innermost thoughts about the Soviet Union. He had come close on occasion—very close— and certainly employed tougher rhetoric than previous administrations, but there was the nagging matter of calling it for what it was: evil. When Reagan was invited to speak before the National Association of Evangelicals in March of 1983, however, events seemed to be conspiring in his favor. By this time, the nuclear freeze movement was gaining a head of steam, particularly among religious groups. It was tantamount to unilateral disarmament as far as the president was concerned. The "moral equivalence" argument—that democratic capitalism and totalitarianism were equally to blame for the Cold War—was starting to gain traction, too. This exasperated Reagan to no end. He couldn't fathom how fairminded people—especially church leaders—put the two on equal footing. But that's what seemed to be happening.

Because it was a speech to evangelicals that mostly dealt with domestic issues, few in the State Department or National Security Council took notice of the various drafts. A "stealth speech" was how one speechwriter described it, for it flew quietly below the radar of the national security apparatus. Years later, Secretary of State George Schultz would confess that he had no advance warning of the phrase, noting that it "had not been planned or developed through any careful or systematic process."[26] Back came the language that was cut from the British Parliament text, only with a twist: to debunk the concept of moral equivalence, the Soviets had to be labeled an evil empire. "I want to remind the Soviets we know what they're up to," he directed his speechwriters. He was determined not to let the few moderates with knowledge of the remarks censor his thinking. This was twenty years in the making. The nuclear freeze crowd, religious groups, Soviet leaders—they were going to hear the truth . . . his truth: "I urge you to beware the temptation of pride—the temptation of blithely declaring yourselves above it all and label both sides equally at fault, to ignore the facts of history and the aggressive impulses of an evil empire, to simply call the arms race a giant misunderstanding and thereby remove yourself from the struggle between right and wrong and good and evil."[27]

* * *

Not surprising, the reaction was volcanic. "It was the worst presidential speech in American history, and I've seen them all," remarked celebrated presidential historian Henry Steele Commager in the *Washington Post*.

New York Times columnist Anthony Lewis called it "primitive" and "outrageous." As far as the *New Republic* was concerned, "the President of the United States was contemplating a holy war." In their estimation, the speech was "not presidential, it's not something a president should say." Even David Gergen, Reagan's communications director, privately thought the evil empire reference was "outrageous." He had tried in vain to expunge the phrase, only giving up "when he discovered that Reagan himself insisted on including the phrase and had actually toughened that section of the speech with some flourishes of his own."[28]

In a sense, the *New Republic* was correct: it wasn't something a president should normally say. Few, if any, had ever used such inflammatory language to denigrate a peacetime adversary—particularly one as powerful as the Soviet Union. It just didn't happen. There were scores and scores of advisors, professional bureaucrats, department staffers, and others to make sure of it. But this wasn't any ordinary situation. Ronald Reagan had been waiting all his life to call the Soviet Union an evil empire. He believed it in his soul, and believed their totalitarian system was teetering on collapse. The fact that few others outside his inner circle shared that opinion didn't bother him in the slightest. He simply couldn't fathom any other outcome except "we win, they lose."

Reflecting back on the era, and Reagan's dogged insistence that the United States was on the verge of triumph, conservative scholar Michael Novak mused, "It really makes you wonder. . . . What did he know that we didn't?" It was certainly different than the leading intellectuals of the day. Months before the speech, renowned historian Arthur Schlesinger acidly observed that "those in the United States who think the Soviet Union is on the verge of economic and social collapse are wishful thinkers." Noted Harvard economist John Kenneth Galbraith saw it similarly. "The Russian system succeeds because, in contrast with the Western industrial economies, it makes full use of its manpower." MIT heavyweight Paul Samuelson took it a step further. "The Soviet model has surely demonstrated that a command economy is capable of mobilizing resources for rapid growth." James Reston of the *New York Times* summed up what many believed: "It's clear that the ideologies of communism, socialism and capitalism are all in trouble."[29]

The reaction inside the Soviet Union to the speech was quite different. Remarked former Soviet dissident Vladimir Bukovsky: "His phrase 'evil empire' became a household word in Russia." Said another dissident, Natan Sharansky: "Finally, the leader of the free world had spoken the truth." Leading Reagan critic and noted Sovietologist Seweryn Bialer, upon returning from the Soviet Union shortly after the speech, noted that "President Reagan's rhetoric has badly shaken the self-esteem and patriotic pride of the Soviet political elites."[30]

Like Ford's pardon of Nixon, distance, reflection, and intervening events have a way of altering opinions over time. While it would be overstating the case to say that Reagan "won" the Cold War, it wouldn't be a stretch to credit him with hastening its demise. As it turns out, their economy was much closer to collapse than anyone—save the true believers in the White House—had suspected. The massive defense spending, guerrilla wars, menacing rhetoric, lack of détente, and refusal to seriously negotiate arms reduction put unrelenting pressure on an already wobbly system. The stress was simply too much. Something had to give.

As for the speech itself, it was only that—a speech; words on paper, nothing more. With it came no doctrinal shift, no new policy, no new programs. But in a flash it had perfectly captured what Reagan believed was the metaphysical essence of the Cold War—good versus evil. Never again, as far as he was concerned, could the United States and the Soviet Union be considered moral equivalents. He had succeeded in branding it evil.

Chapter 15

BARACK OBAMA TAKES ON HEALTHCARE REFORM

Photo by Pete Souza, the newly announced White House photographer.

I begged him not to do this.
—White House Chief of Staff Rahm Emanuel about President Obama's decision to push for an overhaul of the healthcare system in year one

It's not about the 2010 midterms "crippling my presidency," quote unquote. This is about whether we're going to get big things done. I wasn't sent here to do school uniforms.
—President Obama to nervous White House aides who were counseling a scaled-back healthcare bill

If we're able to stop Obama on this, it will be his Waterloo. It will break him.
—Republican Senator Jim DeMint of South Carolina, a vocal critic of the president's healthcare plan

On March 23, 2010, President Obama, flanked by a dozen lawmakers, as well as Regina Kennedy, widow of Senator Ted Kennedy, penned into law a sweeping overhaul of the healthcare system. "The bill I'm signing will set in motion reforms that generations of Americans have fought for and marched for and hungered to see," said the president, adding, "Today we are affirming that essential truth, a truth every generation is called to rediscover for itself, that we are not a nation that scales back its aspirations." The New York Times *called it the "most expansive social legislation enacted in decades." Critics howled that it was nothing less than socialized medicine, the government takeover of a fifth of the economy. For the president and Democrats in Congress, it marked the conclusion of a long, torturous, at times unsteady process that threatened to be derailed at least a half dozen times. The legislation was a personal triumph for the president. Rejecting the counsel of his closest aides, he somewhat recklessly decided to make comprehensive healthcare reform the centerpiece of his agenda, knowing full well that failure could cripple his fledgling administration. It was a big gamble, with potentially a big payoff, and while the politics and substance of it continues to play out, there's no denying that it was one of the boldest first-year gambits since the New Deal.*

* * *

One could credibly argue that it's premature to include President Obama's passage of healthcare reform among the most transformative decisions in presidential history. It will likely be years before the impact of the overhaul is fully understood. It may take that long to appreciate the politics as well. We know it played a role in Republican Senator Scott Brown's victory in Massachusetts, as well as other special elections that year. And don't forget that displeasure with the public option and other aspects of the bill (including the price tag) helped give birth to the Tea Party movement, which doesn't seem to be going away. There are few examples of legislation, or the process of its passage, as polarizing as this one.

This book has been a study in the hows and whys of presidential leadership—the big decisions that shaped the nation, defined legacies, stretched the office, and added to our knowledge of the process. Will healthcare reform come to define President Obama's legacy? Though it's too early to say for sure, it certainly has the potential. Most big legislative achievements—Social Security, Medicare and Medicaid, and Reagan's historic tax cuts—took place during the first two years in office. Aside from the case of the two Roosevelts, very few second terms are as productive as the first. That's not to say that other big things aren't potentially on the horizon for Obama. It's just to offer some perspective.

The same holds true for gauging the lasting impact of the healthcare overhaul. While we don't know what exactly the net result of reform will be—good, bad, indifferent—it's probably a safe assumption that there *will be* some kind of lasting impact. Healthcare is simply too big a part of our economy, and too central to everyday lives, for reform not to be massively disruptive, good or bad. That is not to place a value judgment on the bill—readers can do that for themselves. It's simply recognition that healthcare reform is not a run-of-the-mill item like farm subsidies or tuition tax credits. Its magnitude has few equals.

On the other two points—stretching the office and contributing to the body of knowledge about the institution—there's no doubt that healthcare reform did both. It's hard to recall a president who so persistently and publicly advocated for a cause as Obama did for reform. Wilson comes to mind with the League of Nations, though ultimately that was a failure. Reagan was certainly forceful and effective in selling his tax cuts. Perhaps the closest analogy is Johnson and civil rights, but even then it was for a much shorter duration. Obama stuck with healthcare for the better part of a year, a good portion of that spent nursing it back from life support. On several occasions it looked like it was dead, the most ominous following Scott Brown's special election in January of 2010. If the president was going to lose his nerve, it would have been the days following the Massachusetts Republican's historic upset in the overwhelmingly Democratic state. Certainly that was the conventional wisdom among the Beltway chattering class during their postmortem analysis. Most were expecting the president to dramatically scale back the bill in order to secure passage of something—anything. Many in the White House counseled that way, but the president wasn't buying it. He showed a resilience that resembled Bill Clinton's during the 1992 New Hampshire primary, where he took hit after hit but kept coming. Future presidents might heed the example and ride out the bumpy patches.

In the end, it is uncertain how history will evaluate Obama's presidency, healthcare reform, or anything else for that matter without the sufficient passage of time. Trying to judge it without historical perspective, primary source materials (diaries, memoirs, insider remembrances, etc.), other contemporaneous accounts, and the like would prove difficult and incomplete. We need look no further than some of the decisions in this book to understand how legacies and standing can fluctuate over time. Gerald Ford's pardon of Richard Nixon was so unpopular it cost him the 1976 election; it is now regarded as one of the most courageous acts in the history of the office. Many contemporaries considered JFK's moon challenge to be a colossal waste of time and money, a "moondoggle." In retrospect, it was a defining moment in the century, contributed greatly to morale in the country, and helped inspire a generation of Americans. Ronald Reagan was criticized for calling the Soviet Union an "evil empire." Some considered the harsh rhetoric too antagonistic, too menacing—a slippery slope to World War III. It turns out that Reagan perceived that Soviet communism was in the advance stages of decay, that confrontation would expedite its demise. He was right. Even the Emancipation Proclamation was not met with universal praise at the time. While Lincoln understood its historical significance, few around him grasped its enormity. It's now regarded as a singular achievement in the nation's history.

* * *

In his recent book chronicling President Obama's first year in office, *Newsweek* columnist Jonathan Alter noted that if the "president and Congress pulled it off, health care reform would be more than an achievement on its own terms; it would accomplish something that had eluded presidents for nearly a hundred years and help redeem the promise of the 2008 election."[1] The observation, of course, came *after* the legislation had passed, but the point still rings true: this was a monumental achievement.

Part of what makes Obama's triumph all the more impressive is the trail of failures that preceded it. As the president pointed out in his March 2010 healthcare summit in the East Room of the White House, Teddy Roosevelt was the first to take a stab at universal healthcare—sort of. It wasn't as president, but rather as the Bull Moose Progressive candidate in 1912. In his platform, he called for the "adoption of a system of social insurance adapted to American use" that would protect Americans against "the hazards of sickness, irregular employment and old age."[2] It was TR's belief that the "supreme duty of the Nation is the conservation of human resources through an enlightened measure of social and industrial justice." According to biographer H. W. Brands, what TR envisioned was "pretty much what FDR accomplished with Social Security, but with health insurance added."[3] Of course, Teddy Roosevelt got thumped by Woodrow Wilson, and with him went the promise of universal healthcare.

Next was Franklin Roosevelt. "Whether we come to this form of insurance soon or later on," he said of national healthcare in the fall of 1934, "I am confident that we can devise a system which will enhance and not hinder the remarkable progress which has been made . . . in the professions of medicine . . . in the United States."[4] FDR floated the idea of including some kind of universal healthcare in the Social Security Act but quickly retreated at the first sign of opposition. He made another half-hearted attempt in 1938 but decided to scrap it after the Democrats suffered a poor showing in the midterm elections. Even a leader as skilled as Franklin Roosevelt was no match for the entrenched interests lined up against it.

The most serious push for universal coverage came from Harry Truman following his "upset" victory over Thomas Dewey in the 1948 election. With the political winds at his back, he aggressively lobbied for a single, comprehensive healthcare system but was met with fierce resistance by moderate Democrats and conservative Republicans in Congress. "I consider it socialism. It is to my mind the most socialistic measure this Congress has ever had before it," was Republican Senator Robert Taft's take on the proposal, a refrain that would be repeated some sixty years later.[5] Ironically enough, it was the Democrats in Congress who stalled the measure, as the chairman of the committee responsible for the legislation locked it in committee, where it died, a victim of the burgeoning "Red scare" that would soon turn the nation upside down.

With the passage of Medicare in the summer of 1965, Lyndon Johnson took the first steps toward universal coverage as nineteen million seniors now had access to healthcare. Johnson held the signing ceremony at the Truman Library, where the former president and his wife were given the first two Medicare cards. It's considered his greatest achievement along with civil rights.

And of course there was "HillaryCare," President Clinton's highly visible attempt at universal coverage. The story is familiar but worth repeating. Clinton had campaigned on national healthcare, and like President Obama chose to make it a cornerstone of his first-term agenda. In what would turn out to be a massive misstep, he appointed the First Lady to head the reform taskforce, where she toiled in secrecy and produced a huge one-thousand-page bill. The Republicans in Congress, healthcare interest groups, and grassroots organizations worked relentlessly to kill it, ultimately succeeding when the Democrats in Congress lost confidence in both Clintons. The Republicans parlayed their victory into an unprecedented sweep in the midterm elections, which saw them retake control of Congress for the first time in forty years. The Democrats' defeat was so resounding, so complete, that few believed universal healthcare would ever see the light of day.

* * *

It's easy to understand why Rahm Emanuel, David Axelrod, and others in the president's inner circle opposed making healthcare overhaul the centerpiece of Obama's agenda. True enough, they had campaigned on it during the primary (less so during the general election), but given that the economy was in freefall, nobody was concerned about voter backlash should it be shoved to the backburner. "They'll give you a pass on this one," Vice President Joe Biden astutely counseled the president about abandoning the promise.[6] For Emanuel, a veteran of the Clinton White House, the scar tissue from HillaryCare was a stark reminder of the perils of moving too far, too fast on the issue. The last thing the chief of staff wanted was a repeat of the 1993 debacle and the repercussions that might come with it. "I begged him not to do this," Emanuel revealed to Jonathan Alter for his book.[7] Many inside the White House believed that stabilizing the economy and creating jobs in year one would be plenty enough. White House polling indicated that insurance coverage wasn't a burning priority for the American people; jobs were. Heavyweights in the Senate like Chuck Schumer and Byron Dorgan concurred. The consensus was that healthcare reform could wait.

The president, however, saw things differently. He understood the risk of overhauling the system while the economy was teetering on collapse—"I remember telling Nancy Pelosi that moving forward on this could end up being so costly for me politically that it would affect my chance if I were to run for reelection"—but he also knew that deferring it to future Congresses virtually assured that "it was not going to be done." It was a risk he was willing to take. "We knew," the president would later say, "that it would be all-consuming—in the midst of having to deal with this enormous economic crisis and two wars—and that it would take a lot out of us."[8]

Obama was thinking about legacy as much as anything else. He liked to remind staffers that he came to Washington to get "big things done." Doing "school uniforms," he made a point of noting, wasn't part of the job description. He correctly surmised that he would likely get "one bite at the apple" for an issue as big, complicated, and disruptive as healthcare reform.[9] The best time to tackle it, he concluded, was while he still had the enormous goodwill from the election at his back. Without it, the prospects of achieving reform were much dimmer—even with a Democratic Congress. "Given how difficult fighting the special interests has been on Capitol Hill," reflected Obama toward the end of 2009, "it's clear that if we hadn't decided to make a bold step forward this year, we probably wouldn't have had the political capital to get it done in the future."[10] Once his mind was made up, there would be no turning back.

But it wasn't just about legacy, or reelection, or accomplishing big things for the sake of accomplishing big things. After listening to hundreds—perhaps thousands—of hard-luck stories on the campaign trail and as president from people forced to choose between healthcare and living expenses, the issue became very personal. Every rope line he worked was affixed with dozens of people with unsettling tales, one more heartbreaking than the next. He made a point of highlighting the wrenching notes, letters, e-mails, and personal pleas in his speeches and town hall meetings, both as candidate and later as president. "I'm signing it for eleven-year-old Marcelas Owens, who's also here," said the president at the bill-signing ceremony, referring to a particularly tragic story. "Marcelas lost his mom to an illness. And she didn't have insurance and couldn't afford the care that she needed. So in her memory he has told her story across America so that no other children have to go through what his family has experienced."

There were other considerations as well. The president initially positioned healthcare reform as an economic imperative—"bending the cost curve"—in order to strengthen the nation's long-term solvency. The thinking was that the American people would appreciate the urgency if framed as a matter of "economic security." But for various reasons, including the seemingly astronomical price tag, that message failed to resonate. The White House smartly course-corrected over time, subtly shifting the emphasis to coverage for the uninsured, though even that didn't totally connect with voters. It wasn't until reform became synonymous with an all-out assault on insurance companies that the president finally hit his rhetorical stride.[11] "I just met with some of them [insurance companies]," said the president during one of his weekly Youtube addresses, "and they couldn't give me a straight answer as to why they keep arbitrarily and massively raising premiums—by as much as 60 percent in states like Illinois. If we do not act, they will continue to do this. They will continue to drop people's coverage when they need it. They will continue to refuse coverage based on preexisting conditions. These practices will continue."[12]

Learning from mistakes would be a recurring theme for the president in year one. To be sure, there were ample opportunities to go to school during the healthcare reform process. Asking Congress to craft a bill from scratch with little White House guidance was a doozy. As pundits have been quick to point out, Obama may have "overlearned" the lesson from HillaryCare—avoid plopping a fully baked one-thousand-page bill in the lap of Congress—and reflexively went too far the other way. As it turned out, not having an "Obama plan" from the onset was a devastating, nearly fatal, miscalculation. It put Congress, and its time-honored system of horse-trading, bickering, and messy turf battles front and center for all to see, all the while enabling Republicans to demagogue the most ominous-sounding provisions. The net impact? What the White House hoped would be a several-month process extended indefinitely. As mistakes go, it was colossal.

There were others. The dalliance with the "public option" was a near-crippling misstep, too. The truth of the matter is that the president said exceedingly little about a government-run "public" option during the campaign. There were oblique references here and there, but never was it the cornerstone of his reform plan. During the spring and summer of 2009, however, it somehow got elevated from a "sliver" of the plan, as the president liked to say, to the main attraction. That the White House lost control of the message is understandable given that liberals and conservatives both had a vested interest in harping on it. For progressives, government-run healthcare represented the holy grail of "real" reform, the promised land of nationalized healthcare. For them, it was the public option or bust. There could be no compromise on that point. For Republicans, talk of a government-funded alternative was a gift from above—irrefutable proof that the president, indeed, was a socialist bent on nationalizing the economy. They had to pinch themselves to make sure that their good fortune wasn't just a dream. A combination of poor message management, failure to take the Republicans seriously, liberal intransigence, and plain bad luck kept the public option at the center of the debate for months at a time, and in the process nearly sank the president's hope for reform.

Some in the president's own party contend that it was a rookie mistake to chase the mirage of bipartisanship for so long, that he would have been better served going it alone from the beginning. The issue cuts both ways. He certainly should have recognized sooner that gaining Republican support for a predominantly Democratic bill was at best a long shot, probably not worth pursuing. He wasted precious time and energy tilting at windmills with nothing to show for it. Others maintain that he could have attracted moderate Republicans by including a few of their ideas, such as tort reform and portability of coverage. Alas, it wasn't in the cards.

It turns out that President Obama was much more the gambler than anyone could have predicted. Pinning his presidency on something that had never been done—all the while staving off an economic collapse—would seem like a sucker's bet to most. On a couple of occasions he had the chance to opt out, but chose instead to double down. During the August recess of 2009, as congressional Democrats were getting savaged by angry constituents at town hall meetings for their support of "socialized medicine," Rahm Emanuel suggested the president consider a scaled-back plan. Dubbed the "Titanic strategy" because it covered women and children first, Emanuel's approach was roughly half the size of the original plan and more bipartisan. Obama considered it but ultimately passed. "I understand what Rahm is saying," he told senior staffers in an Oval Office powwow, "and maybe we'll have to scale back, but we don't have to do that now." The consequences were simply too great. "If we do, twenty-two million go uninsured."[13]

Going the "reconciliation route"—the infrequently used, highly controversial process has been typically reserved for mandatory tax or spending programs because it does not allow for unlimited debate or filibuster—was also a roll of the dice. After all, the voters had just spoken (in the Massachusetts special election) with resounding clarity: junk ObamaCare and start anew. Moreover, the president's poll numbers were sagging; Democrats no longer enjoyed a filibuster-proof majority; the White House was in panicked disarray; and a guy named Scott Brown seemed to be the new center of the political universe. The safe play would have been to scrap the bill and start over, incorporate a few Republican ideas, cajole it through Congress, and declare some kind of victory. Using reconciliation (some commentators dubbed it the "nuclear option") seemed farfetched and risky, even though it had been employed on twenty-three prior occasions, seventeen of those times by Republicans.

The president had made a virtue of being "postpartisan," someone with little interest in the back-and-forth sniping of Washington. By railroading the legislation using the draconian reconciliation process, he risked drawing the ire of the public and contradicting his "brand." As it stood, he took a good deal of heat for it, appearing a hypocrite in some quarters. But so be it. He was willing to live with the consequences.

* * *

Obama's healthcare reform is a study in overcoming failure as much as achieving success. It had more missteps, miscalculations, and near-death experiences than any legislation in recent memory. At several key moments—the 2009 August recess and following Scott Brown's victory— the president would have been within his rights to abandon it altogether, or at least dramatically scale it back. But it's also a tale of persistence, of staying the course. Pulling the plug would have been the expedient thing to do, but in the president's mind, the wrong thing. It would have been politically ruinous to ditch the bill and start anew. Had that been the case, it's likely that nothing would have been passed. He had invested too much time, energy, and national attention to simply walk away. As Lyndon Johnson was fond of saying, sometimes you have to go "all in."

In the days following the Brown victory, most pundits assumed that major reform was dead. Perhaps the president would move forward with a bipartisan, piecemeal bill, but that would be the extent of it. There's no way he would stick it out.

Of course, he did. He went the route of reconciliation, which he knew would be highly unpopular and polarizing, but figured the ends justified the means. At the heart of the decision was a daring calculation: would the benefits of reform—both substantive and political—outweigh the unseemly (in the eyes of some) process by which it occurred?[14] Maybe there would be a short-term hit, but the president concluded that the residual anger would dissipate as the reforms eventually took hold. On that score, we may not know the final tally for years.

It's also too soon to postulate how this will affect the president's reelection chances, let alone his legacy. Should it become a sacred entitlement like Social Security and Medicare—both of which were highly controversial in their day—it bodes well for posterity. Should it wreak havoc with the quality of care, fail to control costs, and layer more complexity into the system, as critics contend, it could set the Democrats back for years.

Passage does seem to have altered the trajectory of his presidency, at least through the summer of 2010. Most fair-minded observers gave Obama an "incomplete" grade for year one, recognizing that healthcare still hung in the balance, but stronger grades in year two, reflecting passage of the healthcare bill and financial regulatory reform, among other things. But coming back in the face of the Scott Brown victory, and using the reconciliation process, has revealed a toughness that few knew existed. Will the momentum translate to other victories, or will it stall with the gulf oil crisis and other challenges? Time will tell.

AFTERWORD

This book is meant neither to be an authoritative grouping of the fifteen events, nor a dispositive exposition on their import and impact. Certainly quibbling can be done on both counts. A strong case could be made for including the Monroe Doctrine, which many regard as the defining declaration of the nineteenth century; Jackson's effort to kill the Second Bank of the United States; the annexation of Texas; probably a half dozen actions by Lincoln, including the suspension of habeas corpus; the Spanish-American War; Roosevelt's trust busting and efforts at conservation; Wilson's maneuvering to bring the nation into the Great War; Hoover's failure to mitigate the Great Depression; the entire New Deal program, most notably Social Security; the creation of Medicare and Medicaid; Nixon's cover-up of Watergate; Reagan's tax cuts; Clinton's 1993 budget; or Bush's decision to invade Iraq. The list is almost endless. All are worthy of consideration.

And therein lay the beauty of historical debate. There is no right or wrong answer, no right or wrong interpretation. Everyone is entitled to an opinion. Richard Nixon once remarked that he was dubious about his legacy because, in his estimation, while history would treat him fairly, "historians probably won't because most historians are on the left." Be that as it may, academic historians certainly have unique insights and perspective, but that doesn't make analysis, whether left or right, their exclusive domain. We live in a world where information abounds. Research is at our fingertips—no longer reserved only for those in the ivory tower. The Internet is an amazingly flattening tool. Every day new resources become available. The possibilities for exploring varied points of view are nearly limitless.

If this book does nothing but spark interest in learning more about the fifteen events, or those not included for that matter, my mission is accomplished. If it happens to entertain, even better. Some of the most interesting anecdotes, analysis, and tidbits, in fact, are housed in the endnotes. I encourage readers to sift through the notes, Google search the primary and secondary sources, and explore the material. It will be well worth the effort.

Writing this book was an enormous joy for me (though I'm sure I wasn't a joy to be around as the deadline loomed). I felt like I came to know these characters, or at least aspects of their personalities, leadership styles, decision making, and ultimately their presidencies. Moving from one chapter to the next was challenging at times. It was hard to leave behind giants like Jackson, Lincoln, Teddy Roosevelt, and the others after spending so much time with them, but alas, the goal was to explore fifteen of the biggest decisions of the presidency.

Jackson and Lincoln were particularly enjoyable to write about. In a century where legislators enjoyed primacy over the mostly "caretaker" presidents, they stood out. Part of it was their unyielding commitment to keeping the nation together. The two gave more thought to the "perpetual" nature of the Union than any of their predecessors, mostly because circumstances required it. But their legacies on the issue go beyond just rejecting nullification or prosecuting the Civil War to completion. Through his words, writings, and deeds, Jackson helped seed the idea that since the Union predated the Constitution, it couldn't be summarily disbanded by the states. Lincoln added an eloquence to that simple insight that immortalized it for the ages.

Another chapter that was particularly meaningful to write was that of Roosevelt and Lend-Lease. It was fascinating on so many levels. The relationship between FDR and Churchill is certainly unprecedented in presidential history. The unusual bond between the two men arguably had more to do with the defeat of Nazi Germany than any other factor. Lend-Lease would not have happened without Churchill's constant prodding of Roosevelt. Very few men could have steered the country from isolationist to interventionist in such a short period of time the way Roosevelt did. England might have surrendered to Hitler were it not for America's "peacetime" support. There are so many wonderful books on Churchill and Roosevelt that discuss their relationship in great detail. The endnotes in that chapter are particularly interesting.

As mentioned in the introduction, I hope that this book sparks an even greater curiosity about the presidency and its office holders. By learning from the past, we can become more educated and better citizens.

NOTES

Chapter 1

1. It's befitting that Alexander Hamilton is one of only two nonpresidents to appear on paper currency—his face adorns the $10 bill. The other is Benjamin Franklin ($100 bill).

2. Though Madison and Jefferson strongly opposed the debt-assumption component of the plan, they ultimately relented as part of a compromise whereby Hamilton agreed to allow the capital to be relocated from Philadelphia to Washington instead of his beloved New York City. Jefferson and the other antifederalists insisted on having the capital city in the South. Willard Sterne Randall, *Alexander Hamilton: A Life* (New York: HarperCollins, 2003), p. 394.

3. Francis Graham Wilson, *The American Political Mind: A Textbook in Political Theory* (New York: McGraw-Hill, 1949), p. 153.

4. Ron Chernow, *Alexander Hamilton* (New York: Penguin Books, 2005), p. 300.

5. Forrest McDonald, *Alexander Hamilton: A Biography* (New York: W. W. Norton, 1982), p. 170.

6. Said the celebrated senator Daniel Webster years later of Hamilton's financial genius: "The fabled birth of Minerva from the brain of Jove was hardly more sudden or more perfect than the financial system of the United States as it bursts forth from the conception of Alexander Hamilton." Ibid., p. 302.

7. According to Alexander Hamilton's *Report on the Western Country*, which he delivered to President Washington on August 5, 1794, the county instigators included such notables as James Marshall, the register and recorder of the county, David Bradford, deputy attorney general for the state, and Henry Taylor and James Edgar, associate judges, among others. According to Hamilton's report, the county organizers actually published a stern warning in the *Pittsburgh Gazette* to anyone who dared to collect the taxes: "Any person who had accepted or might accept an office under Congress in order to carry it into effect should be considered inimical to the interest of the Country; and recommending to the citizens of Washington County to treat every person who had accepted or might thereafter accept any such office with contempt, and absolutely refuse all kind of communication or intercourse with the officers and to withhold from them all aid support or comfort." Steven Boyd, ed., *The Whiskey Rebellion: Past and Present Perspectives* (Westport, CT: Greenwood, 1985), p. 33.

8. William Hogeland, *The Whiskey Rebellion* (New York: Scribner, 2005), pp. 20–21. One poor soul was tarred and feathered for simply remarking that "the inhabitants of the county could not reasonably expect protection from a government, whose laws they so strenuously opposed." Ibid., p. 36.

9. Mari-Lynn Evans, Holly George-Warren, and Robert Santelli, *The Appalachians: America's First and Last Frontier* (New York: Random House, 2004), p. 256; Thomas Slaughter, *The Whiskey Rebellion* (Oxford: Oxford University Press, 1986), p. 119.

10. Joseph J. Ellis, *After the Revolution: Profiles of Early American Culture* (New York: W. W. Norton, 2002), p. 103.

11. Boyd, *Whiskey Rebellion*, pp. 33–36.

12. George Washington, State of the Union address, October 25, 1791. Available at http://www.infoplease.com/t/hist/state-of-the-union/3.html.

13. George Washington, Presidential Proclamation of September 15, 1792. Available at http://www.presidency.ucsb.edu/ws/index.php?pid=65427.

14. John C. Hamilton, ed., *The Works of Alexander Hamilton* (New York: John F. Trow, Printer, 1850), p. 313.

15. Hogeland, *The Whiskey Rebellion*, p. 124.

16. How bad did the new wave of attacks become? In one instance, the local mob tarred and feathered a tavern owner who made the mistake of renting a room to one of the tax collectors. They later tore down his tavern. Ibid., p. 144.

17. John C. Fitzpatrick, ed., *The Writings of George Washington from the Original Manuscript Sources 1745–1799*, vol. 33: July 1, 1793–October 9, 1794 (Washington, DC: Government Printing Office, 1940), pp. 505–507.

18. Thomas Langston and Michael G. Sherman, *George Washington* (Washington, DC: CQ Press, 2003), p. 159. In the August 7 proclamation, Washington was careful to couch the threat of military force as a measure of last resort: "It is my judgment necessary under the circumstances of the case to take measures for calling forth the militia in order to suppress the combination aforesaid, and to cause the laws to be duly executed; and I have accordingly determined to do so, feeling the deepest regret for the occasion, but withal the most solemn conviction that the essential interests of the Union demand it, that the very existence of government and the fundamental principles of social order are materially involved in the issue, and that the patriotism and firmness of all good citizens are seriously called upon, as occasions may require, to aid in the effectual suppression of so fatal a spirit."

19. Hogeland, *Whiskey Rebellion*, pp. 186–87.

20. Michael Hoover, US Department of Treasury, "The Whiskey Rebellion." Available at http://www.ttb.gov/public_info/whisky_rebellion.shtml#4.

21. Fitzpatrick, *Writings of George Washington*, p. 465.

Chapter 2

1. Joseph J. Ellis, *American Sphinx: The Character of Thomas Jefferson* (New York: Random House, 1998), p. 243.

2. David Mayer, *The Constitutional Thought of Thomas Jefferson* (Charlottesville: University of Virginia, 1994), p. 119. Jefferson viewed his victory not so much a revolution but more a reaffirmation of the "original intent" of the revolution of 1776. "The storm through which we have passed," he wrote John Dickinson, a fellow alumnus of the Second Continental Congress, "has been tremendous indeed. The tough sides of our Argosie have been thoroughly tried. Her strength has stood the waves into which she was steered, with a view to sink her. We shall put her on the republican track, and she will now show by the beauty of her motion the skill of her builders." R. B. Bernstein, *Thomas Jefferson* (Oxford: Oxford University Press, 2003), p. 137.

3. Ellis, *American Sphinx*, p. 212.

4. With a near-hysteria sweeping through the Federalist camp over Jefferson's rumored plan to scrap the Constitution and dismantle the government, the one Federalist who stuck up for him, ironically enough, was Alexander Hamilton. It was a long, somewhat tortured defense, replete with a laundry list of insults, but Hamilton admitted that although Jefferson's "policies are tinctured with fanaticism, that he is too much in earnest in his democracy, that he has been a mischievous enemy to the principal measures of the past administration, that he is crafty and persevering in his objects, that he is not scrupulous about the means of success, nor very mindful of truth, and is a contemptible hypocrite," he was also likely to "temporize" his views, and the "result of such a temper is the preservation of systems, though originally opposed, which being once established, could not be overturned without danger to the person who did it. . . . A true estimate of Mr. J's character," Hamilton concluded, "warrants the expectation of a temporizing rather than a violent system." Hamilton couldn't have been more prescient. Ibid., p. 213.

5. Jefferson's First Inaugural. Available at http://avalon.law.yale.edu/19th _century/jefinau1.asp.

6. Ellis, *American Sphinx*, p. 226.

7. Ibid., p. 220.

8. Rita Mullin, *Thomas Jefferson: Architect of Freedom* (New York: Sterling Publishing, 2007), p. 85.

9. Letter from Lord Hawkesbury, British foreign secretary, to Rufus King, May 7, 1802. Fred Israel, ed., *Major Presidential Decisions* (New York: Chelsea House, 1980), p. 36.

10. Thomas Jefferson to Robert L. Livingston, April 18, 1802. Israel, *Major Presidential Decisions*, p. 38.

11. Forrest McDonald, *The Presidency of Thomas Jefferson* (Lawrence: University of Kansas Press, 1975), p. 64.

12. George Herring, *From Colony to Super Power: U.S. Foreign Relations since 1776* (Oxford: University of Oxford Press, 2008), p. 106. Just how big a role did Leclerc's defeat in Haiti play in the sale of the Louisiana Territory? According to Jefferson biographer John Ellis, a huge one: "If, then, one ever wished to construct a monument in New Orleans memorializing the Louisiana Purchase, Jefferson would have to be a central figure, but he would also need to be flanked by busts of Toussaint and his fellow black insurrectionaries, plus perhaps a tribute to the deadly mosquito." Ellis, *American Sphinx*, p. 247.

13. Letter from Thomas Jefferson to Pierre Samuel du Pont de Nemours, April 25, 1802. Israel, *Major Presidential Decisions*, p. 40. Jefferson's offer was to purchase both New Orleans and Florida, which the United States believed was part of the retrocession from Spain. Jefferson considered Florida much more valuable than the Louisiana Territory.

14. Letter from Pierre Samuel du Pont de Nemours to Thomas Jefferson, April 30, 1802. Ibid., p. 44.

15. Thomas Flemming, *The Louisiana Purchase* (New York: John Wiley & Sons, 2003), p. 59.

16. McDonald, *Presidency of Thomas Jefferson*, p. 67.

17. Letter from Robert Livingston and James Monroe to James Madison, May 13, 1803. Israel, *Major Presidential Decisions*, p. 63.

18. Noble Cunningham Jr., *In Pursuit of Reason: The Life of Thomas Jefferson* (Baton Rouge: Louisiana State University, 1987), p. 265.

19. James Parton, *Life of Thomas Jefferson* (Boston: Houghton, Osgood and Company, 1878), p. 654.

20. McDonald, *Presidency of Thomas Jefferson*, p. 69.

21. Letter from Thomas Jefferson to Albert Gallatin, January 1803, Israel, *Major Presidential Decisions*, p. 164; Mayer, *Constitutional Thought of Thomas Jefferson*, p. 245.

22. Mayer, *Constitutional Thought of Thomas Jefferson*, p. 245; letter from Thomas Jefferson to Senator John Breckinridge of Kentucky, August 12, 1802, Israel, *Major Presidential Decisions*, p. 165; letter from Thomas Jefferson to Attorney General Levi Lincoln, August 30, 1803, Israel, *Major Presidential Decisions*, p. 168.

23. Letter from Thomas Jefferson to Senator Wilson Cary Nicholas of Virginia, September 7, 1803, Israel, *Major Presidential Decisions*, p. 170.

24. Mayer, *Constitutional Thought of Thomas Jefferson*, p. 250.

25. Moncure Conway, *The Life of Thomas Paine*, vol. 2 (New York: G. P Putnam's Sons, 1908), p. 332.

26. Albert Ellery Bergh, ed., *The Writings of Thomas Jefferson*, vol. 11 (Washington, DC: Thomas Jefferson Memorial Association, 1907), pp. 418–22.

Chapter 3

1. The following passage in the Kentucky Resolution of 1798 made the most forceful case in favor of nullification: "that in cases of an abuse of the delegated powers, the members of the general government, being chosen by the people, a change by the people would be the constitutional remedy; but, where powers are assumed which have not been delegated, a nullification of the act is the rightful remedy: that every State has a natural right in cases not within the compact, (casus non fœderis) to nullify of their own authority all assumptions of power by others within their limits: that without this right, they would be under the dominion, absolute and unlimited, of whosoever might exercise this right of judgment for them: that nevertheless, this commonwealth, from motives of regard and respect for its co-States, has wished to communicate with them on the subject: that with them alone it is proper to communicate, they alone being parties to the compact, and solely authorized to judge in the last resort of the powers exercised under it." The full text of the Kentucky Resolution can be found online at http://www.constitution.org/cons/kent1798.htm.

2. Because he was vice president when the Alien and Sedition Acts were passed, Thomas Jefferson kept his authorship of the Kentucky Resolution a secret for fear of being labeled a traitor to the administration or worse. It remained that way for over two decades until he finally owned up to writing it in 1821. B. B. Oberg, ed., *The Papers of Thomas Jefferson*, vol. 30: 1 January 1798 to 31 January 1799 (Princeton, NJ: Princeton University Press, 2003), pp. 529–56. Available at http://www.princeton.edu/~tjpapers/kyres/kyednote.html.

3. Orrin Leslie Elliott, *The Tariff Controversy in the United States, 1789–1833* (Palo Alto: Stanford University Press, 1892), p. 57.

4. Frederick Jackson Turner, *Chapter XIV: The Tariff of 1824*, http://historion.net/rise-new-west-1819–1829/chapter-xiv-tariff-1824–1820–1824?page=2.

5. The Tariff of 1824 dramatically increased the federal government's annual revenues from approximately $24 million (the average revenues in the four years prior to the tariff) to nearly $29 million (the average revenues in the four years after

the tariff). Andrew Stewart, *The American System: Speeches on the Tariff System and Internal Improvements* (Philadelphia: Henry Carey Baird Publishing, 1872), p. 34.

6. Said Henry Clay of Andrew Jackson: "I cannot believe that killing 2,500 Englishmen at New Orleans qualifies for the various, difficult, and complicated duties of the Chief Magistracy." Glyndon Garlock Van Deusen, *The Life of Henry Clay* (Westport, CT: Greenwood Press, 1979), p. 183.

7. Six men have served as both secretary of state and president—all prior to the Civil War: Thomas Jefferson served as Washington's secretary of state; James Madison served as Jefferson's secretary of state; James Monroe served as Madison's secretary of state; John Quincy Adams served as Monroe's secretary of state; Martin Van Buren served as Andrew Jackson's secretary of state; and James Buchanan served as James K. Polk's secretary of state. Will Hillary Clinton be the next?

8. *South Carolina Historical and Genealogical Magazine* 3 (January 1902): 186; Daniel Walker Howe, *What Hath God Wrought: The Transformation of America, 1815–1848* (Oxford: Oxford University Press, 2007), p. 250.

9. Howe, *What God Hath Wrought*, p. 250.

10. Andrew Lenner, *The Federal Principle in American Politics, 1790–1833* (Lanham, MD: Rowman & Littlefield, 2001), p. 167.

11. Herman V. Ames, *State Documents on Federal Relations* (New York: Longmans, Green & Co. 1911), pp. 152–55. Available at http://www.constitution.org/hames/sdfr.htm; Frederic Bancroft, *Calhoun and the South Carolina Nullification Movement* (Baltimore: John Hopkins Press, 1928), pp. 14–16.

12. The election of 1828 would not mark the end of John Quincy Adams's political career. He would go on to serve as a distinguished member of the House of Representatives from 1831 until his death in 1848—the only former president to serve in that body. Robert Vincent Remini, *John Quincy Adams* (New York: Times Books, 2002), p. 131.

13. F. W. Taussig, *The Tariff History of the United States* (New York: G. P. Putnam's Sons, 1892), p. 88.

14. H. W. Brands, *Andrew Jackson: His Life and Times* (New York: Doubleday, 2005), pp. 440–42; Bancroft, *Calhoun and the South Carolina Nullification Movement*, pp. 41–44.

15. Robert V. Remini, *Andrew Jackson and the Course of American Freedom, 1822–1832*, vol. 2 (New York: Harper & Row, 1981), pp. 175–76; John Meacham, *American Lion: Andrew Jackson in the White House* (New York: Random House, 2008), pp. 57–58.

16. Ibid., Brands, *Andrew Jackson*, pp. 434–35. "Historic Speeches: 1829 State of the Union Address," http://www.presidentialrhetoric.com/historicspeeches/jackson/stateoftheunion1829.html.

17. The debate created one of the most memorable rhetorical flourishes in Senate history. Said Webster of preserving the Union: "When my eyes shall be turned to behold for the last time the sun in heaven, may I not see him shining on the broken and dishonored fragments of a once glorious Union; on States dissevered, discordant, belligerent; on a land rent with civil feuds, or drenched, it may be, in fraternal blood! Let their last feeble and lingering glance rather behold the gorgeous ensign of the republic . . . not a stripe erased or polluted, nor a single star obscured, bearing for its motto, no such miserable interrogatory as 'What is all this worth?' nor those other words of delusion and folly, 'Liberty first and Union afterwards'; but everywhere, spread all over in characters of living light, blazing on all its ample folds, as they float over the sea and over the land, and in every wind under the whole heavens, that other sentiment, dear to every true American heart,—Liberty *and* Union, now and for ever, one and inseparable!" Brands, *Andrew Jackson*, p. 443.

18. J. K. Brennan, *The World's Progress* (Chicago: Delphian Society, 1913), p. 66.

19. Remini, *Andrew Jackson*, 2:233.

20. Ibid., pp. 233–35; Brands, *Andrew Jackson*, p. 435.

21. Regarding the toasts, Jackson would later confide that he could not bear to hear the "dissolution of the Union spoken of lightly." Remini, *Andrew Jackson*, 2:233; Meacham, *American Lion*, p. 135; Brands, *Andrew Jackson*, p. 445; Richard B. Latner, *The Presidency of Andrew Jackson* (Athens: University of Georgia Press, 1979), p. 70. The Democratic Party's annual fundraising gala is now called the Jefferson-Jackson Day gala in honor of Thomas Jefferson, founder of the Democratic-Republicans, and Andrew Jackson, founder of the modern-day Democratic Party.

22. Merrill D. Peterson, *The Great Triumvirate: Webster, Clay and Calhoun* (Oxford: Oxford University Press, 1987), pp. 214–15.

23. John Spencer Bassett, ed., *Correspondence of Andrew Jackson*, vol. 4 (Washington, DC: Carnegie Institution of Washington, 1929), p. 374.

24. Remini, *Andrew Jackson*, 2:332. Remini writes eloquently about Jackson's restraint and statesmanship during the merchant episode: "The wisdom Jackson displayed in this single, minor episode demonstrated clearly his steady emergence as a statesman of the first rank. He understood the gravity of the issue but he did not rush to hasty action. He also understood the duty of enforcing the law. He showed conviction and determination in complying with his duty, which he conveyed to the public and the press" (p. 333).

25. Richard Ellis, *The Union at Risk: Jacksonian Democracy, States' Rights, and the Nullification Crisis* (Oxford: Oxford University Press, 1987), p. 4.

26. In the Fort Hill address, Calhoun reiterated that the Constitution was

little more than a "compact" between the states, and cited Jefferson's and Madison's Kentucky and Virginia Resolutions as controlling authority: "The Constitution of the United States is, in fact, a compact, to which each State is a party. . . . States, or parties, have a right to judge of its infractions; and in case of a deliberate, palpable, and dangerous exercise of power not delegated, they have the right, in the last resort, to use the language of the Virginia Resolutions, 'to interpose for arresting the progress of the evil, and for maintaining, within their respective limits, the authorities, rights, and liberties appertaining to them.'" Available at http://www.thevrwc.org/Calhoun.pdf.

27. The relevant passage of Jackson's annual Message to Congress, where he called for tariff reduction (delivered on December 6, 1831): "The confidence with which the extinguishment of the public debt may be anticipated presents an opportunity for carrying into effect more fully the policy in relation to import duties which has been recommended in my former messages. A modification of the tariff which shall produce a reduction of our revenue to the wants of the Government and an adjustment of the duties on imports with a view to equal justice in relation to all our national interests and to the counteraction of foreign policy so far as it may be injurious to those interests, is deemed to be one of the principal objects which demand the consideration of the present Congress. Justice to the interests of the merchant as well as the manufacturer requires that material reductions in the import duties be prospective; and unless the present Congress shall dispose of the subject the proposed reductions can not properly be made to take effect at the period when the necessity for the revenue arising from present rates shall cease. It is therefore desirable that arrangements be adopted at your present session to relieve the people from unnecessary taxation after the extinguishment of the public debt. In the exercise of that spirit of concession and conciliation which has distinguished the friends of our Union in all great emergencies, it is believed that this object may be effected without injury to any national interest." Available at http://www.synaptic.bc.ca/ejournal/JacksonThirdAnnualMessage.htm.

28. Bassett, *Correspondence of Andrew Jackson*, 4:374.

29. Latner, *Presidency of Jackson*, pp. 146–47; Remini, *Andrew Jackson*, 2:361.

30. Remini, *Andrew Jackson*, 2:361.

31. Ibid.

32. Merrill D. Peterson, *Olive Branch and Sword—The Compromise of 1833* (Baton Rouge: Louisiana State University Press, 1982), p. 39.

33. Remini, *Andrew Jackson*, 2:361.

34. Meacham, *American Lion*, p. 222.

35. Remini, *Andrew Jackson*, 3:28. The South Carolina state legislature assumed that the Nullification Ordinance would receive a positive reception

from the other Southern states. It didn't. Georgia lawmakers called it "rash and revolutionary"; Alabama found the doctrine "unsound in theory and dangerous in practice"; "reckless precipitancy" was how the Mississippi legislature described it. Ibid., p. 42.

36. Brands, *Andrew Jackson*, p. 475.

37. Jackson biographer Robert V. Remini may have summed it up best (in describing the legacy of the proclamation): "Jackson never so much deserved the trust and confidence and love of the American people as he did at this moment. It was a superb state paper. Little in it needed improvements. Indeed, Abraham Lincoln later extracted from it the basic argument he needed to explain and justify his intended course of action to meet succession in 1861. The proclamation is a major statement in constitutional law. It came about only because Jackson was a statesman of the first rank." Remini, *Andrew Jackson*, 3:23.

38. Brands, *Andrew Jackson*, p. 477; Remini, *Andrew Jackson*, 3:12–13; Joel Poinsett to Jackson, November 16, 1832, Bassett, *Correspondence of Andrew Jackson*, 4:486.

39. Jackson to Lewis Cass, December 17, 1832, Bassett, *Correspondence of Andrew Jackson*, 4:502; Remini, *Andrew Jackson*, 3:26.

40. Remini, *Andrew Jackson*, 3:20–21; Brands, *Andrew Jackson*, p. 478.

41. Remini, *Andrew Jackson*, 3:20.

42. Jackson's second inaugural is widely considered among the finest in history and worth reading in its entirety. Available at Yale Law School, Avalon Project: Documents in Law, History and Diplomacy, http://avalon.law.yale.edu/19th_century/jackson2.asp.

Chapter 4

1. Letter from John Jay to R. Lushington, March 15, 1786; Henry Johnston, ed., *The Correspondence and Public Papers of John Jay*, vol. 3 (New York: G. P. Putnam's Sons, 1891), p. 185.

2. Gordon S. Wood, *The Americanization of Benjamin Franklin* (New York: Penguin Group, 2004), p. 227. Of all the founders, Franklin by far held the most progressive views on slavery and race. Beyond just emancipation, he believed in a sort of affirmative action to help assimilate freed slaves into society. Emancipation was a good first step, he wrote, but it was critical "to instruct, and advise, and qualify those, who have been restored to freedom, for the exercise and enjoyment of civil liberty, to promote in them habits of industry, to furnish them with employments suited to their age, sex, talents and other circumstances, and

to procure their children an education calculated for their future situation in life." Ibid.

3. Letter from Patrick Henry to Robert Pleasants, January 18, 1783; Gary B. Nash, *The Unknown American Revolution: The Unruly Birth of Democracy and the Struggle to Create America* (New York: Penguin Group, 2005), p. 118.

4. Lawrence B. Evans, ed., *The Writings of George Washington* (New York: G. P. Putnam's Son, 1908), p. 525. In his 1786 letter to Lafayette, Washington goes on to mention how "some petitions were presented to the Assembly, at its last session, for the abolition of slavery, but they could scarcely obtain a reading. To set them afloat at once would, I really believe, be productive of much inconvenience and mischief; but by degrees it certainly might, and assuredly ought to be effected; and that too by legislative authority." Ibid.

5. R. B. Berstein, *The Founding Fathers Reconsidered* (Oxford: Oxford University Press, 2009), pp. 97–99.

6. Technically, the Missouri Compromise was the second time Congress had banned slavery from a new territory. Under the Articles of Confederation, Congress banned slavery from the Northwest Territories in 1787, which the following Congress (in adherence to the newly created Constitution) adopted with several minor modifications.

7. Letter from Thomas Jefferson to John Holmes, April 22, 1820. Available at http://www.loc.gov/exhibits/jefferson/159.html. Jefferson's letter to Holmes is remarkably clairvoyant and worth reading in its entirety: "I thank you, Dear Sir, for the copy you have been so kind as to send me of the letter to your constituents on the Missouri question. It is a perfect justification to them. I had for a long time ceased to read the newspapers or pay any attention to public affairs, confident they were in good hands, and content to be a passenger in our bark to the shore from which I am not distant. But this momentous question, like a fire bell in the night, awakened and filled me with terror. I considered it at once as the knell of the Union. It is hushed indeed for the moment. But this is a reprieve only, not a final sentence. A geographical line, coinciding with a marked principle, moral and political, once conceived and held up to the angry passions of men, will never be obliterated; and every new irritation will mark it deeper and deeper. I can say with conscious truth that there is not a man on earth who would sacrifice more than I would, to relieve us from this heavy reproach, in any *practicable* way. The cession of that kind of property, for so it is misnamed, is a bagatelle which would not cost me in a second thought, if, in that way, a general emancipation and *expatriation* could be effected: and, gradually, and with due sacrifices, I think it might be. But, as it is, we have the wolf by the ear, and we can neither hold him, nor safely let him go. Justice is in one scale, and self-preservation in the other. Of one thing I am certain, that as the passage

of slaves from one state to another would not make a slave of a single human being who would not be so without it, so their diffusion over a greater surface would make them individually happier and proportionally facilitate the accomplishment of their emancipation, by dividing the burthen on a greater number of co-adjutors. An abstinence too from this act of power would remove the jealousy excited by the undertaking of Congress, to regulate the condition of the different descriptions of men composing a state. This certainly is the exclusive right of every state, which nothing in the constitution has taken from them and given to the general government. Could congress, for example say that the Non-freemen of Connecticut shall be freemen, or that they shall not emigrate into any other state? I regret that I am now to die in the belief that the useless sacrifice of themselves, by the generation of 1776, to acquire self-government and happiness to their country, is to be thrown away by the unwise and unworthy passions of their sons, and that my only consolation is to be that I live not to weep over it. If they would but dispassionately weigh the blessings they will throw away against an abstract principle more likely to be affected by union than by scission, they would pause before they would perpetrate this act of suicide on themselves and of treason against the hopes of the world."

8. For a complete ranking of the presidents, see my book *President's Most Wanted* (Virginia: Potomac Books, 2008).

9. Michael Johnson, ed., *Abraham Lincoln, Slavery, and the Civil War, Selected Writings and Speeches* (New York: St. Martin's Press, 2001), p. 23.

10. Ibid., pp. 46–47.

11. Ibid., p. 47.

12. Ibid., p. 49.

13. Roy P. Basler, ed., *Abraham Lincoln, His Speeches and Writings* (Cleveland: De Capo Press, 2001), p. 333.

14. Johnson, *Abraham Lincoln: Selected Writings*, p. 58.

15. Basler, *Abraham Lincoln*, p. 426.

16. Johnson, *Abraham Lincoln*, p. 72.

17. Ibid.

18. Marion Mills Miller, ed., *Great Debates in American History*, vol. 5, *States' Rights (1798–1861), Slavery (1858–1861)* (New York: Current Literature Publishing Company, 1913), p. 127. Douglas seized on Lincoln's theme of equality to portray him as a radical abolitionist out of touch with the majority of Illinois residents: "I ask you, are you in favor of conferring upon the negro the rights and privileges of citizenship? Do you desire to strike out of our State Constitution that clause which keeps slaves and free negroes out of the State, and allow the free negroes to flow in, and cover your prairies with black settlements? Do you desire to turn this beautiful State into a free negro colony, in order that

when Missouri abolishes slavery she can send one hundred thousand emancipated slaves into Illinois, to become citizens and voters, on an equality with yourselves? If you desire negro citizenship, if you desire to allow them to come into the State and settle with the white man, if you desire them to vote on an equality with yourselves, and to make them eligible to office, to serve on juries, and to adjudge your rights, then support Mr. Lincoln and the Black Republican party, who are in favor of the citizenship of the negro. For one, I am opposed to negro citizenship in any and every form. I believe this Government was made on the white basis. I believe it was made by white men, for the benefit of white men and their posterity forever, and I am in favor of confining citizenship to white men, men of European birth and descent, instead of conferring it upon negroes, Indians, and other inferior races."

19. Johnson, *Abraham Lincoln*, p. 74.

20. Ibid., p. 75.

21. Ibid., pp. 79–80.

22. Richard D. Heffner, *A Documentary History of the United States* (New York: Signet, 2002), p. 172.

23. Allen Guelzo, *Lincoln's Emancipation Proclamation: The End of Slavery in America* (New York: Simon & Schuster, 2004).

24. William Klingaman, *Abraham Lincoln and the Road to Emancipation* (New York: Viking, 2001), p. 127.

25. David Herbert Donald, *Lincoln* (New York: Simon & Schuster, 1995), p. 347.

26. Ibid., p. 347; Herbert Mitgang, ed., *Abraham Lincoln: A Press Portrait* (Chicago: Quadrangle Books, 1971), p. 290.

27. "Oh how I wish the Border States would accept my proposition," Lincoln lamented to two allies in Congress. Then "all of us would not have lived in vain!" Donald, *Lincoln*, p. 362.

28. Ibid., p. 352.

29. Guelzo, *Lincoln*, p. 99.

30. James Horton and Lois Horton, *Slavery and the Making of America* (Oxford: Oxford University Press, 2005), p. 179.

31. Guelzo, *Lincoln*, p. 122.

32. Donald, *Lincoln*, p. 363.

33. Stephen Oates, *With Malice Toward None: A Life of Abraham Lincoln* (New York: HarperCollins, 1977), p. 321.

34. Donald, *Lincoln*, pp. 367–68; Harry J. Maihafer, *War of Words: Abraham Lincoln and the Civil War Press* (Dulles, VA: Brassey's, 2001), pp. 80–81; Mark Scroggins, *Hannibal: The Life of Abraham Lincoln's First Vice President* (Lanham, MD: University Press of America, 1994), p. 189; Guezlo, *Lincoln*, p. 178.

35. Klingaman, *Abraham Lincoln*, p. 198; Donald, *Lincoln*, pp. 377–80.

36. Klingaman, *Abraham Lincoln*, p. 200.

37. Guelzo, *Lincoln*, p. 206.

38. Ibid., p. 186; Allen C. Guelzo, *Lincoln: A Very Short Introduction* (Oxford: Oxford University Press, 2009), p. 106; Henry Jarvis Raymond and Francis Bicknell, *The Life and Public Services of Abraham Lincoln* (New York: Derby and Miller, 1865), p. 764.

Chapter 5

1. Edmund Morris, *Theodore Rex* (New York: Random House, 2001), p. 351.

2. Alexander Missal, *Seaway to the Future: American Social Visions and the Construction of the Panama Canal* (Madison: University of Wisconsin, 2008), p. 21; Fred J. Haskin, *The Panama Canal* (New York: Doubleday, Page & Company, 1913), p. 195.

3. Lindley M. Keasbey, *The Nicaragua Canal and the Monroe Doctrine* (New York: G. P. Putnam's Sons, 1896), p. 120.

4. Missal, *Seaway to the Future*, p. 22. German poet Johann Goethe, inspired no doubt by the writings of his countryman Alexander von Humboldt, made a Nostradamus-esque prediction in 1827 about America's role in a future isthmus crossing. "I would be surprised if the United States would miss the chance to get such a work [the canal] into her hands. It is to be foreseen that this young State, with its decided tendency toward the West, will in thirty to forty years have also taken possession, and will have populated the large areas of land on the side of the Rocky Mountains. It is furthermore to be foreseen that in this entire coast of the Pacific Ocean, where nature had already created the most roomy and safest harbors, in course of time very important commercial towns will carry on a large traffic between China and the East Indies with the United States. . . . I therefore repeat that it is entirely indispensable for the United States to make a passage from the Gulf of Mexico to the Pacific Ocean, and I am certain that she will accomplish it." Richard H. Collin, *Theodore Roosevelt's Caribbean: The Panama Canal, the Monroe Doctrine, and the Latin American Context* (Baton Rouge: Louisiana State University, 1990), p. 128.

5. William Kennish, *The Practicability and Importance of a Ship Canal to Connect the Atlantic and Pacific Oceans* (New York: George F. Nesbitt & Company, 1855), p. 76.

6. David Bushnell, *The Making of Modern Colombia: A Nation in Spite of Itself* (Los Angeles: University of California Press, 1993), p. 99; Missal, *Seaway*, p. 22.

7. Ralph Avery, *America's Triumph at Panama* (Chicago: L. W. Walter Company, 1913), p. 58.

8. Initially found guilty of fraud and sentenced to prison, Ferdinand de Lesseps's verdict was overturned by the Court de Cessation on the grounds that the three-year statute of limitations had expired. He would die a broken and disgraced figure. James MacGregor Burns, *Transforming Leadership* (New York: Grove Press, 2003), p. 129.

9. Henry Hendrix, *Theodore Roosevelt's Naval Diplomacy: The U.S. Navy and the Birth of the American Century* (Annapolis: Naval Institute Press, 2009), p. 11.

10. Interestingly, Roosevelt's *Naval War of 1812* was so well regarded by the naval brass and so persuasive in its conclusions that the seas held the key to America's future that it convinced the navy to spend $1.3 million on three state-of-the-art warships in 1882. Nathan Miller, *Theodore Roosevelt: A Life* (New York: William Morrow and Company, 1992), p. 129.

11. Hendrix, *Theodore Roosevelt's Naval Diplomacy*, p. 8.

12. Ibid., p. 10.

13. Ibid.

14. Miller, *Theodore Roosevelt*, p. 250.

15. Missal, *Seaway*, p. 33; Miller, *Theodore Roosevelt*, p. 251.

16. Miller, *Theodore Roosevelt*, p. 257.

17. The "Strenuous Life" speech, available at http://www.bartleby.com/58/1.html; David McCullough, *The Path between the Seas: The Creation of the Panama Canal 1870–1914* (New York: Simon & Schuster, 1977), p. 254; Miller, *Theodore Roosevelt*, p. 330.

18. Joseph B. Bishop, *Theodore Roosevelt and His Times* (New York: Charles Scribner's Son's, 1920), pp. 143–44. McCullough, *Path between the Seas*, pp. 256–57.

19. Morris, *Theodore Rex*, pp. 25–26; McCullough, *Path between the Seas*, p. 259; Miller, *Theodore Roosevelt*, p. 400.

20. McCullough, *Path between the Seas*, p. 261.

21. Ibid., p. 264.

22. Matthew Parker, *Panama Fever: The Battle to Build the Canal* (London: Hutchison, 1988), p. 253; Miller, *Theodore Roosevelt*, p. 404; Morris, *Theodore Rex*, p. 718.

23. McCullough, *Path between the Seas*, p. 319.

24. Parker, *Panama Fever*, p. 185.

25. Morris, *Theodore Rex*, p. 116.

26. Miller, *Theodore Roosevelt*, p. 405. Congress authorized Roosevelt to spend $40 million to purchase the French assets and rights, making it the most expensive land acquisition in United States history up to that point. He was given another $130 million in construction funds. Morris, *Theodore Rex*, p. 116.

27. *Hearings on the Rainey Resolution before the Committee on Foreign Affairs of the House of Representatives* (Washington: Government Printing Office, 1913), p. 673; Letter from Arthur Beaupre to John Hay, May 4, 1903, *Theodore Roosevelt Collection*; McCullough, *Path between the Seas*, p. 333.

28. *Hearings on the Rainey Resolution*, p. 342; Morris, *Theodore Rex*, p. 240.

29. *Hearings on the Rainey Resolution*, p. 345; Morris, *Theodore Rex*, p. 242; McCullough, *Path between the Seas*, p. 334.

30. McCullough, *Path between the Seas*, p. 339; Morris, *Theodore Rex*, p. 263; *Hearings on the Rainey Resolution*, pp. 352–54.

31. Henry Pringle, *Theodore Roosevelt: A Biography* (New York: Mariner Press, 2003), p. 311; McCullough, *Path between the Seas*, p. 340; Morris, *Theodore Rex*, p. 264; Bishop, *Theodore Roosevelt and His Times*, p. 276.

32. John Bassett Moore Memorandum of August 1903; Dwight Carroll Minor, *The Fight for the Panama Route* (New York: Octagon Books, 1966), p. 427.

33. Bishop, *Theodore Roosevelt and His Times*, pp. 278–79; Morris, *Theodore Rex*, p. 268; McCullough, *Path between the Seas*, p. 341.

34. Morris, *Theodore Rex*, p. 268.

35. Theodore Roosevelt, *Theodore Roosevelt: An Autobiography* (New York: Charles Scribner's Son, 1913), pp. 514–16.

36. Parker, *Panama Fever*, p. 231; McCullough, *Path between the Seas*, p. 351.

37. McCullough, *Path between the Seas*, p. 351.

38. Ibid., p. 354. Interestingly, Hay left Bunau-Varilla with a parting gift that day, the latest book by adventure writer Richard Harding Davis. It was about a young American who runs off to Central America to join a revolutionary army under the command of a charismatic French leader. Bunau-Varilla devoured it on the train ride back to New York, his confidence in US support growing with each passing page. Morris, *Theodore Rex*, p. 277.

39. Ibid., p. 281.

40. Ibid., p. 297.

41. McCullough, *Path between the Seas*, p. 381; Morris, *Theodore Rex*, p. 295.

42. Morris, *Theodore Rex*, p. 297.

43. Theodore Roosevelt, State of the Union address, January 4, 1904; *Hearings on the Rainey Resolution*, p. 578.

44. Missal, *Seaway to the Future*, p. 42.

45. Bishop, *Theodore Roosevelt and His Times*, p. 308.

46. Walter Lafeber, *Panama Canal: Crisis in Historical Perspective* (Oxford: Oxford University Press, 1978), p. 49. The Senate eventually ratified a new treaty with Colombia in 1921 that included the $25 million indemnification but did not contain a formal apology. In the intervening years since the canal

opened, Colombia had become a major oil-producing nation, and American companies were eager to do business in the country.

47. Bishop, *Theodore Roosevelt and His Times*, p. 308.

Chapter 6

1. With 27 percent of the popular tally and eighty-eight electoral votes, Theodore Roosevelt registered the highest totals of any third-party candidate since the advent of the two major parties. Taft turned in the worst performance of any incumbent president in history with 23 percent of the popular vote and just eight electoral votes.

2. Helen Thomas and Craig Crawford, *Listen Up, Mr. President: Everything You Always Wanted Your President to Know and Do* (New York: Scribner, 2009), p. 25.

3. One of Wilson's first acts as president was to overturn a law passed by the previous Congress (which had large Democratic majorities in both chambers) that exempted US ships from paying any tolls to pass through the Panama Canal. In 1912, Taft had signed the bill into law over Great Britain's protestation. Wilson agreed with Great Britain that this policy was unfair and, with some twisting of arms in Congress, had the provision repealed. J. Holland Rose and E. A. Benians, *The Cambridge History of the British Empire*, vol. 3 (Cambridge: Cambridge University Press, 1959), p. 331.

4. Woodrow Wilson, *The Messages and Papers of Woodrow Wilson*, vol. 1 (New York: Review of Reviews Corporation, 1924), p. 372.

5. John Milton Cooper, *The Warrior and the Priest: Woodrow Wilson and Theodore Roosevelt* (Cambridge, MA: Harvard University Press, 1983), p. 310.

6. Woodrow Wilson's Flag Day address of June 14, 1917; Wilson, *Messages and Papers*, p. 412.

7. Wilson, *Messages and Papers*, p. 411. Wilson may have understood the Allied Powers' desire for vengeance, but it didn't mean that he agreed with it: "England and France have not the same views with regard to peace that we have by any means," he told Edward "Colonel" House, a close advisor. "If there is to be an interchange of views at all, it ought to be between us and the liberals in Germany, with no one else brought in." John Milton Cooper, *Woodrow Wilson: A Biography* (New York: Alfred A. Knopf, 2009), p. 417.

8. Woodrow Wilson's Fifth Annual Message to Congress, December 4, 1917; Wilson, *Messages and Papers*, pp. 443–53; Cooper, *Woodrow Wilson*, p. 420.

9. H. W. Brands, *Woodrow Wilson* (New York: Times Books, 2003), p. 89; Cooper, *Wilson*, p. 419.

10. "Wilson's Address to Congress, Stating the War Aims and Peace Terms of the United States," January 8, 1918; Wilson, *Messages and Papers*, p. 464; Cooper, *Wilson*, p. 422.

11. Cooper, *Wilson*, p. 422; Wilson, *Messages and Papers*, p. 472.

12. Cooper, *Wilson*, p. 424.

13. "Wilson's Address to Congress, Analyzing German and Austrian Peace Utterances," February 11, 1918; Wilson, *Messages and Papers*, p. 479.

14. Cooper, *Wilson*, pp. 429, 439.

15. "Wilson's Address at Mount Vernon, Voicing the War Objects of the Associated People of the World," July 4, 1918; Wilson, *Messages and Papers*, p. 500.

16. "Wilson's Address Opening the New York Campaign for the Fourth Liberty Loan," September 27, 1918; Wilson, *Messages and Papers*, pp. 523–25.

17. Cooper, *Wilson*, p. 442.

18. Ibid., p. 448.

19. Peter Neville, *Hitler and Appeasement: The British Attempt to Prevent the Second World War* (London: Hambledon Continuum, 2006), p. 1; Cooper, *Wilson*, p. 451.

20. Cooper, *Wilson*, p. 445; John Milton Cooper, *Breaking the Heart of the World: Woodrow Wilson and the Fight for the League of Nations* (Cambridge: Cambridge University Press, 2001), p. 35.

21. Ibid., p. 457.

22. Ibid, pp. 474–75; Cooper, *Breaking the Heart of the World*, p. 54.

23. Joseph Hernon, *Profiles in Character: Hubris and Heroism in the U.S. Senate* (Armonk, NY: M. E. Sharpe, 1997), p. 142; Cooper, *Wilson*, p. 477.

24. Cooper, *Wilson*, p. 507.

25. Ibid., p. 511.

26. Ibid., p. 514.

27. Ibid., pp. 520–22.

28. Ibid., pp. 527–28.

29. Ibid., p. 529.

Chapter 7

1. While the Johnson Act banned private Americans from making loans to debtor countries, it did not prevent the United States government from loaning to countries in default. Edwin Borchard, *State Insolvency and Foreign Bondholders* (New Haven, CT: Yale University Press, 1961), p. 175.

2. Congress was heavily influenced by Walter Millis's 1935 bestselling

book, *Road to War: America, 1914–17*, in which he posited that America, by virtue of its wartime trade with the Allied Powers, had become a "silent partner of the Entente." The book concluded that the only way to prevent America from being drawn into another European conflict was through strict neutrality laws that banned all trade with belligerent nations. Robert Dalleck, *Franklin Roosevelt and American Foreign Policy, 1932–1945* (New York: Oxford University Press, 1979), p. 102. "By the mid-thirties," writes historian Robert Dalleck, "America generally believed that involvement in World War I had been a mistake, that Wilson's freedom to take unneutral steps had pushed the country into fighting, and that only strict limitations on presidential discretion could keep this from happening again." Ibid., p. 109.

3. Ibid., p. 110.

4. Ibid., p. 144.

5. Ibid.

6. Barbara Rearden Farnham, *Roosevelt and the Munich Crisis: A Study of Political Decision Making* (Princeton, NJ: Princeton University Press, 1997), p. 61.

7. Ibid., p. 101.

8. Conrad Black, *Franklin Delano Roosevelt: Champion of Freedom* (New York: Public Affairs, 2003), p. 451.

9. Dalleck, *Franklin Roosevelt and Foreign Policy*, p. 140.

10. Quarantine Speech, Chicago, Illinois, October 5, 1937; B. D. Zevin, ed., *Nothing to Fear: The Selected Addresses of Franklin D. Roosevelt* (New York: Houghton Mifflin Company, 1946), p. 110.

11. Wayne S. Cole, *Roosevelt and the Isolationists: 1932–1945* (Lincoln: University of Nebraska Press, 1983), pp. 246–47.

12. Dalleck, *Franklin Roosevelt and Foreign Policy*, p. 106.

13. While the British public initially hailed Chamberlain for averting another total war, Winston Churchill—still a backbencher at this point—was a bit more circumspect. "Do not suppose that this is the end," said Churchill shortly after the Munich summit. "This is only the beginning of reckoning. This is only the first sip, the first foretaste of a bitter cup which will be proffered to us year by year unless, by a supreme recovery of moral health and martial vigor, we arise again and take our stand for freedom as in the olden time." Dalleck, *Franklin Roosevelt and Foreign Policy*, p. 171.

14. Ibid., p. 172.

15. Ibid., p. 181.

16. Cole, *Roosevelt and the Isolationists*, p. 306.

17. The American Presidency Project: Excerpts from the Press Conference in Warm Springs, Georgia, March 31, 1939. Online reference: http://www.presidency.ucsb.edu/ws/index.php?pid=15733.

18. The American Presidency Project: Excerpts from the Press Conference in Warm Springs, George, April 8, 1939. Online reference: http://www.presidency.ucsb.edu/ws/index.php?pid=15735.

19. The American Presidency Project: Address to the Governing Board of the Pan-American Union, April 14, 1939. Online reference: http://www.presidency.ucsb.edu/ws/index.php?pid=15740&st=pan+american&st1=; Dalleck, *Franklin Roosevelt and Foreign Policy*, p. 185.

20. Ibid., p. 187.

21. Cole, *Roosevelt and the Isolationists*, p. 315; Dalleck, *Franklin Roosevelt and Foreign Policy*, p. 191.

22. Dalleck, *Franklin Roosevelt and Foreign Policy*, p. 198.

23. Black, *Franklin Delano Roosevelt*, p. 532.

24. "Address Delivered by President Roosevelt to Congress," September 21, 1939; Zevin, *Nothing to Fear*, p. 183. Available at http://teachingamericanhistory.org/library/index.asp?document=706.

25. Black, *Franklin Delano Roosevelt*, p. 537.

26. Franklin Roosevelt, State of the Union address, January 3, 1940. Available at http://stateoftheunion.onetwothree.net/texts/19400103.html.

27. Doris Kearns Goodwin, *No Ordinary Time* (New York: Simon & Schuster, 1994), p. 41.

28. Jon Meacham, *Franklin and Winston: An Intimate Portrait of an Epic Friendship* (New York: Random House, 2003), p. 48.

29. Ibid., p. 49.

30. Ibid.

31. Address before a joint session of the Senate and House of Representatives asking additional appropriations for national defense, May 16, 1940. Available at http://www.ibiblio.org/pha/7-2-188/188-16.html.

32. David Reynolds, *From Munich to Pearl Harbor: Roosevelt's America and the Origins of the Second World War* (Chicago: Ivan R. Dee, 2001), p. 78.

33. Goodwin, *No Ordinary Time*, p. 61.

34. Ibid.

35. Ibid., p. 64; Meacham, *Franklin and Winston*, p. 53.

36. George Marshall, the army chief of staff, was hesitant to classify the military supplies as "surplus materials" but relented under intense pressure from Roosevelt. "It was the only time that I recall that I did something that there was a certain amount of duplicity in it," said Marshall. Goodwin, *No Ordinary Time*, p. 66.

37. Winston S. Churchill, *Never Give In! The Best of Winston Churchill's Speeches* (London: Easton Press, 2003), p. 218.

38. John Grafton, ed., *Franklin Roosevelt: Great Speeches* (Mineola: Dover, 1999), p. 76.

39. Meacham, *Franklin and Winston*, pp. 60–61.

40. Reynolds, *From Munich to Pearl Harbor*, p. 86; Goodwin, *No Ordinary Time*, p. 142; Meacham, *Franklin and Winston*, pp. 72–73. Writing of the destroyer-for-bases swap, the *Louisville Courier Journal* wrote that "we haven't had a better bargain since the Indians sold Manhattan Island for $24 in wampum and a demi john of hard liquor." Wrote the *Washington Post*: "The President's bargain was the first major expansion of the American frontier since the Spanish American war." Goodwin, *No Ordinary Time*, p. 149.

41. Meacham, *Franklin and Winston*, p. 72; Goodwin, *No Ordinary Time*, p. 148.

42. Thomas Parris, *To Keep the British Isles Afloat: FDR's Men in Churchill's London, 1941* (New York: HarperCollins, 2009), p. 106.

43. Meacham, *Franklin and Winston*, p. 76.

44. Black, *Franklin Delano Roosevelt*, p. 604.

45. Meacham, *Franklin and Winston*, p. 78.

46. Goodwin, *No Ordinary Time*, p. 193.

47. Franklin Roosevelt, press conference, December 17, 1940. Available at http://docs.fdrlibrary.marist.edu/odllpc2.html; Goodwin, *No Ordinary Time*, p. 194; Black, *Franklin Delano Roosevelt*, p. 605.

48. Franklin Roosevelt, radio address, December 29, 1940. Available at http://docs.fdrlibrary.marist.edu/122940.html.

49. Goodwin, *No Ordinary Time*, p. 196.

50. Franklin Delano Roosevelt, State of the Union address, January 6, 1941. Available at http://www.americanrhetoric.com/speeches/fdrthefourfreedoms.htm.

51. Goodwin, *No Ordinary Time*, p. 214. Lindbergh produced audible gasps from the hearing room when he stated his preference "to see neither side win." Dalleck, *Franklin Roosevelt and Foreign Policy*, p. 417.

52. The debate over H.R. 1776 didn't lack for vitriol or rancor. "It is a measure of aggressive warfare," is how Democrat Hugh Peterson described it. "You can dress this measure up all you please," said Republican Dewey Short, "you can sprinkle it with perfume and pour powder on it, masquerade it in any form you please with these innocuous and meaningless amendments that have been offered, but it is still foul and it stinks to high heaven." Congressman George Tinkham called it a "war bill of monstrous implications." Senator Robert Taft of Ohio worried that the bill could give Roosevelt the "power to carry on a kind of undeclared war all over the world." Nonetheless, the House passed H.R. 1776 by a margin of 260–165, with the Senate approving by an equally lopsided margin, 60–31. Charles A. Beard, *President Roosevelt and the Coming of the War: A Study in Appearances and Reality* (New Haven, CT: Yale University Press, 1948), pp. 60–68.

53. Goodwin, *No Ordinary Time*, p. 214.

54. Finlo Rohrer, "What Is a Little Debt between Friends?" *BBC News Magazine*, May 10, 2006. Available at http://news.bbc.co.uk/2/hi/uk_news/magazine/4757181.stm.

Chapter 8

1. Albert Einstein, letter to Franklin Roosevelt, August 2, 1939. Available at http://hypertextbook.com/eworld/einstein.shtml#first. In the meeting with Sachs to discuss the Einstein letter, Roosevelt got the gist quickly: "Alex, what you are after is to see that the Nazis don't blow us up." Responded Sachs: "Precisely." Richard Rhodes, *The Making of the Atomic Bomb* (New York: Simon & Schuster, 1986), p. 314.

2. Jennet Conant, *Tuxedo Park: A Wall Street Tycoon and the Secret Palace of Science That Changed the Course of World War II* (New York: Simon & Schuster, 2002), p. 12.

3. F. G. Gosling, *The Manhattan Project: Making the Atomic Bomb* (Washington, DC: Department of Energy, 1999), p. 6.

4. Franklin Roosevelt, "Address before the Eighth Pan-American Scientific Congress," May 10, 1940. Available at http://www.presidency.ucsb.edu/ws/index .php?pid=15948; Rhodes, *Making of the Atomic Bomb*, p. 336.

5. Gosling, *Manhattan Project*, p. 10; Rhodes, *Making of the Atomic Bomb*, p. 387.

6. Franklin Roosevelt, radio address, December 9, 1941; Russel D. Buhite and David W. Levy, *FDR's Fireside Chats* (Norman: University of Oklahoma Press, 1992), p. 204.

7. David McCullough, *Truman* (New York: Simon & Schuster, 1992), p. 440.

8. Rhodes, *Making of the Atomic Bomb*, p. 406.

9. McCullough, *Truman*, p. 341.

10. Ibid., p. 342.

11. "The Truman Memoirs," *Life*, September 26, 1955, p. 99.

12. McCullough, *Truman*, pp. 298, 320.

13. Ibid., p. 355.

14. The "Truman Committee" was responsible for saving taxpayers $15 billion in fraudulent and wasteful government contracts. It earned him the cover of *Time* magazine in 1943. James Ciment, ed., *The Home Front Encyclopedia: The United States, Britain and Canada in World Wars I and II* (Santa Barbara, CA: ABC-CLIO, 2007), p. 1017.

15. McCullough, *Truman*, pp. 349–50. David McCullough, in his wonderful biography of Harry Truman, points out that for those who knew Truman, there was little doubt about his ability to handle the job. "Truman is honest and patriotic and has a head full of good horse sense," wrote John Nance Garner, Roosevelt's first vice president. "Besides, he has guts." Speaker of the House Sam Rayburn concurred, telling reporters that Truman would do just fine because he had "the stuff in him" to get the job done. To Republican Arthur Vandenberg, Truman was "a grand person with every good intention and high honesty of person" who could "swing the job." After meeting with Truman, Assistant Secretary of State Dean Acheson (who would later serve as Truman's secretary of state) noted in a letter to his son that Truman was "straightforward, decisive, simple, entirely honest." Acheson was convinced that he would "learn fast and inspire confidence," and counted it as a "blessing" that Truman—and not Henry Wallace—was president. Ibid., pp. 350–51.

16. Harry Truman, *Memoirs*, vol. 1, *Year of Decisions* (New York: Doubleday & Company, 1955), p. 10.

17. The Russian threat was very real. A report from the Office of Strategic Services (OSS), produced just days before Roosevelt's death, predicted—with amazing accuracy as it turned out—that "Russia will emerge from the present conflict as by far the strongest nation in Europe and Asia—strong enough, if the United States should stand aside, to dominate Europe and at the same time establish her hegemony over Asia. Russia's natural resources and manpower are so great that within relatively few years she can be much more powerful than either Germany, or Japan has ever been. In the easily foreseeable future Russia may well outrank even the United States in military potential." McCullough, *Truman*, p. 372.

18. Melvyn Leffler and David S. Painter, eds., *Origins of the Cold War: An International History* (New York: Routledge, 1994), p. 66. Available at Harry S. Truman Library: The Decision to Drop the Bomb, http://www.truman library.org/whistlestop/study_collections/bomb/large/documents/index.php?documentdate=1945–04–24&documentid=9–14&studycollectionid=&page number=1.

19. Memorandum discussed with the president, April 25, 1945. Available at http://www.gwu.edu/~nsarchiv/NSAEBB/NSAEBB162/3a.pdf; McCullough, *Truman*, p. 378.

20. Truman, *Memoirs*, p. 87.

21. Burton Folsom, *New Deal or Raw Deal: How FDR's Economic Legacy Damaged America* (New York: Simon & Schuster, 2008), p. 318.

22. McCullough, *Truman*, pp. 390–91.

23. Gosling, *Manhattan Project*, pp. 45–46.

24. Harry Truman, diary entry, June 17, 1945. Available at http://www.nuclear files.org/menu/library/correspondence/truman-harry/corr_diary_truman.htm.

25. Robert Ferrell, *Harry S. Truman: A Life* (Columbia: University of Missouri Press, 1994), p. 213.

26. McCullough, *Truman*, pp. 400–401.

27. Rhodes, *Making of the Atomic Bomb*, p. 686.

28. McCullough, *Truman*, p. 432.

29. Rhodes, *Making of the Atomic Bomb*, p. 688.

30. McCullough, *Truman*, p. 437.

31. William O'Neill, *A Democracy at War: America's Fight at Home and Abroad during World War II* (Cambridge, MA: Harvard University Press, 1993), p. 442.

32. Harry Truman, diary entry, July 25, 1945. Available at http://www .trumanlibrary.org/whistlestop/study_collections/bomb/ferrell_book/ferrell_boo k _chap5.htm; McCullough, *Truman*, p. 444; Rhodes, *Making of the Atomic Bomb*, p. 690.

33. Statement by the President Announcing the Use of the Atomic Bomb on Hiroshima, August 6, 1945. Available at http://www.trumanlibrary.org/ calendar/viewpapers.php?pid=100.

34. Richard Frank, *Downfall: The End of the Imperial Japanese Empire* (New York: Penguin Group, 1999), p. 296.

35. Truman, *Memoirs*, p. 419.

36. McCullough, *Truman*, p. 458.

37. Michael Lacey, ed., *The Truman Presidency* (Cambridge: Cambridge University Press, 1989), p. 176; Letter on Japanese Brutality, http://www.nuclear files.org/menu/library/correspondence/truman-harry/corr_truman_1945–08– 11.htm.

38. Lacey, *Truman Presidency*, pp. 176–77. Truman's Message to Congress on the Atomic Bomb, October 3, 1945. Available at http://www.jewishvirtual library.org/jsource/ww2/abomb.html.

39. Kai Bird and Martin Sherwin, *American Prometheus: The Triumph and Tragedy of J. Robert Oppenheimer* (New York: Random House, 2005), p. 332.

40. Stewart Udall, *The Myths of August: A Personal Exploration of Our Tragic Cold War Affair with the Atom* (New York: Pantheon Books, 1994), p. 96.

41. Ferrell, *Harry S. Truman: A Life*, p. 214.

42. Monte Poen, *Strictly Personal and Confidential: The Letters Harry Truman Never Mailed* (Columbia: University of Missouri Press, 1999), pp. 34–36.

43. Letter from Harry S. Truman to Mrs. Haydon Klein, August 4, 1964. Available at http://www.trumanlibrary.org/whistlestop/study_collections/bomb/ large/documents/index.php?documentdate=1964–08–04&documentid=9 –16&studycollectionid=&pagenumber=1.

44. Ferrell, *Harry S. Truman*, p. 214.

45. O'Neill, *Democracy at War*, p. 422.

Chapter 9

1. William Safire, *Safire's Political Dictionary* (Oxford: Oxford University Press, 2008), p. 338.

2. Robert J. Donovan, *The Presidency of Harry Truman: 1949–1953* (New York: W. W. Norton, 1982), p. 303.

3. David McCullough, *Truman* (New York: Simon & Schuster, 1992), p. 949.

4. Dean Acheson, *Present at the Creation: My Years in the State Department* (New York: W. W. Norton, 1969).

5. Steve Neal, *Harry and Ike: The Partnership That Remade the Postwar World* (New York: Touchstone, 2001), p. 212.

6. McCullough, *Truman*, p. 998.

7. Ibid., p. 999.

8. Ibid., p. 1000.

9. Robert Donovan, *The Presidency of Harry Truman* (New York: W. W. Norton, 1967), p. 359.

10. Richard Rovere and Arthur Schlesinger, *General MacArthur and President Truman* (New Brunswick, NJ: Transaction, 1992), p. 227.

11. Robert Beisner, *Dean Acheson: A Life in the Cold War* (Oxford: Oxford University Press, 2006), p. 429.

12. McCullough, *Truman*, p. 1000.

13. David Halberstam, *The Coldest Winter: America and the Korean War* (New York: Hyperion, 2007), p. 719.

14. David Oshinsky, *A Conspiracy So Immense: The World of Joe McCarthy* (Oxford: Oxford University Press, 2007), p. 197.

15. Neal, *Harry and Ike*, p. 239.

16. Harry Truman, televised address, April 16, 1951. Available at http://usinfo.org/ docs/democracy/58.htm.

17. McCullough, *Truman*, p. 1017.

Chapter 10

1. David Oshinsky, *A Conspiracy So Immense: The World of Joe McCarthy* (New York: Oxford University Press, 2005), p. 229. According to Gallup, Eisen-

hower led Harry Truman 40–20 among Democrats, and Senator Robert Taft, the leading Republican candidate, 30–22. Another poll showed Eisenhower besting Taft in the senator's home city of Cincinnati. Ibid.

2. Fred Israel, *The State of the Union Messages of the Presidents: 1790–1966*, vol. 3 (New York: Chelsea House, 1966), p. 3026. Dwight Eisenhower, State of the Union address, January 7, 1954. Available at http://www.infoplease.com/t/hist/ state-of-the-union/166.html.

3. Stephen Ambrose, *Eisenhower: Soldier and President* (New York: Simon & Schuster, 1990), p. 312.

4. Matthew Brzezinski, *Red Moon Rising:* Sputnik *and the Hidden Rivalries That Ignited the Space Age* (New York: Times Books, 2007), p. 172.

5. Ibid.

6. Ibid., p. 171; http://history.nasa.gov/sputnik/15.html. White House spinning didn't stop with just the press release downplaying the significance of *Sputnik*. Eisenhower aide Maxwell Rabb said it was "without military significance." Charlie Wilson called it a "neat technical trick." Sherman Adams, the White House chief of staff, referred to the satellite as a "hunk of iron that almost anyone could launch." Press Secretary Jim Haggerty reiterated that the White House wasn't about to get lured into "an outer space basketball game." Ibid., p. 171. For a wonderful recounting of the early space race, read Matthew Brzezinski's *Red Moon Rising*.

7. William B. Breuer, *Race to the Moon: America's Duel with the Soviets* (Westport, CT: Praeger Publishers, 1993), p. 148.

8. Much of the quotes from this section are attributed to Brzezinski, *Red Moon Rising*, pp. 171–73; Matthew Von Bencke, *The Politics of Space: A History of the U.S.-Soviet/Russian Competition and Cooperation in Space* (New York: Westview Press, 1997), pp. 19–20.

9. Von Bencke, *Politics of Space*, p. 2.

10. Ibid., pp. 20–21; Brzezinski, *Red Moon Rising*, pp. 174–75.

11. Brzezinski, *Red Moon Rising*, p. 215.

12. Presidential News Conference, October 9, 1957. Available at http://www.presidency.ucsb.edu/ws/index.php?pid=10924.

13. Breuer, *Race to the Moon*, p. 150.

14. Brzezinski, *Red Moon Rising*, p. 216.

15. Breuer, *Race to the Moon*, p. 155.

16. Ibid., p. 159.

17. There had been a long association between the Kennedys and Joe McCarthy. Joe Kennedy, the clan's volatile head, was a big donor to McCarthy's campaigns and publicly supported his Red-hunting crusade. Younger brother Bobby served on McCarthy's staff, and sister Pat dated the Wisconsin senator on occasion. As for John Kennedy, he was the only Democratic senator to attend both McCarthy's wedding and funeral. Oshinsky, *A Conspiracy So Immense*, pp. 33–34.

18. Eligar Sadeh, *Space Politics and Policy: An Evolutionary Perspective* (Norwell: Kluwer Academic Publishers, 2002), p. 66.

19. Breuer, *Race to the Moon*, p. 2.

20. Stephen Ambrose, *Nixon*, vol. 1, *The Education of a Politician, 1913–1962* (New York: Simon & Schuster, 1987), p. 586; Breuer, *Race to the Moon*, p. 2.

21. Von Bencke, *Politics of Space*, p. 20. Kennedy hammered at this theme of the United States falling behind the Soviet Union in the eyes of the world. "Mr. Nixon," he thundered on the campaign trail just a week before the election, "has stated on many occasions that he believes that our prestige is at an all time high, and that of the Communists at an all time low. Now, yesterday the newspapers carried the report of a survey made by the United States Government in ten countries of the world, and they asked them the question, 'Do you believe the Soviet Union or the United States is first in military power and science?' And a majority of the people in ten countries said the Soviet Union was first." Kennedy speech, October 26, 1960. Available at http://www.jfklibrary.org/Historical+Resources/Archives/Reference+Desk/Speeches/JFK/JFK+Pre-Pres/1960/002PREPRES12SPEECHES_60OCT26a.htm.

22. White House Historical Association, "John F. Kennedy and the Space Race." Available at http://www.whitehousehistory.org/whha_classroom/ classroom_9–12-visionary-kennedy.html; Breuer, *Race to the Moon*, p. 3.

23. Breuer, *Race to the Moon*, pp. 3, 163.

24. White House Historical Association, "John F. Kennedy and the Space Race"; Ben Evans, *Escaping the Bonds of Earth: The Fifties and Sixties* (Chichester, UK: Praxis Publishing, 2009), p. 26.

25. Roger Launius and Howard McCurdy, eds., *Spaceflight and the Myth of Presidential Leadership* (Chicago: University of Illinois Press, 1997), p. 56.

26. Memo from John F. Kennedy to Lyndon Johnson, April 20, 1960. Available at http://www.perno.com/amer/docs/JFK%20to%20LBJ%20on%20the%20Space%20Program.htm.

27. Memo from Lyndon Johnson to John F. Kennedy, April 28, 1961. Available at http://www.perno.com/amer/docs/JFK%20to%20LBJ%20on%20the%20Space%20Program.htm; Launius and McCurdy, *Spaceflight*, pp. 55–57.

28. Launius and McCurdy, *Spaceflight*, pp. 59–60.

29. Ibid., p. 60.

30. Ibid. In his wonderful biography of John F. Kennedy, historian Robert Dallek adds a humorous footnote to Shepard's historic flight. In the days leading up to it, there had been some concern over the live television coverage—a disaster could have been a mortal blow to the space program. Everyone at the White House—most notably the president—was relieved when it went off without a hitch. While riding with Johnson to an event a few weeks after

Shepard's orbital trip, Kennedy couldn't help but rib the vice president. "You know, Lyndon, nobody knows that the Vice President is the Chairman of the Space Council. But if that flight had been a flop, I guarantee you that everybody would have known that you were the Chairman." Everyone in the car had a good laugh with the notable exception of Johnson. Robert Dallek, *John F. Kennedy: An Unfinished Life* (New York: Little, Brown, and Company, 2003), p. 394.

31. John F. Kennedy, Special Message to Congress, May 25, 1961. Available at http://www.presidency.ucsb.edu/ws/index.php?pid=8151.

32. Ibid.

33. Tim Naftali and Aleksandr Fursenko, *One Hell of a Gamble: The Secret History of the Cuban Missile Crisis* (New York: W. W. Norton, 1997), p. 129; Howard E. McCurdy, *Space and the American Imagination* (Washington, DC: Smithsonian Institution Press, 1997), p. 97.

34. Launius and McCurdy, *Spaceflight*, pp. 42–43.

35. Ambrose, *Eisenhower*, p. 554; Launius and McCurdy, *Spaceflight*, pp. 42–43.

36. John F. Kennedy, speech at Rice University, September 12, 1962. Available at http://www.jfklibrary.org/Historical+Resources/Archives/Reference+Desk/Speeches/JFK/003POF03SpaceEffort09121962.htm.

37. Dallek, *John F. Kennedy*, p. 652.

38. John F. Kennedy, speech at Rice University, September 12, 1962. Available at http://er.jsc.nasa.gov/seh/ricetalk.htm.

39. Francis X. Clines, "Going Out of Business Sale for Soviet's Space Program," *New York Times*, August 8, 1993.

Chapter 11

1. Irwin Unger and Debi Unger, *LBJ: A Life* (New York: John Wiley & Sons, 1999), p. 27.

2. Robert Dallek, *Flawed Giant: Lyndon Johnson and His Times, 1961–1973* (Oxford: Oxford University Press, 1998), p. 24. Dalleck recounts a story from LBJ's 1948 Senate campaign where the underdog Johnson refused to begin speaking at a campaign event until black attendees were allowed to sit along side whites in the audience. "How many votes you think I'll get there?" an aide recalled LBJ asking. "I held up both hands: ten votes," said the aide. "He said, 'Oh no' and held up two fingers."

3. Unger and Unger, *LBJ: A Life*, p. 36.

4. Dallek, *Flawed Giant*, p. 6. In her biography of Lyndon Johnson, Doris

Kearns Goodwin takes a stab at discovering the origins of LBJ's relentless ambition and obsession with mastering the political process. "Certainly, most participants in public life are not as intensely 'political' as Lyndon Johnson was," she writes. "His obsessive single-mindedness was an aspect of his nature that had evolved from the inner need to protect himself from the perplexing hazards of his childhood. Whatever its source, this quality was an invaluable asset in his public career. . . . This may help explain the frenzied quality of Johnson's enterprising activity, his scrupulous avoidance of tranquility. More and more, he depended upon his skills in politics to stave off the consequences of inner conflicts, and provide him a surrogate for love and acceptance." Doris Kearns Goodwin, *Lyndon Johnson and the American Dream* (New York: Harper & Row, Publishers, 1976), p. 79.

5. Unger and Unger, *LBJ: A Life*, p. 38.

6. Ibid., p. 139.

7. Robert Caro, *The Years of Lyndon Johnson: Master of the Senate* (New York: Alfred A. Knopf, 2002), p. 954; p. 954; Dallek, *Flawed Giant*, p. 717. Robert Parker, the former maitre d' of the Senate dining room, pulled no punches in his autobiography, *Capitol Hill in Black and White*, about how cruel Johnson could be. "For years," writes Parker, "he [Johnson] called me 'boy,' 'nigger,' or 'chief,' never by my name. . . . He especially liked to call me nigger in front of southerners and racists like Richard Russell." Parker surmised that it was "LBJ's way of being one of the boys." In private, Parker noted, Johnson "softened a bit," and in a moment of candor once confessed his motives: "I can't be too easy with you. I don't want to be called a nigger lover." Ibid., p. 717. Robert Parker, *Capitol Hill in Black and White* (New York: Dodd, Mead & Company, 1986), p. 261.

8. Robert Caro, *The Years of Lyndon Johnson: Master of the Senate* (New York: Alfred A Knopf, 2002), p. 832.

9. Goodwin, *Lyndon Johnson and the American Dream*, p. 148. According to historian Robert Caro, LBJ was shameless in portraying the 1957 Civil Rights Act in a much different light depending on the audience. To Northern senator Paul Douglas, he counseled the civil rights advocate to "be reasonable" about a jury trial provision if "we're going to have any civil rights bill at all." To North Carolina Senator Sam Ervin, he warned him to "be ready to take up the Nigra bill again." He lamented to Mississippi Senator John Stennis that the cause was lost: "Let's face it, our ass is in a crack—we're gonna have to let this nigger bill pass." Caro, *Years of Lyndon Johnson*, p. 954.

10. In defending the watered-down 1957 civil rights bill to liberal critics in the media and the Senate, Johnson let it be known that more reform was on the horizon. "It's just a beginning. We've shown that we can do it. We'll do it again,

in a couple of years." Caro, *Years of Lyndon Johnson*, p. 1003. Caro believes that Johnson purposefully misled his Southern cohorts during the process of the 1957 Civil Rights Act to satisfy his future ambition of becoming president. "Misled they certainly were. Did he intend to mislead them?—we don't know. But if we take him at his word—his word that at Cotulla, 'I swore then and there that if I ever had a chance to help those underprivileged kids I was going to do it'—then Lyndon Johnson was misleading the southern senators deliberately. . . . He was planning to betray, and to betray on a very large scale, the men, some of them very clever men, who were, for years, not only his most loyal but his most important supporters." Ibid., p. 870.

11. Gary Donaldson, *The First Modern Campaign: Kennedy, Nixon, and the Election of 1960* (Lanham, MD: Rowman and Littlefield, 2007), p. 151.

12. Unger and Unger, *LBJ: A Life*, p. 260.

13. Dallek, *Flawed Giant*, p. 26.

14. Remarks of Vice President Lyndon Johnson, Memorial Day Weekend, Gettysburg, Pennsylvania, May 30, 1963. Available at http://www.lbjlib.utexas .edu/johnson/archives.hom/speeches.hom/630530.asp.

15. John F. Kennedy, Civil Rights address, June 11, 1963. Available at http://www.americanrhetoric.com/speeches/jfkcivilrights.htm.

16. Dallek, *Flawed Giant*, p. 37; Robert Dallek, *An Unfinished Life: John F. Kennedy* (New York: Little, Brown and Company, 2003), p. 650.

17. Dalleck, *An Unfinished Life*, p. 650.

18. Nick Kotz, *Judgment Days: Lyndon Baines Johnson, Martin Luther King, Jr, and the Laws That Changed America* (New York: Houghton Mifflin Company, 2005), p. 113.

19. Goodwin, *Lyndon Johnson and the American Dream*, p. 191.

20. Dallek, *Flawed Giant*, p. 112.

21. Lyndon Johnson, Address before a Joint Session of Congress, November 27, 1963. Available at http://www.lbjlib.utexas.edu/johnson/archives .hom/speeches.hom/631127.asp.

22. Kotz, *Judgment Days*, p. 38. Beyond just threats, Johnson tried to reason with the Southern senators about giving up the filibuster. "You've got a Southern president," he reminded them. "If you want to blow him out of the water, go right ahead and do it, but you boys will never see another one again. We're friends on the q.t. Would you rather have Nixon or Scranton? You have to make up your mind." Ibid., p. 39.

23. Kotz, *Judgment Days*, p. 133.

24. Ibid., p. 97.

25. In the speech announcing his decision to join with Democrats to invoke cloture, Senator Dirksen, noting that it was the one hundredth anniversary to the

day of Lincoln's nomination for a second term as president, famously quoted French novelist Victor Hugo: "Stronger than all the armies is an idea whose time has come." He added, "The time has come for equality of opportunity in sharing in government, in education, and in employment. It will not be stayed or denied. It is here!" Peter Schweizer and Wynton Hall, *Landmark Speeches of the American Conservative Movement* (College Station: Texas A&M Press, 2007), p. 23.

26. Dallek, *Flawed Giant*, p. 6.

27. Ibid., p. 24.

Chapter 12

1. Monica Crowley, *Nixon in Winter: The Final Revelations* (New York: I. B. Tauris, 1998), p. 159.

2. Dennis McDougal, *Privileged Son: Otis Chandler and the Rise and Fall of the* LA Times *Dynasty* (New York: Perseus Publishing, 2001), p. 177. "Of course, I knew Jerry Voorhis wasn't a communist, but I had to win," is how Nixon would later explain his behavior during the 1946 campaign.

3. Rick Perlstein, *Nixonland: The Rise of a President and the Fracturing of America* (New York: Scribner, 2008), p. 34. Douglas did get some measure of revenge against Nixon for his smear tactics. It is widely believed that she popularized the nickname "Tricky Dick."

4. Douglas Brinkley, *Dean Acheson: The Cold War Years, 1953–1971* (New Haven, CT: Yale University Press, 1992), p. 263.

5. Stephen A. Ambrose, *Nixon: The Education of a Politician, 1913–1962* (New York: Simon & Schuster, 1987), p. 349. According to Ambrose, Eisenhower was embarrassed by Nixon's fusillades against his successor, so much so that he penned a testy note to his hatchet man, though he ultimately decided not to send it in favor of a face-to-face meeting. "I quite understand the impulse—particularly before a partisan audience—to lash out at our political opponents," wrote Eisenhower, "but I am constantly working to produce a truly bipartisan approach, and I rather think that keeping up the attacks . . . will hamper our efforts." Ike kept the letter to himself, but in Ambrose's words took Nixon "to the woodshed" when he returned to Washington. The scolding resulted in a promise from the chastened vice president to "delete such references" from any future speeches.

6. Helen Thomas and Craig Crawford, *Listen Up, Mr. President: Everything You Always Wanted Your President to Know and Do* (New York: Scribner, 2009), p. 74.

7. Richard Nixon, *The Memoirs of Richard Nixon* (New York: Grosset & Dunlap, 1978), p. 344.

8. Richard Nixon, "Asia after Vietnam," *Foreign Affairs* 46 (October 1967): 121–24; Nixon, *Memoirs*, p. 285.

9. Nixon, *Memoirs*, pp. 282, 273.

10. Nixon biographer Elizabeth Drew puts Nixon's dislike of the State Department more bluntly. "Not only did Nixon distrust the foreign policy bureaucracy," she writes, "he remarked that he didn't want foreign policy run by the 'striped-pants faggots in foggy bottom'—he also didn't want a strong Secretary of State, such as Eisenhower's powerful John Foster Dulles." Nixon chose his longtime friend William Rogers for the position, whom he childishly pitted against the more talented and unscrupulous Kissinger from the beginning. Nixon would confess years later that his treatment of Rogers had been "terrible." Elizabeth Drew, *Richard M. Nixon* (New York: Times Books, 2007), p. 63. Monica Crowley, *Nixon in Winter*, p. 293.

11. Nixon, *Memoirs*, p. 341.

12. Margaret MacMillan, *Nixon and Mao: The Week That Changed the World* (New York: Random House, 2008), p. 57. Nixon made a somewhat oblique reference to normalizing relations with China in his inaugural address. "We seek an open world . . . a world in which no people, great or small, will live in angry isolation." He used similar language in his *Foreign Affairs* article two years earlier. Nixon, *Memoirs*, p. 545.

13. Gao Wenqian, *Zhou Enlai: The Last Perfect Revolutionary* (New York: Public Affairs, 2007), p. 4.

14. Walter Isaacson, *Kissinger* (New York: Simon & Schuster, 1992), p. 337.

15. Robert Dallek, *Nixon and Kissinger: Partners in Power* (New York: HarperCollins, 2007), p. 264.

16. Isaacson, *Kissinger*, p. 338. Nixon was convinced that it was important for China to be an active member of the world community. "Maybe that role won't be possible for five years, maybe not even ten years. But in 20 years it had better be, or the world is in mortal danger. If there is anything I want to do before I die, it is to go to China. If I don't, I want my children to." Henry Kissinger, *The White House Years* (New York: Little, Brown and Company, 1979), p. 699.

17. Isaacson, *Kissinger*, p. 339.

18. Dallek, *Nixon and Kissinger*, pp. 268–69.

19. Isaacson, *Kissinger*, pp. 340–41.

20. Richard Reeves, *President Nixon: Alone in the White House* (New York: Simon & Schuster, 2001), p. 329.

21. Dallek, *Nixon and Kissinger*, p. 290.

Chapter 13

1. The Republicans only picked up twelve net seats, even though Nixon carried forty-nine states with 60 percent of the vote (the second-largest landslide in history after LBJ's trouncing of Goldwater in 1964).

2. Gerald Ford was not on the top of Richard Nixon's list. Nixon's preferred choice for vice president was Democrat-turned-Republican John Connolly, the former governor of Texas, but the prickly Connolly had few allies in Congress and stood little chance of winning confirmation. Nixon gave consideration to New York's liberal governor Nelson Rockefeller, and California's conservative governor Ronald Reagan, but neither had enough appeal with the opposite wing of the party. It came down to George H. W. Bush, who at the time was serving as Republican National Committee chairman, and Gerald Ford. Ford won out because he was the safest choice—easily confirmable, moderate on the issues, unlikely to make waves, a man of integrity—and he breezed through the confirmation process.

3. Deborah Strober and Gerald Strober, *The Nixon Presidency: An Oral History of the Era* (New York: HarperCollins, 1994), p. 191.

4. Yanek Mieczkowski, *Gerald Ford and the Challenge of the 1970s* (Lexington: University of Kentucky Press, 2005), p. 28.

5. Douglas Brinkley, *Gerald R. Ford* (New York: Times Books, 2007), p. 67.

6. *Time*, September 9, 1974; Douglas Brinkley, *Gerald R. Ford* (New York: Times Books, 2007), p. 67.

7. Brinkley, *Gerald R. Ford*, pp. 39–40.

8. Richard A. Brody, *Assessing the President: The Media, Elite Opinion, and Public Support* (Stanford, CA: Stanford University Press, 1991), p. 39.

9. "Gerald Ford Off to a Fast, Clean Start," *Time*, August 26, 1974. Available at http://www.time.com/time/magazine/article/0,9171,944928,00.html.

10. Gerald Ford, *A Time to Heal* (New York: Harper & Row, 1979), p. 178.

11. Upon becoming president, Gerald Ford asked for the portraits of his three favorite presidents—Lincoln, Truman, and Eisenhower—to be placed in the Cabinet Room. "He had guts, he was plain-talking, he had no illusion about being a great intellectual, but he seemed to make the right decisions" is how Ford described Truman. Mieczkowski, *Gerald Ford and the Challenges of the 1970s*, p. 25.

12. The stress of Watergate and the resignation took an extraordinary toll on Nixon's physical and mental well-being. Some aides, including Len Garment, feared that he could be suicidal in the aftermath of the resignation. After meeting with Nixon in California to discuss the condition of his pardon, Ford's special

counsel, Benton Becker, reported back to Ford that he wasn't sure if Nixon would be alive much longer. "I'm not a medical doctor, but I have serious questions in my mind whether that man is going to be alive at the time of the election," Becker told Ford. "Well, 1976 is a long time away," responded Ford. "I don't mean 1976. I mean 1974," said Becker. Barry Werth, *31 Days: The Crisis That Gave Us the Government We Have Today* (New York: Doubleday, 2006), pp. 213, 311.

13. Nixon had 46 million pieces of paper and 950 reels of tape (4,000 hours of recordings) for which legal ownership had to be sorted out. The collection of tape reels was so heavy, in fact, that it was feared that the weight of the tapes would collapse the second floor of the Old Executive Office Building, where they sat in storage. Ibid., p. 33.

14. Ford, *A Time to Heal*, p. 159.

15. John T. Woolley and Gerhard Peters, *The American Presidency Project* (Santa Barbara, CA). Available at http://www.presidency.ucsb.edu/ws/?pid=4671.

16. Ford, *A Time to Heal*, p. 158. Ford told aides that he had wanted to hold a press conference every several weeks, but became less certain of that after the first one. He feared that they would all turn into Watergate feeding frenzies.

17. Ibid., p. 161.

18. Bob Woodward, *Shadows: Five Presidents and the Legacy of Watergate* (New York: Simon & Schuster, 1999), p. 35

19. Bob Woodward, "Ford, Nixon Sustained Friendship for Decades," *Washington Post*, December 29, 2006, p. A1.

20. According to Bob Woodward and Carl Bernstein, the six options discussed in the Ford-Haig meeting of August 1 were: (1) Nixon could step aside temporarily in accordance with the Twenty-fifth Amendment; (2) Nixon could ride it out a little longer, perhaps holding off on a decision until after the formal impeachment vote in the House of Representatives; (3) The White House could lobby the House of Representatives to go for a censure vote instead of impeachment; (4) Nixon could pardon himself and then resign; (5) Nixon could pardon all the Watergate actors (Haldeman, Mitchell, etc.) and then resign; (6) Nixon could resign and hope that Ford would pardon him. Bob Woodward and Carl Bernstein, *The Final Days* (New York: Simon & Schuster, 1976), p. 325.

21. Ford, *A Time to Heal*, p. 4.

22. Seymour Hersch, "The Pardon," *Atlantic*, August 1983, p. 3.

23. Ibid. Robert Hartmann, Ford's chief of staff (and whom Haig expressly wanted excluded from his meeting with Ford), had an intensely visceral reaction upon learning of Haig's inappropriate overture. Seymour Hersch, quoting Hartmann's own memoir, writes: "'Jesus!' I [Robert Hartmann] said aloud. To myself: So that's the pitch Haig wouldn't make with me present. Aloud again: 'What did

you tell him?' 'I didn't tell him anything. I told him I needed time to think about it.' 'You what?' I fairly shouted. It was almost the worst answer Haig could have taken back to the White House. Far from telling nothing, Ford had told Haig that he was at least willing to entertain the idea—probably all that Haig and Nixon wanted to know. Hartmann quoted himself as telling Ford, "I think you should have taken Haig by the scruff of the neck and the seat of his pants and thrown him the hell out of your office. . . . And then you should have called an immediate press conference and told the world why." According to the *Pittsburgh Post-Gazette*'s reporting on a 1999 C-SPAN panel discussion involving several of Ford's former aides, Robert Hartmann called the pardon "an extremely selfish decision," one that was nothing more than Ford "doing himself a big favor. Ford wanted to get rid of him." "Behind the Long National Nightmare," *Los Angeles Times*, January 7, 2007.

24. Ford, *A Time to Heal*, p. 13.

25. Andrew Downer Crain, *The Ford Presidency* (Jefferson, NC: McFarland and Company, 2009), pp. 24–26.

26. Robert T. Hartmann, *Palace Politics: An Inside Account of the Ford Years* (New York: McGraw-Hill, 1980), p. 270.

27. Stanley I. Kutler, *The Wars of Watergate: The Last Crisis of Richard Nixon* (New York: W. W. Norton, 1990), pp. 512–15. The "smoking gun" tape of June 23, 1972—just a week after the Watergate break-in—left no doubt that Nixon had personally engaged in a criminal conspiracy to obstruct justice and thwart a criminal investigation. The White House was forced to release the full transcript of the tape after the Supreme Court unanimously ruled against Nixon's claim of executive privilege in late July of 1974. It was at this point that Nixon began to seriously consider resignation.

28. In a 1997 interview with Bob Woodward for his book *Shadows: Five Presidents and the Legacy of Watergate*, Ford made his strongest case yet that there simply wasn't the need for any pardon deal. "Another aspect of it that people fail to realize," he told Woodward, "I was going to be president anyhow. At that point, I didn't have to make a deal if I wanted to be president. The die was cast. It was inevitable that he was either going to have to resign or he was going to be impeached so there was no incentive for me to make a deal. Didn't have to." Bob Woodward, "Gerald R. Ford," in *Profiles in Courage for Our Time*, ed. Carole Kennedy (New York: Hyperion, 2002), p. 309. Ford confessed, however, that in retrospect—after discussing it with Robert Hartmann, Bryce Harlow, and other aides—he could understand how Haig's overture could be viewed as a deal offer, though he insisted that it was never consummated because "I never accepted." Ibid., p. 306. Writing of Ford's admission, Woodward—in characteristic fashion—boasts "and so there it was. He had finally acknowledged, on the record,

that he had been offered a deal. It was something that many had suspected all along, but it had been a long, roundabout road, to finally getting there."

29. Werth, *31 Days*, p. 249.

30. Ibid., p. 264. Becker elaborates: "The pardon is an act of forgiveness: We are forgiving you—the president, the King, the executive—is forgiving you for what you've done, your illegal act that you've either been convicted of, or what you've been accused of, or that you're being investigated for, or that you're on trial for. And you don't have to accept it—you can refuse this." Ibid., p. 265.

31. James Cannon, "Character above All," excerpts from an essay on PBS.org: http://www.pbs.org/newshour/character/essays/ford.html. There is some debate as to whether Ford is the only sitting president to testify before Congress. Some historians maintain that in 1862, Abe Lincoln appeared before the House Judiciary Committee to disquiet rumors that his wife, Mary Todd Lincoln, had leaked his State of the Union address to the *New York Herald* newspaper, which at the time had caused an uproar. There is no congressional record of the appearance, though accounts of it appear in several books and articles, the most descriptive being in David Herbert Donald's acclaimed *Lincoln* (New York: Simon & Schuster, 1995), pp. 323–24.

32. Woodward, *Shadows*, p. 37. In his essay for Caroline Kennedy's *Profiles in Courage for Our Times*, Woodward writes in even greater detail about his changed opinion on the pardon. "By the time of my interviews with Ford in 1997 and 1998 [for his book *Shadows*], I had come almost full circle in my conclusions about the pardon. I was close to thinking that Ford had done the right thing in pardoning Nixon. After the interviews, I was completely convinced. Ford was wise to act. What at first and perhaps for many years looked like a decision to protect Nixon was instead largely designed to protect the nation. Watergate was a poison that would not go away. There was more to it than I saw at the time." "Gerald R. Ford," p. 310.

33. Anthony Lewis, "Abroad at Home; For Gerald Ford," *New York Times*, August 5, 2000.

34. Richard Reeves, "I'm Sorry, Mr. President," *American Heritage*, 1996. Available at http://www.americanheritage.com/articles/magazine/ah/1996/8/1996_8_52.shtml.

35. The award read in full: "President Gerald Ford was honored for his courage in making a controversial decision of conscience to pardon former President Richard M. Nixon. On September 8, 1974, President Ford granted a 'full, free and absolute pardon' to former President Nixon 'for all offenses against the United States which he . . . has committed or may have committed or taken part in' while he was president. Nixon accepted the pardon. The response from the press, Congress, and the general public was overwhelmingly negative.

Appearing before the US House Committee on the Judiciary, President Ford explained under oath, in the first sworn congressional testimony ever given by a sitting president, that there were no deals connected with the pardon. Ford wrote in his autobiography that Nixon's pardon 'wasn't motivated primarily by sympathy for his plight or by concern over the state of his health. It was the state of the country's health at home and around the world that worried me.' In 1976, President Ford lost the White House to Jimmy Carter in one of the closest elections in American history. Many historians believe Ford's pardon of Nixon contributed to his defeat." John F. Kennedy Library Foundation, http://www.jfk library.org/Education+and+Public+Programs/Profile+in+Courage+Award/Award+Recipients/Gerald+Ford/.

36. Nick Ragone, "Some Legacies Are Re-built after Leaving the White House," *Star-Ledger*, February 15, 2009. http://blog.nj.com/njv_guest_blog/2009/02/some_legacies_are_rebuilt_afte.html.

Chapter 14

1. Ronald Reagan had his own take on what made him a "great communicator." He expounded on it during his farewell address to the nation. "And in all of that time I won a nickname, 'The Great Communicator.' But I never thought it was my style or the words I used that made a difference: It was the content. I wasn't a great communicator, but I communicated great things, and they didn't spring full bloom from my brow, they came from the heart of a great nation— from our experience, our wisdom, and our belief in principles that have guided us for two centuries. They called it the Reagan revolution. Well, I'll accept that, but for me it always seemed more like the great rediscovery, a rediscovery of our values and our common sense." Ronald Reagan, Address to the Nation, January 11, 1989. Available at http://old.nationalreview.com/document/reagan2004 06052132 .asp.

2. "Why Reagan Was the Great Communicator," *USA Today*, June 6, 2004. Available at http://www.usatoday.com/news/opinion/editorials/2004–06–06 -cannon_x.htm.

3. Reagan biographer Richard Reeves makes the humorous observation that although Reagan formally started writing his inaugural speech the day after defeating Carter, in reality he had been working on it for twenty-five years. "Reagan," he writes, "who took pride in the fact that he wrote or at least carefully edited most of his own speeches before and after he became a politician . . . had actually been working on it (his inaugural speech) . . . beginning on the day in 1954 when he was hired by General Electric to translate his fading name into

being the company's traveling spokesperson and morale booster." Richard Reeves, *President Reagan: The Triumph of Imagination* (New York: Simon & Schuster, 2006), p. 6.

4. Ben Smith, "Transformation, Like Reagan," Politico, January 16, 2008, http://www.politico.com/blogs/bensmith/0108/Transformation_like_Reagan.html.

5. Steven Hayward, *The Age of Reagan: The Conservative Counter-Revolution, 1980–1989* (New York: Random House, 2009), p. 102.

6. Ibid.

7. Reeves, *President Reagan*, p. 109.

8. Reagan's approach was not lost on the leading "Sovietologist" of the day, Stephen Cohen, a well-respected professor at Princeton University and outspoken Reagan critic. "All evidence indicates that the Reagan administration has abandoned both containment and détente for a very different objective: destroying the Soviet Union as a world power and possibly even its communist system," wrote Cohen shortly after the evil empire speech. Dinesh D'Souza, *Ronald Reagan: How an Ordinary Man Became an Extraordinary Leader* (New York: Free Press, 1997), p. 3.

9. Hayward, *Age of Reagan*, p. 27.

10. Ibid., p. 4.

11. With fifty-nine electoral votes, even Herbert Hoover fared better than Jimmy Carter's forty-nine.

12. Ronald Reagan, press conference, January 29, 1981. Available at http://www.presidency.ucsb.edu/ws/index.php?pid=44101.

13. Ronald Reagan, interview with Walter Cronkite, March 3, 1981. Available at http://www.presidency.ucsb.edu/ws/index.php?pid=43497.

14. Just how much did Reagan increase defense spending? As a percentage of discretionary (or nonentitlement) spending, defense appropriations increased from 48.7 to 62.2 percent—a 35 percent increase during his watch. http://www.truthandpolitics.org/military-relative-size.php.

15. Reeves, *President Reagan*, p. 104.

16. Ibid., p. 111.

17. Ronald Reagan, Speech to National Television Audience, October 27, 1964. Available at http://www.nationalcenter.org/ReaganChoosing1964.html. The word "evil" to describe other countries came back in vogue in 2002 with President George W. Bush's infamous "axis of evil" phrase in his State of the Union address to describe North Korea, Iraq, and Iran. The term harkened back to the "Evil Empire" speech, but as Bush speechwriter David Frum notes, its inspiration came from Franklin Roosevelt's "Day of Infamy" speech where the United States declared war on Japan. "For FDR," writes Frum in his memoir of his White House days, "Pearl Harbor was not only an attack—it was

a warning of future and worse attacks from another, even more dangerous, enemy. The soft-on-Iraq lobby promised that Saddam Hussein could be deterred forever. But if deterrence always worked, there would never have been a Pearl Harbor." David Frum, *The Right Man: An Inside Account of the Bush White House* (New York: Random House, 2005), p. 234. In the days following Bush's State of the Union Speech, the "axis of evil" phrase became the focus of intense media attention, similar to that of the "evil empire" line some nineteen years earlier. It certainly branded the three regimes as threats to the United States, though in the case of the war in Iraq, to much different results than the Cold War and the demise of the Soviet Union. In the end, Reagan's use of the word *evil* has come to symbolize the fall of the Soviet Union, while Bush's has become synonymous with what many consider a failed war.

18. Ronald Reagan, Speech at the Commencement Exercises at the United States Military Academy, May 27, 1981. Available at http://www.presidency .ucsb.edu/ws/index.php?pid=43865.

19. Ronald Reagan, Commencement Address at the University of Notre Dame, May 17, 1981. Available at http://old.nationalreview.com/document /reagan200406091024.asp.

20. Hayward, *Age of Reagan*, p. 241.

21. Ronald Reagan, Speech before the British Parliament, June 8, 1982. Available at http://teachingamericanhistory.org/library/index.asp?document=449.

22. Reeves, *President Reagan*, p. 110.

23. Robert Schlesinger, *White House Ghosts: Presidents and Their Speechwriters* (New York: Simon & Schuster, 2008), p. 326; Reeves, *President Reagan*, p. 111.

24. Reeves, *President Reagan*, p. 134.

25. Ibid.

26. Hayward, *Age of Reagan*, p. 288.

27. Ronald Reagan, Address to National Association of Evangelicals, March 8, 1983. Available at http://www.nationalcenter.org/ReaganEvilEmpire1983.html; Schlesinger, *White House Ghosts*, pp. 328–29; Reeves, *President Reagan*, p. 140.

28. Hayward, *Age of Reason*, pp. 288–89; Schlesinger, *White House Ghosts*, pp. 328–29.

29. D'Souza, *Ronald Reagan*, pp. 2–3.

30. Hayward, *Age of Reason*, p. 289.

Chapter 15

1. Jonathan Alter, *The Promise: President Obama, Year One* (New York: Simon & Schuster, 2010), p. 116.

2. Theodore Roosevelt, *Progressive Principles: Selections from Addresses Made during the Presidential Campaign of 1912* (New York: Progressive National Service, 1913), pp. 323–25.

3. Alexander Lane, "Teddy Roosevelt First Called for Healthcare Reform Nearly a Century Ago," *St. Petersburg Times*, March 5, 2009. Available at http://www.politifact.com/truth-o-meter/statements/2009/mar/05/barack-obama/ Obama-goes-back-to-his-Republican-roots-on-health-/.

4. Nancy Altman, *The Battle for Social Security: From FDR's Vision to Bush's Gamble* (New York: John Wiley & Sons, 2005), p. 56.

5. Monte Poen, *Harry Truman versus the Medical Lobby* (St. Louis: University of Missouri Press, 1979), p. 88.

6. Alter, *The Promise*, p. 244.

7. Ibid., p. 395.

8. Ibid., p. 244.

9. Ibid., p. 399.

10. Scott Wilson, "Obama Lists Financial Rescue as 'Most Important Thing' of His First Year," *Washington Post*, December 23, 2009. Available at http://www.washingtonpost.com/wp-dyn/content/article/2009/12/22/ AR2009122202101.html?sid=ST2009122202132.

11. Linda Felderman, "Healthcare Reform Bill Signed, Obama Ramps Up Big Sell," *Christian Science Monitor*, March 23, 2010. Available at http://www.cs monitor.com/USA/Politics/2010/0323/Healthcare-reform-bill-signed-Obama -ramps-up-big-sell.

12. Barack Obama, Youtube address, March 6, 2010. Available at http:// politicalticker.blogs.cnn.com/2010/03/06/obama-singles-out-insurance -companies/?fbid=reZnTQ4frnw.

13. Alter, *The Promise*, p. 395.

14. The reconciliation process has been employed twenty-three times since its inception in 1980. On seventeen occasions, Republican presidents have signed a bill into law using reconciliation as the means. Jason M. Breslow, "Healthcare Reform's Next Steps: 23rd Use of Reconciliation?" PBS, February 26, 2010; available at http://www.pbs.org/newshour/updates/politics/jan-june10/reconciliation _02-26.html.

INDEX